How to Sell Anything on eBay . . . and Make a Fortune!

OTHER BOOKS BY DENNIS L. PRINCE

Unleashing the Power of eBay

*How to Sell Anything on eBay . . .
and Make a Fortune! Organizer*

101 Ways to Boost Your Fortune on eBay

With Lynn Dralle
*How to Sell Antiques and Collectibles on eBay . . .
and Make a Fortune!*

With William M. Meyer
*How to Sell Music, Collectibles, and Instruments
on eBay . . . and Make a Fortune!*

With Sarah Manongdo and Dan Joya
*How to Buy Everything for Your Wedding
on eBay . . . and Save a Fortune!*

How to Sell Anything on eBay . . . and Make a Fortune!

Revised and Expanded Edition

Dennis L. Prince

McGraw-Hill

New York   Chicago   San Francisco
Lisbon   London   Madrid   Mexico City   Milan
New Delhi   San Juan   Seoul   Singapore
Sydney   Toronto

ISBN-13: 978-0-07-148013-0
ISBN-10: 0-07-148013-7

Prince, Dennis L.
    How to sell anything on eBay . . . and make a fortune! / Dennis L. Prince.—2nd ed.
        p. cm.
    Includes index.
    ISBN 0-07-148013-7
  1. eBay (Firm) 2. Internet auctions. I. Title.
    HF5478.P753   2007
658.8'7—dc22   2006036388

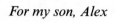

For my son, Alex

Contents

Introduction

These days it seems as if the Internet has been at our beck and call . . . well . . . forever. The truth is, it's been serving our needs, desires, and impulses only since around 1995. Sure, the origins of the Internet date back much further than that, but in the context of *treasure hunting* and *fortune finding,* we've been able to log on and riffle through a sea of important, intriguing, and outright insane offerings only since Labor Day 1995—the day eBay went live.

As an early adopter of the eBay site and its unique approach to merchandising goods to the four corners of the earth, I'm in a select group that embraced its approach in its infancy and worked within the online community to make it a better place to buy and sell goods in the compelling auction format. At the time, it was as much about the gamesmanship of the auction as it was about the incredible items being offered for bid. Those who sought rare items, long-lost nostalgia goods, and even a spare body part or two (yes, someone actually tried to auction a perfectly functioning kidney) needed to look no further than the Web site that was all the buzz at office break stations and supermarket checkout lines.

Impassioned collectors found the site to be a treasure trove of all the items they so desperately sought, for which they no longer had to scour classified ads, pore over trade papers, or crisscross the country to race through the collector's shows; most everything these people were looking for was typically up for auction at eBay. More important, those who had the goods to satisfy these enthusiastic shoppers quickly discovered the goldmine element of eBay. As demand spiked, sellers responded, listing all manner of goods, and gleefully watched the high bids roll in. From coveted collectibles to shabby chic, from high-end treasures to bottom-of-the-barrel baubles, from the practical to the whimsical, from the unimaginable to the unmentionable, eBay has been host to almost everything and anything, all on display, all for sale, and all brought forth by its legions of sellers, traders, and hagglers who have found it to be *the* place to test their entrepreneurial prowess and create a business outlet that suits their own unique needs. Now hosting over 80 million active registered users, amateurs and professionals alike, these savvy folk have found their success—their *fortune*—on their own terms. Why not join them?

Back in the early days of eBay, the sellers who stepped in to carve out their personal fortunes weren't *eBay experts*—there was no such thing, since all of them were learning the tricks of this new trade. Those pioneering sellers, though, learned in one of the best ways available: through hard work, experimentation, and perseverance. Sometimes by applying brick-and-mortar principles, often by going the route of trial and error, these brave new merchants learned to tame the realm of online auctioning and sales and have rightly earned their "expert" status as a result. You, too, can become an expert seller, but you shouldn't have to take that long, hard road to riches.

Here's an easier way.

If you're new to eBay, first, don't feel embarrassed if you *still* haven't begun working this online moneymaking machine; there are many, many others just like you. And this is the book you've always wanted but perhaps never thought to read. Many folks like you are overwhelmed at first encountering eBay (it's *big*), while others are uncertain about dealing online with total strangers (there are *millions* of them). Nevertheless, you know that regular people just like you—some professional, some semiskilled, some bona fide novices—are making thousands upon thousands of dollars on eBay every day, and that's likely why you've finally decided to peek inside this book to see just how daunting the task might be.

The good news: eBay is not really daunting if you know the steps involved (which I spell out for you in this book), and it's definitely feasible for you to join in the online opportunity. We've been waiting for you, and we're glad you've finally arrived.

ABOUT THIS REVISED EDITION

With over 75,000 copies of the first edition of this book having been sold, it's rewarding to know that readers have been well served by its content and intent. The mail I've received from readers has confirmed that the book achieved what I intended: to show how anyone can become successful at eBay and how practically anything can be sold to help build a fortune. That first edition has done its job well, but now it's time to give it a new coat of paint.

As is the nature of the Internet, change is constant online and eBay is a site that has continually evolved to make online trading easier and safer. The site has rolled out many new features and functions, some of which you should definitely take advantage of and others you might want to keep at arm's length. The purpose of this revised and expanded edition, then, is to explain the eBay experience to you and identify the most beneficial aspects the site has to offer. Since 1999, I've been writing about eBay to help others get the most from it just as I have. But, rather than make you endure the painstaking process of learning as you go, I'm able to give you the benefit of my experiences—my many successes and few setbacks—to save you time, trouble, and money.

As with any Internet site, eBay is constantly changing and evolving. While the first edition of this book was able to lead tens of thousands of newcomers through the site, enough change has occurred that it's time to bring this text up to date. Herein you'll find new screen shots, updated specifications, and revised techniques that will ensure you can quickly interpret and apply the best methods to forge your own success within the auction place.

Beyond revised screen layouts and a few rule changes, understand that other adjustments made on the site are evidence that eBay is in the business to make money—and why shouldn't they be? While I continue to be a staunch eBay supporter, know that my allegiance has always been to the users, not to the site itself. I fully support eBay and its undeniable value to us all, but I've recognized that some aspects of the site are intended to suit its needs over its community.

To that end, this new edition continues where the previous one left off: to show you how to harness the best the site has to offer, to get you in the game and up to speed as quickly as possible, and to help you maximize your own profits, even when those seem to run counter to what eBay might recommend. I'm in it for you and your fortune, and, believe me, your fortune is just a few keystrokes and mouse-clicks away.

FORTUNE OR FOLLY?

Webster defines fortune as "a prosperity attained," "the turns and courses accompanying one's progress," "riches," and "wealth." Each of us adds our own flavor to those definitions, personalizing the concept and developing a unique meaning that fits our individual wants, needs, and beliefs. But regardless of how we slice it, dice it, or quantify it, we tend to agree on this basic underlying precept: *fortune* means *success.* Irrespective, then, of how you define fortune for yourself, if fortune is your goal, eBay is your gateway. Even though the online marketplace is maturing and the original luster of eBay's novelty has faded somewhat, it's no longer a quirky little Web hangout; it's a serious endeavor and a reliable enterprise where you can set your own stake in the ground and open up shop for yourself, sell anything and everything that suits your fancy, and earn a tidy profit or even an honest-to-goodness fortune. Of course, there is still a bit of quirkiness to eBay; it never runs short of those peculiar curiosities and odd artifacts that pique the interest and often tickle the funny bone; these are the real-world testimonies that you *can* sell anything at eBay and often for far more than you would ever have previously dared to imagine.

And though eBay continues to host sellers who dabble in fun and sometimes frivolous goods that lend character and allure to the site, it's equally teeming with legions of sellers who recognize it as the best arena for breaking into the world of small business, for enabling a global reach to established brick-and-mortar proprietors, and for genuinely serving as a viable sales channel to major manufacturers and retailers. Rarely will you find a business model so adaptable to uniquely suit your needs—whoever you are, wherever you are, whatever your goals.

YOUR PATH TO SUCCESS IN ONLINE SELLING

Your goals at eBay, then, are likely to include establishing your business identity or broadening the visibility of an existing identity, attaining and perhaps surpassing your bottom-line aspirations, increasing your ever-important customer base, and enabling yourself to function as a full-fledged enterprise regardless of whether you work alone or are part of a greater team. Accordingly, this book's goal is to help you hit your targets head-on by revealing the mindset and methodologies that can best support your personal view of success, your definition of fortune.

The good news for you is that I've already seen or done just about everything that either handsomely pays off or unceremoniously flops in the online marketplace. Whether you're curious about buying in bulk for resale, listing sparingly for maximum sales price, going offline to salvage missed opportunities, or keeping ahead of the undesirable element that would rob you blind and waste your time, I've been there, sold that, and closed the deal—and I don't mind sharing with you what I've learned.

As one of the original members of the eBay community, having first navigated the fledgling site back in December 1995, I was initially struck by the fun and fancy the online trading post offered, and I loaded up on the nostalgic knickknacks and doodads that greeted me at every click of the mouse. Quickly, I realized the potential for selling off my own stockpile of trinkets and memorabilia to the mere thousand-strong enclave of the day. And though I reaped a modest profit from my initial sales at the site, the earliest fortune I gained, I now realize, was to have been fortunate enough to grow in pace with eBay, evolving my business savvy and reinvesting what I had earned and learned back into my auctioning efforts—the same approach eBay itself was applying to its own growth. With my first fortune ("good fortune," I like to call it) in the bag, I saw my quantifiable fortunes clearly laid in front of me.

In the years since, eBay became the ready-when-I-need-it virtual storefront that has given me the freedom to earn as much or as little as I want, to work as often or infrequently as I choose, and to apply what I've learned however it best suits me as a recognized PowerSeller, shrewd buyer, and seasoned professional (not to mention this ongoing stint of writing about eBay and auctioning for the past seven years).

A PROMISE TO YOU

Before you begin reading this book, know this: I firmly believe that time is money. My time is valuable; your time is valuable; our time equates to an opportunity to make money and otherwise amass fortune. As it is a most precious commodity, I won't waste your time, just as I wouldn't have you waste my money. This book will move ahead quickly, covering the critical information you want and need to get your auctioning moving from the start.

If you're new to eBay and online auctioning, don't worry that you might be left in the dust, but by the same token, recognize that I'll refrain from detouring heavily into the cutesy little details and potential distractions you'll sometimes encounter at eBay. The site has much to offer, but quite frankly I'm most interested in *your* success and, therefore, steering you to the best features of eBay while perhaps passing by some of the less-effective attractions. With so many features to wrangle, if it's key to making you successful, you'll read about it here. If it's potentially beneficial and of possible interest, I'll direct you to where you can learn more about it on your own. But if it's potentially a time waster or not a great way to boost your income, you won't be seeing it in these pages. We've got a fortune to make, right? So why waste time? I assure you we won't.

THIS BOOK, AT YOUR SERVICE

Over the years of guiding people in the best ways to use eBay, I've learned that most folks want specific direction and uncomplicated answers to their immediate questions about buying and selling in the online auction format. With so much to teach, though, I've also learned that folks need to be able to quickly refer back to previously covered information without having to wade through a sea of text to find an elusive answer. To that end, I've arranged this book in a very natural flow and one that follows the eBay experience, start to finish. As a quick preview, here's how the information has been conveniently broken up into four sections for you.

Part I: Getting Started

This first section provides a quick history of eBay and then wastes no time in taking you on a tour of the site and getting you registered and ready to go. From here, it's on to search the site, bid on an item or two, and *win*. Sure, *selling* is the focus of this book, but some of the best sellers, you'll learn, are likewise some of the best buyers—those who know a great deal when they see it, can skillfully ferret out a hidden treasure, and can equally assess the person they'll be dealing with to ensure the experience is beneficial in the end.

Part II: The Fundamentals of Selling on eBay

Now it's your turn to offer the goods, and this part of the book gets you off and running on the right foot. Besides learning the fundamentals of listing items for auction, you'll also learn the ins and outs of getting paid, getting items shipped, and managing any customer problems that might arise.

Part III: Surefire Ways to Increase Your Sales

This is it, the fount of knowledge that is the product of years of mining the online auction space. Here is where you learn how to easily create professional-looking listings, how to use item images and other enhancements to boost your profits, and how to wisely reinvest in more inventory when your closet, attic, or basement runs dry.

Part IV: Taking Your eBay Business to the Next Level

By this point you have become an expert seller and accomplished auctioneer, but why stop there? This final section guides you in ways of improving your efficiency, increasing your output, and beefing up your bottom line. Here, you're ready to go beyond just auctions and will learn how to create a virtual store of your own to the point where you can venture outside the confines of eBay and become an online businessperson in your own right.

YOUR CHANCE TO SOUND OFF

Whenever I share best practices with up-and-coming eBayers, I recognize that each of us brings our unique nuances to the experience. The eBay business model is adaptable and can become specific to each of us who utilizes it. Chances are that you'll take what I share here and you'll morph it—maybe a little, maybe a lot—to suit your individual needs or goals.

That's the beauty of eBay, and it's what I enjoy most about helping others get proficient using it. I always invite folks to share their experiences with me, then, whatever they may encounter. I welcome your thoughts, observations, and comments about your experiences at eBay, so feel free to drop me a line at dlprince@bigfoot.com. I've always enjoyed and respected the community element of eBay and will continue to keep my virtual door open to maintain ongoing discussions with others. After all, we're all friends here, right?

The bottom line is this: eBay is positioned to stay. It is a staple in our lives and livelihoods and an immediately recognizable brand. Its potential is being tapped every minute of every day by businesspersons from all professions, from all levels of experience, and from all over the globe. For fun or profit, eBay delivers. There's a fortune waiting out there—let's go get you some.

Acknowledgments

While I'm so pleased to present this updated version to the eBay faithful and those newcomers eager to begin carving out their fortunes, I have to pause to acknowledge the fine people who have made this book possible.

At McGraw-Hill, I'm blessed to maintain my working relationship with editor extraordinaire Donya Dickerson. She makes my work so much easier and ensures the outcome is the best it can be with her unfailing faith, guidance, and enthusiasm for this material. It continues to be my privilege to write books under her watchful eye. Also, I must thank the rest of the terrific McGraw-Hill team with whom I've had the pleasure to work: Mary Glenn, Ruth Mannino, Bettina Faltermeier, Anthony Sarchiapone, Jeff Weeks, and all the fine folks who serve as the creative and inspirational heart of the McGraw-Hill Sales and Marketing teams. Thanks to each of you.

Next, my thanks to Virginia Carroll and Christine Furry for the excellent copyedit. I appreciate their insightful observations. Their enthusiasm for this particular project is likewise appreciated.

Of course, I must acknowledge all the readers who've written to me in response to the first edition of this book, sharing their experiences, observations, and tales of fortune, helping me maintain the content and tone in this revised edition, which they indicated were important to their success. In the true spirit of the original eBay community, my readers and I have worked together to our mutual success, and because of that, I never stop enjoying writing for them. I thank them for their ongoing support—all of them—and for keeping me on my toes to ensure the information I pass along is relevant and ultimately rewarding.

PART I

GETTING STARTED

1

---

eBay and Auctions: Then and Now

While there's undeniable excitement about jumping right into eBay and about the buying and selling opportunity, you can actually profit from understanding the history of the site and its methods. There was a time, you know, when ARPANET was the veritable Sputnik to what would become cyberspace, when the Commodore PET was a breakthrough in minicomputers, and when Atari's Super Pong was all the rage with home video gamers. We've come a long way.

Looking back on the evolution of technology is not only interesting but also fun. By doing so, we gain perspective, insight, and an appreciation for how much has changed in a very short time as well as how essential—perhaps vital—technology and the Internet have become in our everyday lives. From the perspective of online commerce and eBay in particular, a quick look back is useful in understanding how trading and haggling have emerged from the earliest days of recorded history and been transformed into the online realm of new opportunity for anyone who has goods to sell. So in this chapter you'll get a high-speed tour of the tradition of auctioning, the creation of the Internet, and the ultimate birth of eBay.

AUCTIONS 101

To acquire a truly instinctive feel for what auctions are, how they came to be, and why they're a staple of our longstanding bartering system, it's worthwhile to understand the origins of the bid-and-sell technique. Fear not—you're not in danger of being tricked into a protracted historical lecture; this will be brief. Yet if ever you've heard or wondered "How do auctions really work?" here's the quick answer.

Set the Wayback Machine to about 500 BC and you'll encounter the earliest known auctions: those held in Babylon, employed for the distribution of eligible maidens. Skip ahead to ancient Rome and you'll find yourself at the *atrium auctionarium,* the designated gathering place for the toga-clad masses, where triumphant returning soldiers would auction land and other spoils of their successful battles. Proven an efficient method to garner the highest prices for wares offered (the *market value* of the day), auctions found their way to Great Britain around 1595 and are most notably documented during the seventeenth century with the emergence of the historic Sotheby's and Christie's auction houses. Within short order, the favored format crossed the big pond and was put to continual use within America as well.

The point here is this: auctions have been an effective and time-proven method of distributing goods in the dynamic market of supply and demand, ages before eBay or the Internet were ever conceived. Who would have ever thought?

ONLINE SELLING: THE EARLY YEARS

While 1979 is of future shock status when compared to the dusty days of 500 BC Babylon, it's ancient history when considering the overall life and growth of the Internet. Although the Internet began in the late 1960s (as the Department of Defense's ARPANET), the creation a few years later of the Unix User Network, or *Usenet,* was what got people connected and ready to do business. Termed a *store-and-forward* network where individuals could post news, views, and other communications to be read by others, the Usenet was quickly adopted as a high-tech classified advertising circular. Usenet categories (known as *newsgroups*) were established to help Usenet visitors quickly home in on those areas where items were being posted for sale. While the Usenet is still heavily active in this fashion of person-to-person trading, it was in September of 1995 when a new sort of for-sale listing began popping up, similar to this:

> For Sale: Rare Art Deco piece—now taking bids for this great vintage piece. See it at www.ebay.com/aw.

The rest, as they say, is history.

AUCTIONWEB AT eBAY

For many, eBay is a hobby. Fittingly, it started as precisely that—a hobby. Launching the site on Labor Day 1995, its founder, 27-year-old Pierre Omidyar, introduced a simple trading post called Auction Web to online pioneers. Omidyar's motivation: he sought what he called the emergence of a "perfect market" and a "level playing field" within which individuals, as buyers and sellers, could connect directly with one another, as opposed to being relegated to more controlling and often manipulative centralized sources.

Besides, as cyberlore has it, his fiancée, Pam Wesley, an avid Pez collector, wanted to meet and trade with other collectors of similar passion. In addition to bridging geographical boundaries (something that would help Pam fill in her family of Pez), Omidyar's notion of an open trading space would truly enable buyers to make fully informed decisions, since everyone would have the same access to prices and offerings, while sellers would all have an equal opportunity to present their wares to the masses.

> **eBay TIP:** Did you know that the whole legend of how a passion for Pez launched the now multi-billion-dollar eBay is a ruse? It's true! That is, it's true that it was a lie. In the eBay-authorized book *The Perfect Store: Inside eBay,* author Adam Cohen revealed that the tale is completely untrue, an imaginative myth—practically *urban legend*—from eBay's first public relations perpetrator, Mary Lou Song.
>
> Yes, Pam Wesley *did* want to connect with other Pez collectors, but her motivation to do so was shared with Song, not hubby-to-be Pierre. Immediately, Song realized she had a story with legs, one that was able to capture the attention of the media (they thought AuctionWeb was rather boring up to this point) and result in a new-age love story: a man develops a breakthrough in commerce, driven by his desire to woo his betrothed. It was a lie, but it worked!

Ultimately, Omidyar's theory of the perfect market motivated him to create a situation where supply would meet demand and where price would be determined at the precise (and dynamic) point at which these longstanding economic fundamentals intersect. About as stylish as a simple Usenet listing, AuctionWeb was unveiled with its modest gray-screened, simple text design (see Figure 1.1).

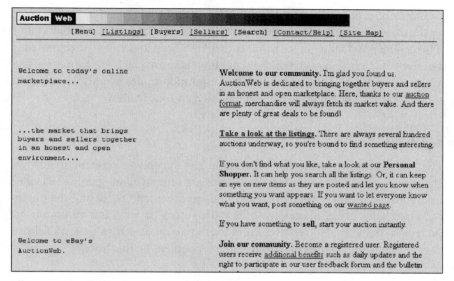

Figure 1.1 These days, screen grabs of Pierre Omidyar's original AuctionWeb site are extremely scarce.

Omidyar had developed and now hosted his creation on a personal computer (PC) in his back bedroom. He poised his brainchild for success, based largely upon the reliance on his fundamental belief in the goodness of people (users or employees) and their limitless abilities to solve problems in a self-governing environment. AuctionWeb's community was founded on the tenet of "power to the people" in a genuinely free and open market. While it's fun to snicker at the fact that the site's inaugural auction consisted of an awkward listing for a broken laser pointer, the useless gadget sold for $14 all the same, and Auction Web was off and running.

Ultimately, the AuctionWeb moniker was dropped and the site became known simply as eBay. Although Omidyar had no formal training in auctions as a market mechanism, his instincts told him that people would naturally be drawn to a destination that offered fair market value for goods, benefiting buyers and sellers alike.

A FAST LESSON ON eBAY AUCTION FORMATS

As auctions have evolved through the centuries, so have auction methods. Most folks envision the venerable auction dialogue that goes something like this: "I have twenty, who'll make it twenty-five? Twenty-five, who'll give me thirty?

Going once, going twice, SOLD to the man in the brown tweed jacket!" Known as the *ascending-price* auction, this is the most common format for auctioning. There are a good many other formats that have been and still are being used in different auction venues. Thankfully, at eBay there are just a few formats in use, yet you'll find they'll suit your needs and aspirations quite handily. Here are the methods you'll encounter when you bid, buy, and sell at eBay.

The Ascending-Price Auction

Historically known as the *English* auction and the *open-outcry* auction, this is the most widely used format at eBay. Items are offered at an opening bid value and additional bids of incremental value are accepted, increasing the potential final sales price. Successive bids must satisfy at least the minimum *bid increment* but can also represent a bidder's *maximum bid* value (you'll learn more about these two terms in subsequent chapters of this book).

The Dutch Auction

A format new to many users is eBay's *Dutch* auction. This likewise longstanding auction format allows sellers to quickly dispense of multiple, identical items. Here, bidders bid the price they're willing to pay while also specifying *how many* of the item they're contesting for. Dutch auctions aren't as tricky as they might sound; however, the strategy for winning this type of auction is a bit complex and will also be explained more fully later in this book.

Reserve-Price Auctions

This is a slight variation of the ascending-price auction whereby the seller establishes a minimum price at which the item will be sold but which bidders aren't able to see. That is, if the competitive bidding fails to reach or eclipse the seller's reserve price, the seller is not required by eBay's rules to sell the item. This variation is especially useful to sellers who are uncertain whether competitive bidding will return a price that either suits their needs or ensures recovery of their original investment. Unfortunately, this format variation is sometimes abused by greedy sellers, as you'll later learn.

Fixed-Price Auction

If you have a price in mind for which you'll sell an item outright, this format (which eBay terms "Buy-It-Now") allows the willing buyer to dispense of the competitive bidding and offer the seller's asking price, thus ending the auction immediately. There are several ways to manage this feature at eBay, and these will also be discussed later.

Private Auctions

Got some erotica or other adult-themed items to sell? Want to prevent other sellers from seeing who's bidding on your stuff? Whatever your motivation, private auctions allow bidders' identities (user IDs) to remain concealed from all except the seller.

Restricted-Access Auctions

A close cousin of the private auction, this format was designed to help users easily locate or summarily avoid adult items. Bidders searching for restricted-access items must provide credit card information for age verification. Items of this sort, corralled in the "Mature Audiences" category, are not listed in general search results and require adult verification logon to access, thus shielding those of us who are easily embarrassed.

GROWING, GROWING . . . AND STILL GROWING

With the formats established, the community values in place, and the lure of online bargaining ready to peak, eBay grew exponentially, practically overnight. Although Omidyar had intentions of providing AuctionWeb as a free-of-charge service site, his mounting server bills pushed him into levying fees. Upon initiating his *final-value fees,* he culled a meager $250 in his first month. Still, this was enough to pay his monthly service provider bill. Just two short months after that, he collected $2,500 in fees, and each month thereafter earned still more as word of AuctionWeb quickly spread across the cybernetic landscape. Of course, eBay has since become a billion-dollar venture.

Along the way, Omidyar turned over the CEO reins to former Hasbro leader Meg Whitman. Under her watch, eBay successfully navigated the dot-com bust of the 1990s and established it as one of the most prolific online destinations to have survived the cyber maelstrom. The site now hosts over 80 million active registered users and has developed worldwide awareness and even pop culture status.

Today, eBay operates country-specific sites in Canada, New Zealand, the United Kingdom, and more (26 total international sites) and is frequently referenced in film and television. It's also well on its way to becoming a verb:

how many times have you heard a disgruntled gift recipient proclaim, "Ah, I guess I'll *eBay* it?"

The company is here to stay just as is the Internet itself, and, for you, this is reassurance that you'll be working with an online platform that will serve your needs and connect you with millions of people around the world, 24-7, as you step up to claim your own fortune.

WOULD YOU LIKE TO KNOW MORE?

Clearly, this was something of a short-and-sweet tour of how we got from ARPANET to making fortunes on eBay. This is all some people really need to know, since those untapped riches await them at the turning of the page. Yet I suspect this will merely whet the appetite of others who are eager to immerse themselves in the minutiae of *exactly* how we got here. Having been one of those curious folk myself, here are a few books I recommend for spare-time reading:

- *Auction: The Social Construction of Value* by Charles W. Smith (University of California Press, 1989). If you truly wish to be a student, and master, of the auction, Smith's book will fill your head with the intricacies of the dynamic pricing. Beware: this one is about as dry as a cold piece of toast, but it compensates for it in the good information within.
- *Fire in the Valley: The Making of the Personal Computer* by Paul Freiberger and Michael Swaine (McGraw-Hill, 1999). If thinking back to 1974 only conjures up painful memories of Nixon, Watergate, and the energy crisis, look deeper and see what geeks like Steve Jobs, Bill Gates, and Paul Allen were busying themselves with in their cluttered garages.
- *The Perfect Store: Inside eBay* by Adam Cohen (Back Bay Books, 2002). *Time* magazine journalist Cohen convinced the powers that be at eBay to grant him total access to the story behind the scenes of the big dog of auction sites. Though Cohen's style rarely breaks free of the magazine article mold, his is an interesting documentation of the activities both in front of and behind the home page we lovingly know as eBay.com.
- *Collectible Microcomputers* by Michael Nadeau (Schiffer Publishing, 2002). Don't toss that old Commodore 64 or Apple Lisa before you've read Nadeau's book. As many of us expected, technology has become quite collectible (see Figure 1.2). Heavily illustrated and sim-

Figure 1.2 One last look back: anyone remember where they left their Super Pong? This sort of funky tech treasure is gold on eBay and often garners hundreds of dollars in bids (really!).

ply fun to leaf through, this is a great pictorial jaunt through the hallowed halls of computer history.

- *F'd Companies: Spectacular Dot-Com Flameouts* by Philip J. Kaplan (Simon & Schuster, 2002). If irreverence is your bag and you simply revel in listening in on the acidic attacks made on some of the biggest flops of the dot-com era, Kaplan has the tabloid tales sure to entertain. An extension of his wildly popular Web site F****dCompany.com, this book chronicles the stories that broke on his site as the bad news for Web businesses were unfolded daily, often with those in the companies' employ learning of their imminent demise on Kaplan's site before the boss ever distributed pink slips. A fun read but not to be taken too seriously.

2

Gearing Up: Hardware, Software, and Net Results

If you're like most people, the task of updating your business tools—your PC, software, and so on—is likely low on your priority list. Further, the notion of being in continual change mode to keep up with the tech world makes many cringe, especially considering the time and effort that would be drained away from your bidding and selling activities. Yet, realistically speaking, there comes a time when operating with inefficient tools is also detrimental to your well-deserved fortune.

With that in mind, you can be well served if you look to upgrade your high-tech gear methodically and piecemeal: a new PC every three years or so, new software applications as often as you deem useful, and upgraded Internet access when it becomes financially prudent (especially as competition continues to be fierce in the realm of high-speed services). Making upgrades one piece at a time will usually cause only minimal disruption to your activity and avoids the potentially overwhelming prospect of gutting the works.

You don't have to be a hard-core gearhead to get the most from the Internet and your eBay business, but you should make sure you've got the tools to run a respectable shop. Although you might already feel secure in your current hardware and software configurations, here's a quick look at the whizbang stuff that drives your online business efforts. This will be a brief checkup of your goods and it won't hurt a bit, I promise. In fact, you'll probably be surprised to find that you are already in good shape.

MAKING SURE YOUR COMPUTER IS UP TO SPEED

If you are interested in online auctions, you probably already have a PC or two in your home. As research in computer ownership and use has become a key statistic that helps online endeavors anticipate and respond to usage trends, Jupiter Research recently published the backward- and forward-looking statistics shown in Table 2.1.

Table 2.1 U.S. Household PC Growth and Penetration

Year	Number (in Millions)	Percent
2001	71.1	67
2002	74.1	69
2003	77.5	71
2004	80.8	73
2005	84.1	75
2006	86.7	77
2007	88.7	78

In addition to Jupiter's research, a *PC Magazine* survey concluded that one-third of American households have at least one personal computer, another third of households have two or more, but a remaining 25 percent have yet to purchase their first magic box (and are likely still fiddling with the remote for their first-ever VCR). The good news is that if you're in one of the two former groups and if you've upgraded your PC within the past 18 months, feel confident that the hardware you now own is more than suitable for an eBay venture. But what if your tech toys are older than that?

Should you be agonizing whether what you've got is good enough to cut the mustard in an online buying and selling marketplace? You'll be happy to know that a desktop or laptop system purchased within the last several years, even if it isn't cutting edge, will probably work perfectly and offer you plenty of power and features to make an eBay experience quite pleasant. Then again, if perhaps you've yet to purchase a PC or maybe you're still not sure the equipment you have is up to par, here are some simple specifications you might follow:

- **Processor/speed.** In older PCs, if the brains of the operation is at least a 450-megahertz Pentium II, you'll be in decent, albeit slightly outdated, shape. Today, though, it's easy to get into the fast lane with an

Intel or AMD dual core processor, quickly becoming standard equipment in current hardware configurations. In the PC world, Microsoft Windows (XP or Vista) is the de facto standard, while the Mac operating system (OS) continues to drive Apple Computer's offerings. Price pressures among the various computer manufacturers spell savings to you, with incredibly impressive upgrades to be had below the $500 price point. If it's been a few years since you've upgraded your computer, feel confident that today's *low-end* offerings will be a significant advance on what you may have been using up to this point.

- **Memory.** Simply enough, try to ensure you're working with at least 512 megabytes (MB) of random-access memory (RAM), but as with the processor, it's easy to surpass this lowest-point benchmark. The upgrade to 1 gigabyte (GB) is cheap in comparison to the tremendous boost in response time you'll see.

- **Storage.** How big is big enough when it comes to your computer's storage space? Well, consider the number of images you might be storing up for selling online wares. Models of several years ago boasted about their delivery of the then-impressive 12 GB, but these days you can slingshot into the realm of 60 or 80 GB of storage at an opening price point offering.

- **Additional drives.** Do you still have a 3.5-inch floppy disk drive in your current PC? If so, that's practically becoming a nostalgic collectible at eBay. (And who recalls 5.25-inch and 8-inch megafloppies?) These days, CD-ROM read/write drives as well as DVD read/write drives are becoming base-model features. Storage to a CD-ROM is cheap and easy and far more reliable than the magnetic floppies of old.

- **Internal modem.** If you go this route, make sure the modem card is at least 56-kilobit; however, keep in mind that in these days of cable modems and DSL connections, internal 56-Kb modems are downright prehistoric by comparison.

- **Monitor.** A 15-inch CRT monitor is fine and a 17-inch model is better yet (more on-screen real estate to work with), but this technology, too, has become outdated, as computer owners are less inclined to wrestle a big, fat monitor onto their desktops. Flat-panel LCD monitors have become much cheaper and are usually thrown in as a free-upgrade incentive. The image quality of these, along with their space-saving design, makes them the better choice. Still, if you love your old CRT and it's performing well for you, there's no need to run out and upgrade just for the sake of doing so. The bottom line is this: if you're satisfied with your online activity today and don't find that your PC is dragging you down, you're probably in good shape and can spare the immediate expense of shopping for a PC. Besides, when it comes to making that fortune, money saved is as good as money earned.

MAKING YOUR WAY THROUGH THE SOFTWARE JUNGLE

The bundled PC solutions of the past several years have been rife with nifty applications, some of which suit your auctioning needs perfectly and others that are, well, generally expendable. The first step in determining whether you need any more applications is to decide what it is you want to *do* with your PC. Here's a simple list of the basic applications that you'll certainly need as an online entrepreneur.

- **Word processor.** Usually a bundled application that came along with the operating system on your computer system. Applications as old as 1995 will work just fine for you, and some folks are still doing great business using a relatively antiquated application.
- **Web browser.** Also embedded into bundled systems, Web browser present you with a choice between Netscape or Internet Explorer. Keep your browser updated (free downloads are available at the Netscape or Microsoft home pages) to ensure you can display and access current design features at eBay and around the Internet.
- **E-mail application.** You can get by with the e-mail tool that accompanies Web browsers, but you might want to upgrade anyway to gain better features. I like both Eudora and MS Outlook.
- **Image editor.** Fear not, because you don't need to master Photoshop to get the images of your auction items into tip-top shape. MS Picture It!, Paint Shop Pro, and even LView are great little packages that will deliver enough features to help you easily manage images. Yes, there are definitely some truly high-end graphics programs out there, but as you'll see later in this book, your eBay needs will be more than adequately met by some of the simpler (and free!) image editing tools.
- **Spreadsheet application.** Don't risk your sales and customer records to scraps of paper that tend to hide when you need them most. Pick a spreadsheet program you like best and get that vital business information safely stored where it'll be easy to retrieve whenever you need it (see Chapter 25 for more details).

- **Antivirus application.** If you've been online for any length of time, you're likely all too familiar with the Love Bug, the Klez worm, and the Blackworm. Virtual viruses are nasty little demons that come to you unexpectedly as you access the Net and communicate with your customers. Protect your business by protecting your PC.

There are additional auction-specific applications that you might also want to use in your eBay exploits. Those will be discussed in greater detail in Chapter 23. For now, however, those just listed are the basic software tools you'll want on board your computer.

YOUR INTERNET CONNECTION

A few years ago it took a concerted effort to catch a cyberwave, but today getting connected to the Internet is practically unavoidable. Go to a library, visit a cybercafé, or just sit in the waiting room at your car dealer's service bay and you'll find the Net up and running, 24-7. For your home, the options are getting better and better every day. If you like choices, you've got choices. Just look at how you can be connected:

- **DSL.** It's fast, and how. Figure the monthly service bill to tally up to about $50, but if you want to prioritize your business costs, put this at the top of your list.
- **Cable.** Playing piggyback on your home cable TV service, this connection uses the same coaxial connection to provide high-speed, always-on Net access. Of course, if you don't have cable TV, see the entry for DSL. The cost is similar to that of DSL.
- **Satellite.** Broadband satellite is also quite fast but requires a dish to gain access and a clear view of the southern sky.
- **Dial-up.** The regular old phone line is stubbornly hanging on, but it appears that its days are numbered. The hassles involved with dial-up services when compared to the high-speed methods already mentioned make dial-up an option only for the most infrequent online surfer. If you're ready to jump into the eBay fray with passion and conviction, forget this cheap alternative outright.

Whatever your choice, getting connected to the Internet is easier than ever. Better still, it's super simple to change up these days, so don't be afraid to upgrade to a different service; if you don't like it, change up again.

ADDITIONAL EQUIPMENT

Of course, there are plenty of additional gadgets and pieces of equipment that you'll need to be thoroughly efficient and successful in your auctioning. From printers to scanners, from digital cameras to all-in-one units, from telephone headsets to office furniture, there's much more needed to establish an optimal auction headquarters. All of these and more will be covered fully in Chapter 23. The intent here is to ensure you have the basics at hand so that you can make your way into the wonderful world of online auctioning. Next stop: eBay!

3

Welcome to the World's Largest Online Marketplace

Even if you've never sold anything on eBay, you've probably at least checked out the site. You've heard the buzz about eBay: the great finds you can buy there and the money to be made by regular folk like you and me. It's rare that I encounter a person who's *never* logged on to the site. If you're a complete newcomer, though, terrific! Welcome to the place that will likely alter your life from this point forward.

Though it may sound a bit sappy, eBay truly is a life-changing phenomenon, just as was television and the Internet itself. eBay is a bustling shopping hub where you'll rub virtual elbows with millions of users from all cultures, from nearly every age category, from practically all points on the globe. Its attraction goes beyond global, though, in terms of meeting the masses. The most remarkable element of eBay is its arguably *individual* appeal, that is, its ability to cater to and satisfy the unique wants, needs, and desires of just about anyone who cares to visit.

Although it's immediately appealing to some, it can likewise be daunting and overwhelming to others. How do people navigate all this? Whether you're new to the site and feel understandably intimidated or you're a repeat visitor who wants to make sure you're hitting all the hot spots, this chapter is your tour of the site, its key features, and its main points of interest that will help you quickly find your fortune.

HOME, SWEET HOME

Mention www.ebay.com, and some folks will bubble over with enthusiasm. For many, this Web destination is like a home—everything they need at their fingertips (literally) and all available any day, any hour, and from the comfort of their own home. Take a look at Figure 3.1 and you'll immediately see that eBay is busy, busy, busy.

Where to begin? Well, before zipping off to hunt for great buys or find a place to list your own merchandise, take a careful look at the home page itself. Notice immediately the Main Toolbar situated across the top of the page (also illustrated in Figure 3.2). The links from this toolbar are the main entryways to the site. In fact, you'll see this toolbar uniformly positioned on just about every eBay screen you visit. You'll also see it's actually two toolbars in one, with Buy, Sell, my eBay, Community, and Help links in the main bar and "home," "pay," "register," and "site map" in the smaller, topmost line of text

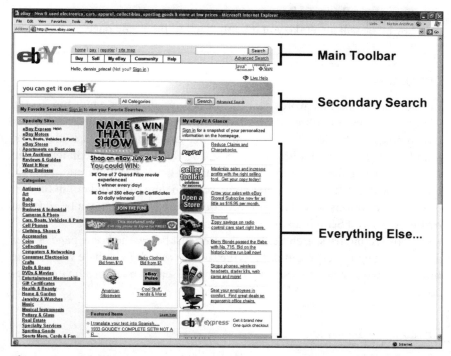

Figure 3.1 The busy eBay home page puts you just a link or two away from finding your fortune.

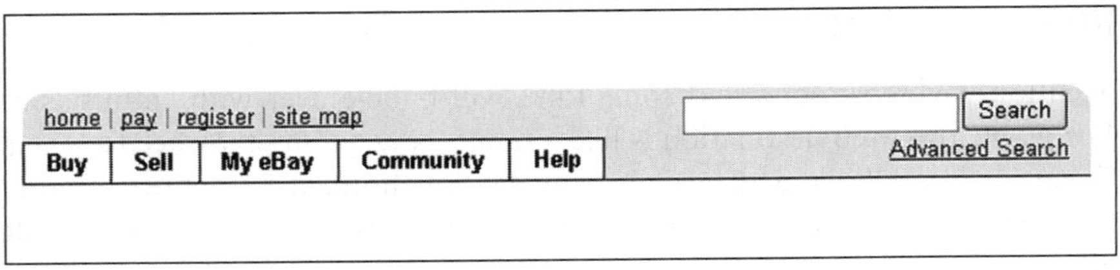

home | pay | register | site map						Search
Buy	**Sell**	**My eBay**	**Community**	**Help**		Advanced Search

Figure 3.2   The eBay toolbar will be a best friend to you. Nearly everywhere you go on the site, you can count on it being there at the top of the page.

links. I'll take you deeper into each link in just a moment. Right now, recognize the convenience of this ever-present toolbar and keep in mind that you'll be making regular use of it.

 eBay TIP: Clicking on the eBay logo on any site page will also take you directly back to the home page.

In Search of . . .

In addition to the link words just mentioned, you'll see a white box to the right on the toolbar, followed by a button labeled "Search" This is the quick search box, which, along with the toolbar text links and buttons, is also to be found on practically all eBay site pages. Use this box to immediately begin combing the site for whatever it is you want or need. Keep in mind, though, that this box searches only for matching words in item titles and not in the text of item descriptions. (We'll cover more complex searches that can be accessed by the Advanced Search text link a little later.)

The secondary search field can be seen just below the home page header area. Although largely redundant to the toolbar search field, here you can use the pull-down selector to restrict your keyword search by a specific item category (see Figure 3.3).

Categorically Speaking

On the left side, running nearly the length of the home page display, are links to Specialty Sites and item Categories. The Specialty Sites are those additional branches of eBay that you might make use of (some more than others)

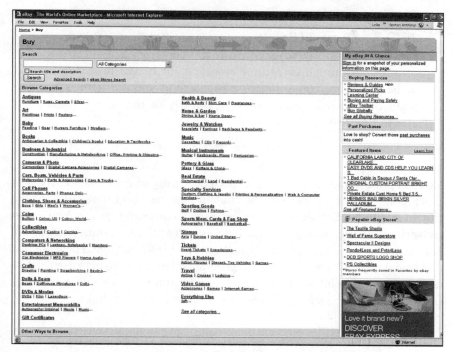

Figure 3.3 Click the Buy button to familiarize yourself with the incredible amount of item categories and subcategories.

and that consist of new spin-offs created by eBay (such as eBay Motors and eBay Express).

The Categories links just below Specialty Sites are your paths into a browsing excursion that is practically unrivaled anywhere else on the Net. These top-level links, each branching further into more specific groupings of goods, ultimately taking you to the various individual listings of products for sale. The sellers decide how their items will be categorized; they choose the category placement that best represents their item and that they believe will be the most likely category to attract the buyers.

Everything Else

The rest of what you see on the home page is really just splash and filler. While there are plenty of useful links here, most of the pages can be accessed from elsewhere within the site. To give the site a feeling of buzz, eBay has

> **eBay TIP:**   Remember, the eBay Search function will
> also bring buyers directly to items from across categories.
> Although categories are great for casual browsing, they
> can be too time consuming to navigate if a specific item is being
> sought out, so most eBay users go directly to the Search function
> (refer to Figure 3.1).

loaded up the home page with the expected offering of eye candy. There is so much going on just inside, and the content changes every time you visit the site. In addition, eBay works on having a fresh marketing appeal. You'll also see various other groupings of item links as well as *thematic* links (such as the baby items or Cool Stuff & Trends auctions) on the home page. These are just additional methods eBay employs to generate interest and to help users determine a starting point for their shopping adventure. As it's just marketing, there's nothing to be missed if you skip over these transient links.

The Bottom Line

The bottom links are what fill up the final quarter of the eBay home page. Here are the partner links and advertisements that eBay thinks might be of interest to you (or by which they have a contractual agreement to put on display).

Finally, there are redundant text links that will take you to many of the same site destinations—such as Site Map and Help—as the main toolbar does. In the world of effective Web design, it's a rule of thumb that a single display page should provide visitors with multiple links to the same most-popular or most-used site features. At the same time, eBay utilizes the screen real estate "above the fold"—that is, the content that appears prior to a visitor having to scroll downward—as you should, too. The keys to your fortune-making success are found within the eBay header area, well above the fold. Already, you've learned how to save time by dismissing the balance of the home page to focus where you really need to.

TAPPING INTO THE TOOLBARS

So what makes those home page toolbars so useful? Glad you asked, because there's more than meets the eye in those simple little labels. In fact, each acts as a useful portal to some key site functions and features. To start, let's look again at the most useful features (see Figure 3.2).

The Buy Button

As its name implies, this button is for those eager to stroll the site's virtual aisles. As with any brick-and-mortar store, shoppers are guided by signposts that identify the different departments—or, in eBay terms, categories—such as music or clothing and accessories. Although the home page lists many category links, the Buy link on the toolbar will take you to the entire listing of category headers on eBay (see Figure 3.3).

ANTIQUES
Antiquities
Architectural & Garden
Asian Antiques
Books, Manuscripts
Decorative Arts
Ethnographic
Furniture
Maps, Atlases, Globes
Maritime
Musical Instruments
Primitives
Rugs, Carpets
Science & Medicine
Silver
Textiles, Linens
Other Antiques

ART
Digital Art
Drawings
Folk Art
Mixed Media
Paintings
Photographic Images
Posters
Prints
Sculpture, Carvings
Self-Representing Artists
Other Art
Wholesale Lots

BABY
Baby Gear
Baby Safety & Health
Bathing & Grooming
Car Safety Seats
Diapering
Feeding
Keepsakes & Baby
    Announcements
Nursery Bedding
Nursery Décor
Nursery Furniture
Potty Training
Strollers
Toys
Other Baby Items
Baby Wholesale Lots

BOOKS
Accessories
Antiquarian & Collectible
Audiobooks
Catalogs
Children's Books
Fiction Books
Magazine Back Issues
Magazine Subscriptions
Nonfiction Books
Textbooks, Education
Wholesale, Bulk Lots
Other

BUSINESS & INDUSTRIAL
Agriculture & Forestry
Construction
Food Service & Retail
Healthcare, Lab & Life Science
Industrial Electrical & Test
Industrial Supply, MRO
Manufacturing & Metalworking
Office, Printing & Shipping
Other Industries

CAMERAS & PHOTO
Bags, Cases & Straps
Binoculars & Telescopes
Camcorder Accessories
Camcorders
Digital Camera Accessories
Digital Cameras
Film
Film Camera Accessories
Film Cameras
Film Processing & Darkroom
Flashes & Accessories
Lenses & Filters
Lighting & Studio Equipment
Manuals, Guides & Books
Photo Albums & Archive Items
Printers, Scanners & Supplies
Professional Video Equipment
Projection Equipment
Stock Photography & Footage
Tripods, Monopods
Vintage
Wholesale Lots

CELL PHONES
Accessories, Parts
Phones Only
Phones with New Plan Purchase
Prepaid Phones & Cards
Wholesale & Large Lots

CLOTHING, SHOES & ACCESSORIES
Infants & Toddler
Boys
Girls
Men's Accessories

Men's Clothing
Men's Shoes
Uniforms
Wedding Apparel
Women's Accessories, Handbags
Women's Clothing
Women's Shoes
Vintage
Wholesale, Large & Small Lots

COINS & PAPER MONEY
Coins: US
Bullion
Coins: Ancient
Coins: World
Exonumia
Paper Money: US
Paper Money: World
Publications & Supplies
Scripophily

COLLECTIBLES
Advertising
Animals
Animation Art, Characters
Arcade, Jukeboxes & Pinball
Autographs
Banks, Registers & Vending
Barware
Bottles & Insulators
Breweriana, Beer
Casino
Clocks
Comics
Cultures, Ethnicities
Decorative Collectibles
Disneyana
Fantasy, Mythical & Magic
Furniture, Appliances & Fans
Historical Memorabilia
Holiday, Seasonal
Housewares & Kitchenware
Knives, Swords & Blades
Lamps, Lighting
Linens, Fabric & Textiles
Metalware
Militaria
Pens & Writing Instruments

Pez, Keychains, Promo Glasses
Photographic Images
Pinbacks, Nodders, Lunchboxes
Postcards & Paper
Radio, Phonograph, TV, Phone
Religions, Spirituality
Rocks, Fossils, Minerals
Science Fiction
Science, Medical
Tobacciana
Tools, Hardware & Locks
Trading Cards
Transportation
Vanity, Perfume & Shaving
Vintage Sewing
Wholesale Lots

COMPUTERS & NETWORKING
Apple, Macintosh Computers
Desktop & Laptop Components
Desktop & Laptop Accessories
Desktop PCs
Drives, Controllers & Storage
Laptops, Notebooks
Monitors & Projectors
Networking
Printers
Printer Supplies & Accessories
Scanners
Software
Technology Books
Vintage Computing Products
Other Hardware & Services

CONSUMER ELECTRONICS
Car Electronics
DVD Players & Recorders
Digital Video Recorders, PVR
   Gadgets & Other Electronics
GPS Devices
Home Audio
Home Theater in a Box
Home Theater Projectors
MP3 Players & Accessories
PDAs/Handheld PCs
Portable Audio
Radios: CB, Ham & Shortwave
Satellite Radio

Satellite, Cable TV
Telephones & Pagers
Televisions
VCRs
Vintage Electronics
Wholesale Lots

CRAFTS
Basketry
Bead Art
Candle & Soap Making
Ceramics, Pottery
Crocheting
Cross Stitch
Decorative, Tole Painting
Drawing
Embroidery
Fabric
Fabric Embellishments
Floral Crafts
Framing & Matting
General Art & Craft Supplies
Glass Art Crafts
Handcrafted Items
Kids Crafts
Knitting
Lacemaking, Tatting
Latch Rug Hooking
Leathercraft
Macramé
Metalworking
Mosaic
Needlepoint
Paper Crafts
Painting
Quilting
Ribbon
Rubber Stamping & Embossing
Scrapbooking
Sewing
Shellcraft
Spinning
Upholstery
Weaving
Woodworking
Yarn
Wall Décor, Tatouage

Other Arts & Crafts
Crafts Wholesale Lots

DOLLS & BEARS
Bear Making Supplies
Bears
Dolls
Dollhouse Miniatures
Paper Dolls
Wholesale Lots

DVDS & MOVIES
DVD, HD DVD & Blu-ray
Film
Laserdisc
UMD
VHS
VHS Non-US (PAL)
Other Formats
Wholesale Lots

EBAY MOTORS
Motorcycles
Parts & Accessories
Passenger Vehicles
Powersports
Other Vehicles

ENTERTAINMENT MEMORABILIA
Autographs-Original
Autographs-Reprints
Movie Memorabilia
Music Memorabilia
Television Memorabilia
Theater Memorabilia
Video Game Memorabilia
Other Memorabilia

GIFT CERTIFICATES

HEALTH & BEAUTY
Bath & Body
Coupons
Dietary Supplements, Nutrition
Fragrances
Hair Care
Hair Removal
Health Care
Makeup
Nail

Massage
Medical, Special Needs
Natural Therapies
Oral Care
Over-the-Counter Medicine
Skin Care
Tanning Beds, Lamps
Tattoos, Body Art
Vision Care
Weight Management
Wholesale Lots
Other Health & Beauty Items

HOME & GARDEN
Bath
Bedding
Building & Hardware
Dining & Bar
Electrical & Solar
Food & Wine
Furniture
Gardening & Plants
Heating, Cooling & Air
Home Décor
Home Security
Kitchen
Lamps, Lighting, Ceiling Fans
Major Appliance
Outdoor Power Equipment
Patio & Grilling
Pet Supplies
Plumbing & Fixtures
Pools & Spas
Rugs & Carpets
Tools
Vacuum Cleaners & Housekeeping
Window Treatments
Wholesale Lots

JEWELRY & WATCHES
Body Jewelry
Bracelets
Charms & Charm Bracelets
Children's Jewelry
Designer Brands
Earrings
Ethnic, Tribal Jewelry
Hair Jewelry

Handcrafted, Artisan Jewelry
Jewelry Boxes & Supplies
Loose Beads
Loose Diamonds & Gemstones
Men's Jewelry
Necklaces & Pendants
Pins, Brooches
Rings
Sets
Vintage, Antique
Watches
Other Items
Wholesale Lots

MUSIC
Accessories
Cassettes
CDs
Digital Music Downloads
DVD Audio
Records
Super Audio CDs
Other Formats
Wholesale Lots

MUSICAL INSTRUMENTS
Brass
DJ Gear & Lighting
Electronic
Equipment
Guitar
Harmonica
Instruction Books, CDs, Videos
Keyboard, Piano
Percussion
Pro Audio
Sheet Music, Song Books
String
Woodwind
Wholesale Lots
Other Instruments

POTTERY & GLASS
Glass
Pottery & China

REAL ESTATE
Commercial
Land

Manufactured Homes
Residential
Timeshares for Sale
Other Real Estate

SPECIALTY SERVICES
Advice & Instruction
Artistic Services
Custom Clothing & Jewelry
eBay Auction Services
Graphic & Logo Design
Media Editing & Duplication
Printing & Personalization
Restoration & Repair
Web & Computer Services
Other Services

SPORTING GOODS
Athletic Apparel
Athletic Footwear
Airsoft
Archery
Baseball & Softball
Basketball
Billiards
Bowling
Boxing
Camping, Hiking, Backpacking
Canoes, Kayaks, Rafts
Climbing
Cycling
Disc Golf
Equestrian
Exercise & Fitness
Fishing
Football
Go-Karts, Recreational
Golf
Gymnastics
Hunting
Ice, Roller Hockey
Ice Skating
Indoor Games
Inline, Roller Skating
Lacrosse
Martial Arts
Paintball
Racquetball & Squash

Running
Scooters
Scuba, Snorkeling
Skateboarding
Skiing & Snowboarding
Snowmobiling
Soccer
Surfing, Wind Surfing
Swimming
Tennis
Triathlon
Wakeboarding, Waterskiing
Other Sports
Wholesale Lots

Sports Mem, Cards & Fan Shop
Autographs-Original
Autographs-Reprints
Cards
Fan Apparel & Souvenirs
Game Used Memorabilia
Manufacturer Authenticated
Vintage Sports Memorabilia
Wholesale Lots

Stamps
United States
Australia
Canada
Br. Comm. Other
UK (Great Britain)
Africa
Asia
Europe
Latin America
Middle East
Publications & Supplies
Topical & Specialty
Worldwide

Tickets
Event Tickets
Experiences
Other Items

Toys & Hobbies
Action Figures

Beanbag Plush, Beanie Babies
Building Toys
Classic Toys
Diecast, Toy Vehicles
Educational
Electronic, Battery, Wind-Up
Fast Food, Cereal Premiums
Games
Model RR, Trains
Models, Kits
Outdoor Toys, Structures
Pretend Play, Preschool
Puzzles
Radio Control
Robots, Monsters, Space Toys
Slot Cars
Stuffed Animals
Toy Soldiers
Trading Card Games
TV, Movie, Character Toys
Vintage, Antique Toys
Wholesale Lots

Travel
Airline
Cruises
Lodging
Luggage
Vacation Packages
Other Travel

Video Games
Accessories
Games
Internet Games
Systems
Vintage Games
Other
Wholesale Lots

Everything Else
Advertising Opportunities
eBay User Tools
Education & Learning
Funeral & Cemetery
Genealogy
Gifts & Occasions
Information Products

Mature Audiences	Religious Products & Supplies
Memberships	Reward Pts, Incentive Progs
Metaphysical	Test Auctions
Mystery Auctions	Weird Stuff
Personal Security	Other

The Sell Button

Since you're here to make a fortune, the Sell button is your doorway to opportunity. Click this button for a direct path to the Sell Your Item forms, where you'll enter information to list the items you'll be putting up on the auction block. Figure 3.4 shows the initial page from where you'll launch into actually crafting your listing, with numerous other pages to follow, all of which will be covered fully in Chapter 7.

> **eBay TIP:** Don't be alarmed if eBay asks you to sign in before granting you access to the Sell Your Item pages. After all, sellers are required to have an account in good standing before an item can be listed. If you didn't previously sign in to eBay before clicking the Sell button, eBay requires you to do so at this point.

My eBay Is Your eBay

If you've surfed many Web sites of late, you're probably familiar with the "my site" feature, a method that allows regular users to assemble a personal portfolio of their favorite site features, settings, and what have you. The intention of "my site" is to provide each user with a self-configured, self-maintained personal version of the site. This feature makes viewing your favorite spots on the site faster and more straightforward, allowing you to avoid traversing the multiple standard pages upon each visit.

eBay's version (see Figure 3.5) is called My eBay. Here is where you monitor your various activities at the site in a convenient, one-stop page. My eBay helps you easily watch your recent buying and selling activity, set up favorite search criteria to be easily reentered, monitor your account status, follow your feedback rating (tracking comments about you entered by other users), and more. When it comes time to pay for items you've won, collect

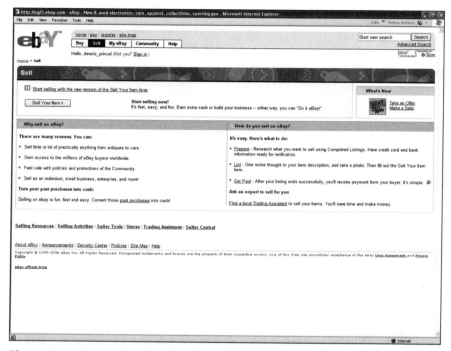

Figure 3.4   The Sell toolbar button starts your selling adventure.

payment for and ship items you've sold, or keep up on feedback given or received, the My eBay page is the control tower from which you can best manage your eBay experience.

The Community Button

Founder Pierre Omidyar envisioned that the underlying success of eBay would be its community of users. Beyond that, he also recognized the opportunity not only to offer a way for users to interact with and help one another but for the site itself to reach out in the spirit of philanthropy by providing assistance to charitable organizations. If you're curious to learn about the various opportunities in the eBay community—both within and outside of the site—set aside some time to explore the different community links you'll find on the eBay Community page (see Figure 3.6).

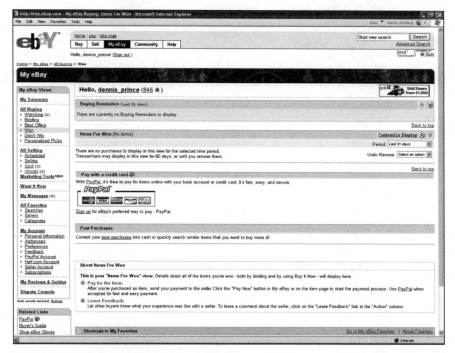

Figure 3.5 There are a number of eBay services at your fingertips when you click on the My eBay toolbar button.

The Help Button

One of the biggest investments eBay has been undertaking is the addition of more useful on-site instruction pages. Click on the Help button and you'll navigate to a vastly improved page (as shown in Figure 3.7), offering active links to eBay pages that will provide an explanation answering any site usage questions you might have. If you can't seem to find the right link, just enter some keywords in the appropriate field to search for links where you'll find answers to your most pressing questions.

WHAT ABOUT THE OTHER TOOLBAR SELECTIONS?

Yes, there are still a few more toolbar selections to consider. For starters, skip past the Home link; it does just what it indicates and returns you to the home page. Then, the Register link is for just that—to register to use eBay if you're

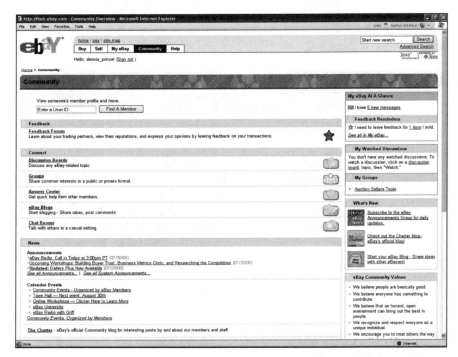

Figure 3.6 The Community button leads you to the site's veritable Welcome Wagon, where you can learn about and interact with the legions of eBay enthusiasts as well as discover how eBay is working to provide assistance to people in need outside of the site.

new to the site (a topic I'll cover fully in Chapter 4) The two remaining links, though, are more intriguing and require further discussion.

The Straightaway to Pay

When you click on the Pay text link, you'll jump immediately to that section of the My eBay page where you'll see what auctions you may have recently won and the payment status of each (see Figure 3.8). If you're an avid bidder—and a frequent winner—clicking the Pay link within the Main Toolbar will allow to you to leap ahead and begin settling your debts. Again, this is where the Main Toolbar is most effective and efficient for your use—allowing you access to the most relevant areas of the site as you manage your bidding (and selling) activity. Time is money, so why waste it meandering through an extended trail of links?

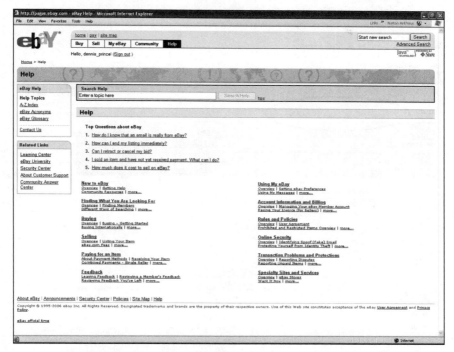

Figure 3.7 The Help button provides a screen that gives you easy access to information, directly or via keyword search.

What a Site to See

The other link to discuss is Site Map. As it implies, this is the link that transports you to the massive eBay site map and allows you to survey the virtual geography of the site from an aerial perspective. Click on the Site Map link and see all that eBay encompasses. Look at Figure 3.9 for a small sample of the entire map.

This is probably the easiest page to navigate if you're looking for a quick link to functional or informational eBay pages. Whether you want tips on buying, need to review policies about selling at the site, want to stay abreast of latest site news and announcements, or are curious about joining the various eBay forum discussions, the site map is the best launching pad to quickly get anywhere and everywhere at eBay.

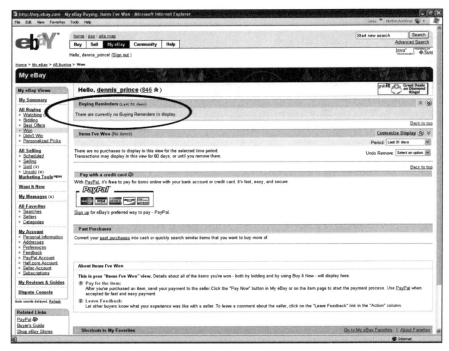

Figure 3.8 The Pay button immediately transports you to the My eBay area, where you can review and pay for the auction items you've won.

> **eBay TIP:** Sometimes, I turn to the site map when I'm managing the items I have up for sale. For example, should I need to end an auction early, the site map is the best place to connect to that otherwise elusive link. You'll likely discover some site functions that are difficult to find—perhaps intentionally—yet the site map will typically get you where you need to go, fast.

EXACTLY WHAT IS eBAY EXPRESS?

One of the newer developments at eBay is the unveiling of eBay Express. Simply put, it's a new sort of distillation of goods, all brand new and all made available for immediate purchase (no bidding, just Buy-It-Now offerings),

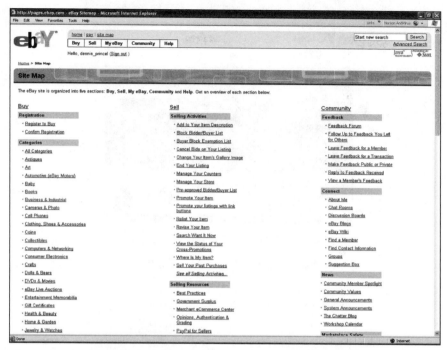

Figure 3.9   If you want a bird's-eye view of this massive site, the Site Map button allows you to see all and find all that makes up the eBay marketplace.

that can be bought in a single shopping experience regardless of the number of sellers actually involved.

Let's say you're shopping to upgrade your eBay office and you need a new PC monitor, a telephone headset, and a wastebasket. At eBay Express, you can push your virtual shopping cart through the online aisles, selectively choosing from items offered by eBay's millions of sellers, arriving at a final checkout point, where you can complete your shopping with a single consolidated purchase—regardless of how many different sellers you actually purchased from. The sellers will be notified to ship the different goods to your specified address, and you're done. This new approach to buying was built with shopper's convenience in mind and doesn't employ any of the traditional auction methods; just find it, buy it, and enjoy it. (See Figure 3.10.)

Perhaps you didn't think it possible, but you've just completed an introductory tour of eBay in less than 30 minutes. By understanding the most impor-

Figure 3.10 The eBay Express feature offers a fast and convenient way for buyers to purchase multiple items from multiple sellers, all with a single checkout transaction.

tant features of the eBay home page up front, you can begin your buying and selling activities quickly and confidently without becoming overwhelmed by everything else the site offers. As you continue through this book, the details will be clarified and the skills and methods will be sharpened to develop your expertise. For now, either take a break and spend a bit of time exploring more of what I've shown to you, or move on to the next chapter and find out what's critical for getting registered and getting ready to harness the site.

4

Getting Registered, Getting Ready, and Getting Yourself Known

Before you can begin bidding or selling at eBay, you'll need to register. Sure, you're free to visit the site and browse the various items up for bid or sale without ever signing in or signing up. Soon, though, you are likely to find something you simply must have. Or, better still, you will discover that you, too, have items that are as good as if not better than those you see other bidders clamoring over. When this happens, you'll be getting registered quickly.

The good news is that registering for an eBay account is fast, simple, and safe—and it's necessary if you want to do business in the online auction marketplace. Once registered, you're free to browse, bid, buy, and—most important—determine how you'll use eBay to boost your personal earnings. Some folks prefer to browse awhile and get more acclimated, while others immediately leap in to buy, buy, buy. Whether you want to shop or you're itching to sell, registration comes first and is key to your learning how the site works and how you can make it work for you. In this chapter, you'll learn the steps to get registered, the methods to ensure some safety and security in your account, and even how to introduce yourself to the rest of the community. In just a few steps, you'll see how easy it is to get started on the right foot.

eBAY REGISTRATION MADE EASY

Starting at eBay's home page, look for the Register text links, found within the trusty Main Toolbar (see Figure 4.1). Click a Register text link to jump to the initial registration screen, pictured in Figure 4.2. In the first part of this registration screen, enter your name, address, phone number, and e-mail address. This information will be stored by eBay and could be provided to other users to help contact you. Don't worry, eBay isn't in the practice of loosely distributing this information, but in an effort to promote and enable safe trading and sort out any issues related to transactions, it does make the information available upon legitimate request.

eBay TIP: The valid e-mail address you provide here is critical in completing the registration process, as eBay will send a confirmation message to that address, providing information you'll need for the final step in registering.

Next, continue on to establish your user ID (click the Check Availability of User ID button to see if your choice is already in use) and establish your account password. Follow this with selecting a secret question and answer—in case you ever forget your password—and specifying your date of birth. Yes, you must be 18 years or older to acquire an eBay account.

eBay TIP: Although you may not have been aware of this, when you registered to use eBay, you simultaneously activated an account at the eBay-owned Half.com. The registration process automatically qualifies you to operate at both the well-loved auction venue and the fixed-price site. You'll learn more about Half.com later in this book.

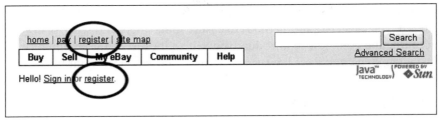

Figure 4.1   The link to registration can be found on the eBay home page Main Toolbar.

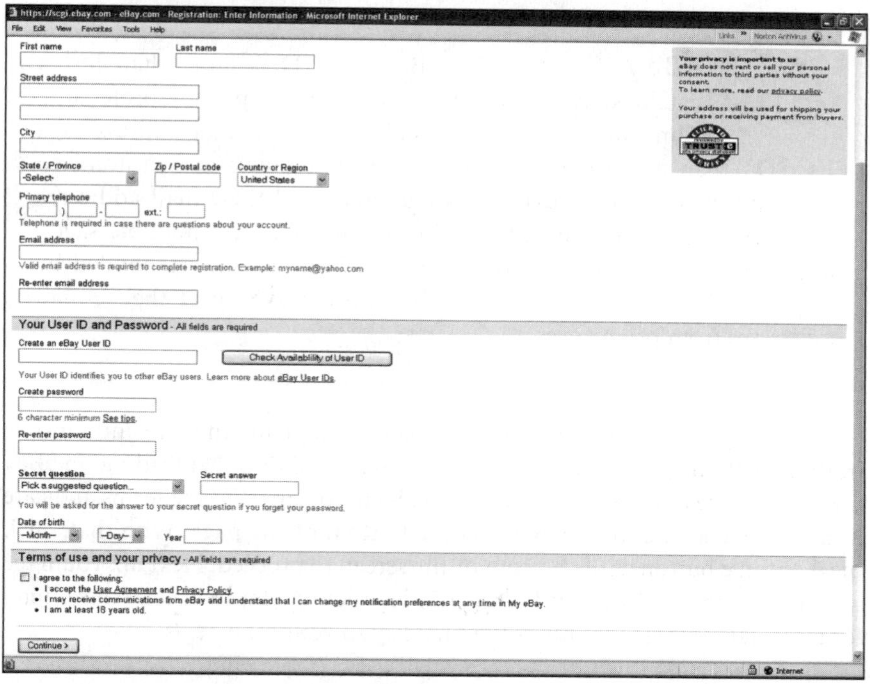

Figure 4.2 Begin the registration process by providing your personal information and determining your user ID.

Last, you'll see the checkbox near the bottom of the registration screen, where you'll indicate that you've read and accepted eBay's User Agreement and Privacy Policy. Although many people will disregard this as the trivial fine print, I advise you to read these agreements carefully so you understand the terms under which you'll be expected to operate and to what degree eBay will bear any responsibility for your encounters.

While there's nothing in the policies that will unjustly ensnare you, understand that eBay stands by its assertion that it is a *venue only* and cannot be held liable for your actions or the actions of others on the site. For many years, this has been a bone of contention among many users who assert that eBay should bear some of the burden for deals that have gone significantly awry. Nevertheless, the text you'll read here is the latest legalese that extricates the venue from liability.

> **eBay TIP:** Your eBay user ID is more than just a catchy screen name; it's also a form of privacy protection.
>
> Time was that eBay would use your e-mail address as a userID—then along came the *harvesters,* individuals and customized *bots* (automated programs) that would collect all the e-mail addresses they could find, using them for addressing unsolicited e-mail messages, annoying sales pitches, and other forms of spam. eBay responded by implementing the user ID, which allows users to protect their e-mail addresses from prying eyes.

Again, nothing here is dangerous, and by applying the safe and sensible trading methods presented later in this book, you'll find that trading on eBay is perfectly safe and appropriately secure. So if you agree to the terms, indicate as much by clicking the checkbox at the bottom of the page. With that, click the Continue button at the bottom of the screen to proceed. Next up, you'll see another screen (as shown in Figure 4.3) instructing you to check your e-mail for a special message that holds the final key to your eBay registration.

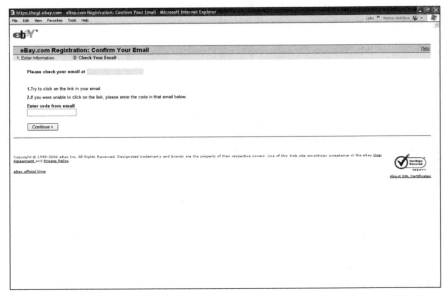

Figure 4.3 The second step in eBay registration is to check your e-mail for a registration key, as prompted by this screen.

The e-mail message you'll receive (as pictured in Figure 4.4) provides an active link, labeled "Activate Your eBay Membership," confirming successful communication to the e-mail address you've provided. Click on the link, and you'll be taken to the eBay site, where you'll be greeted by the screen pictured in Figure 4.5. Armed with your active user ID, you're ready to set out on your quest for great finds and even greater fortunes at eBay. By the way, you might have also seen the pop-up window, also pictured in Figure 4.5, where eBay is curious to learn a bit more about you. Answer only if you want to; this information isn't required to proceed into the site. For the moment, though, congratulations; you're a bona fide eBay community member—it's that easy!

GETTING ACCLIMATED TO THE MARKETPLACE

Before you jump headlong into the fray, I suggest that you take a bit of time to survey the site, sample the wares, and look at what the other buyers and

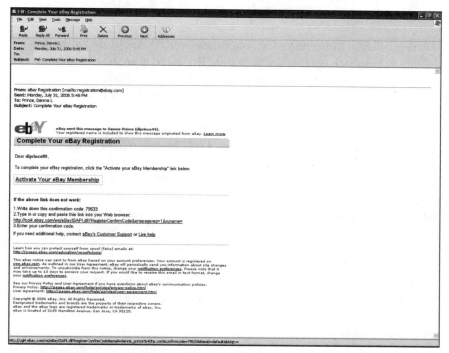

Figure 4.4   The e-mail message you receive from eBay will provide you with an active link and a secret code to complete your registration.

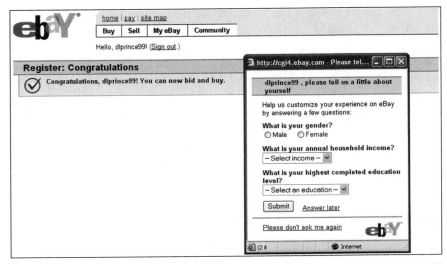

Figure 4.5   Click on the active link you'll find in the eBay confirmation e-mail to complete your registration.

sellers are doing. Many new users, once their user ID is activated, dive into the listings and embark on a veritable feeding frenzy; they are lured to bid on and buy so many items they never knew were available. Unfortunately, their excitement and ambition are often met with a hefty bill to be paid when all is said and done.

When the dust settles, many first-time bidders and buyers discover they've paid too much for an item or have purchased an item of lesser quality than they would have wished, only to see a better example become available shortly thereafter. The excitement is understandable, but at this early stage of eBay use, try to temper your enthusiasm with a sage bit of knowledge: the items you see on eBay tend to pop up time and time again. Even the rarest of pieces generally show up multiple times—maybe within a week, a month, or a year's time, but rarely if ever does a piece surface only once.

Armed with that insight, take time to shop, compare the wares, compare the prices, compare the sellers' sales policies, and get a feel for how the whole business works. If you see an item that truly commands your bid, move ahead to Chapter 5, where you'll learn the best methods for finding and bidding on the items you'll encounter.

SETTING UP YOUR SELLER'S ACCOUNT

Presuming you're here to sell, now is the time to establish your seller's account. Upon your return to the eBay home page and after signing in with your new user ID and password, you'll see within the area labeled "My eBay at a Glance" (see Figure 4.6) a text link to update your account information; click it. The next page you'll see will be the Personal Information section of the My eBay page (see Figure 4.7). Note the part that is circled; this is where you can access the Financial Information relevant to your account.

When you're ready to begin selling at eBay, you'll need to provide full details regarding a valid checking account as well as a credit card account. Why? The fact is, these two items serve as proof-positive identification of you and every other seller actively trading at eBay. To stem fraud that would be committed under alias accounts, every eBay seller is required to provide this level of proof to ensure contact can be made if the need were ever to arise. The playing field is level—in regard to personal information—since all sellers have had to provide these details in order to list, sell, and collect through eBay transactions.

Click on the Edit text link within the Checking Account area to begin establishing your Seller's Account. The screen shown in Figure 4.8 is where you'll find the Create Seller's Account button; click it to get started.

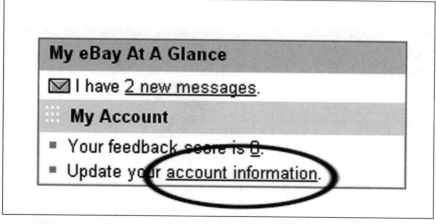

Figure 4.6   Click the Account Information text link from the home page to proceed with completing your eBay account.

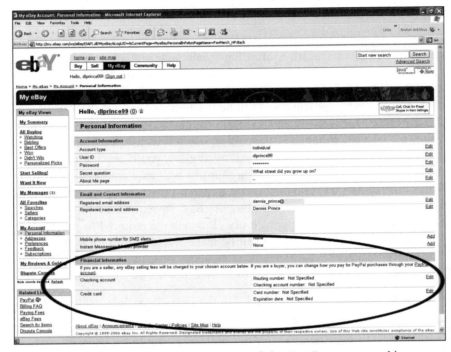

Figure 4.7   The Personal Information area of the My eBay page provides access to financial information necessary for creating a Seller's Account.

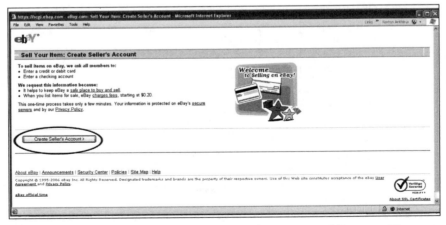

Figure 4.8   Click the Create Seller's Account button to enable your selling ventures at eBay.

> **eBay TIP:** Now is the time that you can infuse added security into the registration process. Before offering your checking account information, ask your financial institution how they protect you from identity theft and misuse of your account. Consider creating a checking account solely for use with your eBay activity, maintaining a reasonably low balance as an added precaution.
>
> When it comes to offering credit card information, ask the card issuer what protections are provided in case of malfeasance. Also, consider establishing a credit card account solely for use in conjunction with your eBay activity and request that a low credit limit be established, not to exceed $3,000.
>
> In general, seek out the sort of protection that provides for assisted dispute of charges and blocking of account activity, both of which are necessary if you ever believe your information has been compromised. These are simple steps you can take to provide an added layer of security on top of eBay's secure data protections.

Your first step in creating your Seller's Account is to provide a credit or debit card to keep on file in your active account. Figure 4.9 shows a sample screen where you'll enter the appropriate information. When complete, click the Continue button.

Next, you'll see a screen like that shown in Figure 4.10, where you'll enter your checking account information. When the information is complete, click the Continue button.

> **eBay TIP:** All of the information you'll enter in this form is protected by the SSL (Secure Sockets Layer) protocol, a secure method whereby sensitive information is transmitted in encrypted format, being unreadable unless a specific *decrypting* key is available. Practically all online transfers of this sort of data are handled via SSL transmission.

Now that eBay has validated your credit card and checking account information, you select which account you'd like to use for paying the fees you'll incur when selling at the site (see Figure 4.11).

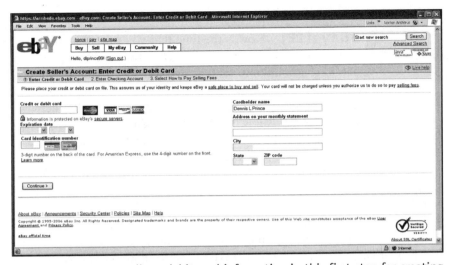

Figure 4.9   Enter credit or debit card information in this first step for creating a Seller's Account.

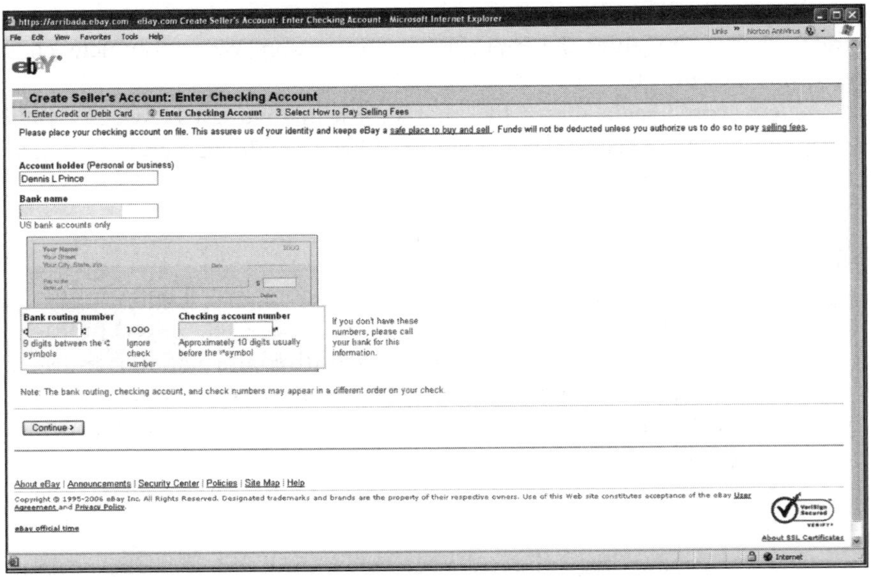

Figure 4.10   Enter checking account information in this second step for creating a Seller's Account.

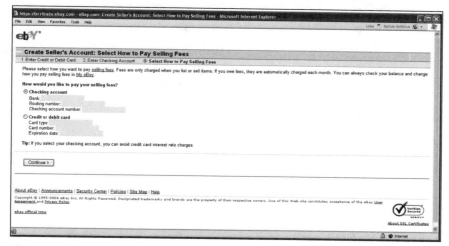

Figure 4.11   Last, select how you would like to pay your eBay fees.

Whenever you list an item for sale, a fee will be assessed. When you select special selling features, additional fees may be assessed. When you sell an item, a sales commission (known as the *final value fee*) will be assessed (incidentally, all of these fees will be discussed in detail in Chapter 7). The fees aren't exorbitant by any means, but you will be charged to list and sell your items in this worldwide marketplace. At the end of each month, you'll need to pay your outstanding balance for the month's accumulated fees, and this last part of the seller's account form is where you indicate whether you wish eBay to automatically deduct the fees from your checking account or if you'd prefer to have your credit card charged instead.

Make your selection and click the Continue button once again.

eBay TIP: How you choose to manage payment is really up to you, but remember that if you accumulate fees on your credit card and fail to pay off that credit card balance at the end of the billing cycle, your card issuer will charge interest on your unpaid balance. In respect to making your fortune, you'll want to be sure the assessment of interest charges doesn't unnecessarily increase your cost of using eBay, thereby reducing your ultimate profit.

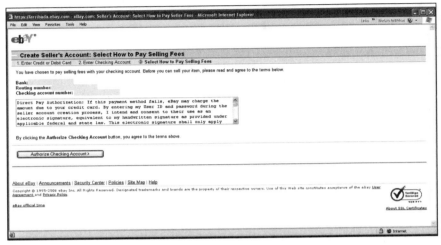

Figure 4.12 Review and accept the Direct Pay Authorization stipulations to complete your Seller's Account creation.

You're almost finished creating your Seller's Account. In the screen depicted in Figure 4.12, you simply agree to allow eBay to access the account you specified for collection of regular site usage fees. After you've read and agree with the Direct Pay Authorization stipulations, click the authorization button at the bottom of the screen. When you do this, you'll be taken immediately to a new screen, where you can immediately begin listing your first item for bid or sale (see Figure 4.13). Overall, it's a quick process and quite secure (made even more so if you apply the security tips I mentioned earlier in this chapter). Congratulations, you're an eBay seller.

ABOUT ME IS ALL ABOUT YOU

Your setup steps are nearly complete. At this point, you have a valid user ID and you've established your seller's account, so what could be left to do? Though it's not a requirement, consider creating an on-site home page of your own where other users can learn more about you as they prepare to buy from the newest seller to set up shop—*you*.

To make this easy, eBay offers a simple-to-use personal page creation tool called About Me. About Me is an opportunity for you to tell other com-

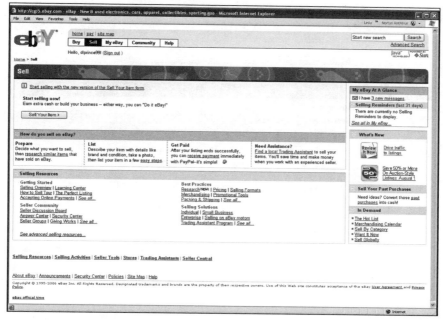

Figure 4.13 Immediately, you're ready to sell. Great work!

munity members about you, your likes, dislikes, and so on. As part of furthering the concept of online community, the About Me page is where you can provide that personal touch and give others a feeling of whom they're dealing with (a definite bonus if you're a seller eager to instill confidence and ease in the minds of your potential customers).

Don't feel you have to create the ultimate About Me page immediately. For starters, you can simply enter some basic information just to lay the foundation. Upon more thought, you can go back and edit your page as you like. To begin creating your About Me page, visit My eBay again and find the About Me section in the Personal Information area (see Figure 4.14); click on the Edit text link.

Clicking the link will take you to a preliminary page explaining the feature. On that page, find and click the "Create and edit your page" button. Figure 4.15 shows the initial page where you'll choose the method by which you'll craft your page—using eBay's simple step-by-step process or through the use

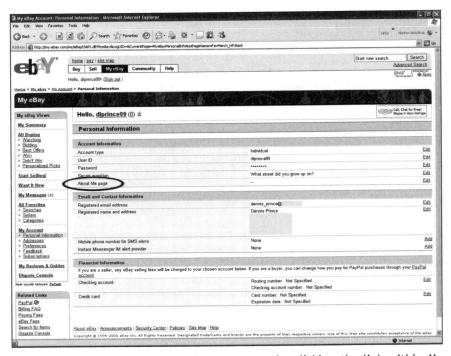

Figure 4.14 Create your own About Me page by clicking the link within My eBay.

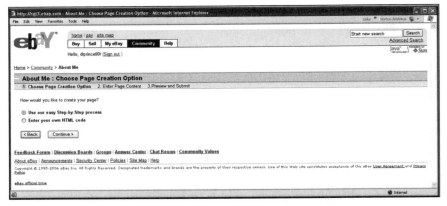

Figure 4.15 Select the method you'd like to use to create your About Me page.

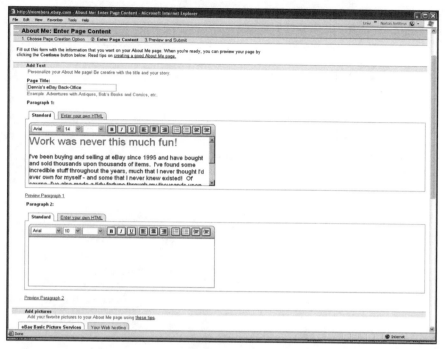

Figure 4.16 Use the step-by-step form to enter text and images for your About Me page.

of some HTML coding of your own (for this example I'll show you the simplicity of the step-by-step option).

Click the Continue button to begin creating your page. Figure 4.16 shows the template in which you can enter your page title, paragraph of information, images, and more. Get as creative as you like and when you're ready click on the Preview & Submit button.

Review the preview layout of your page, as shown in Figure 4.17. Make adjustments as you see fit. When you are satisfied, click the Submit button at the bottom of the screen. (Figure 4.18 shows the outcome of my quick creation.) Again, at this early stage of your eBay experience, a simple page will suffice. Later in this book you'll learn additional ways to utilize your About Me page to maximize your sales.

And now you're a member in good standing at the Net's largest online trading post. Along the way, you likely saw several links that would lead you to different areas of the eBay site or likewise directed you to pages that con-

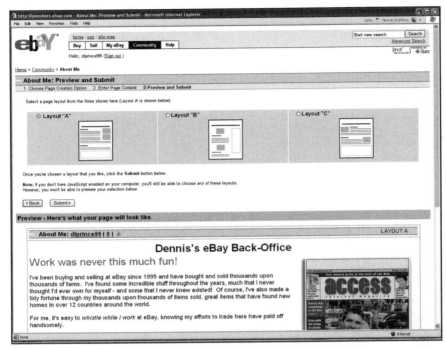

Figure 4.17   Preview your About Me page before you publish it within the eBay community.

tained more information. Feel free to explore those links at your leisure, remembering that the site map can always lead you to the same destinations whenever you choose. But if your goal is to start selling, what's been covered here has established your eBay presence and you can now move forward quickly.

Figure 4.18   A simple About Me page like this can be created in just a few minutes.

5

Find It, Bid It, Win It

Now that you have an active user ID, it's time to begin sifting through the millions of items for sale and up for auction. Recognize that finding great buys on eBay isn't accidental (especially since your goal is to master all the site has to offer). As you begin your journey up and down the virtual aisles, make use of some expert searching methods and approaches that will help you find exactly what you want and uncover some hidden treasures that may have gone unnoticed.

Once you've found a great item (or two or more!), employ additional research methods to ensure you'll be placing your bid with complete confidence, certain that your decision is the most sound and likely to yield the best result (both in terms of quality and price). As you bid and buy, be sure to employ the best bidding strategies around to increase your chances of winning while still paying the best possible price. This is the sort of information you'll find in this chapter—key methods and strategies that will help you quickly become an expert bidder, often enabling you to grab some great bargains for yourself and possibly pave the way for a fast and profitable sale of your own. Read on.

BROWSING THE CATEGORIES

Since it hosts millions of items every day, eBay survives by organizing everything for sale or bid in a logical and intuitive manner. You've already seen how eBay utilizes main categories and subcategories to collate the myriad goods being offered by the legions of sellers. But if you worry that finding a specific item on the site is woefully akin to finding the proverbial needle in a haystack, rest assured the task can be as simple as finding a number in the Yellow Pages (or even simpler). Searching through the categories is a useful activity if you're inclined to simply browse a particular type of item. In fact, browsing rarely goes unrewarded: you're likely to stumble across something you weren't aware would be of interest to you or that you had completely forgotten about but, now that your memory's been jarred, cannot live without.

> **eBay TIP:** I try to make time to browse the categories for two reasons: I, too, stumble across items I had forgotten about and am glad to find them, but more important, as a collector I often find items I was previously unaware existed and which serve as valuable information about my areas of expertise. I recommend that category browsing be added to your regular online regimen.

Browsing the categories is also a useful way to find misplaced gems. Since sellers choose the category under which their items will be listed, it's not uncommon to find items that seem out of place. Of course, to browse the entire site for such mislaid treasures would be an overwhelming task, but it's a useful exercise to do for those who wish to specialize in certain types of goods (a topic to be explored more deeply when the strategies of selling are discussed in Part II of this book). When you understand the sorts of goods that are well suited to a category, you'll understand how to best categorize your own goods for sale as well as be able to effectively spot an out-of-place bargain.

SEARCHES MADE SIMPLE

When you're ready to look for a specific item, eBay has numerous search tools available to help you in your quest. Some of the essentially same tools are found at various places within eBay as a convenience. Other search tools are highly customizable to help you narrow your focus and home in on *exactly* what you're looking for. Expect to make regular use of each tool to help you slice and dice the millions of listings to find just what you want.

10 REASONS TO BUY BEFORE YOU SELL

1. To gain familiarity with eBay functions and features
2. To understand market trends, bidding tendencies, and potential prices
3. To recognize different sales strategies in use
4. To learn how postauction payments work
5. To recognize shipping costs and lead times
6. To learn how to interact effectively with others
7. To determine which seller policies seem to be best
8. To uncover potential sources of goods for resale
9. To identify elements of exceptional customer service
10. To build a reputable feedback rating before selling

THE MAIN SEARCH

The first way to search is quite basic and always at hand. Return to the eBay home page and recall the search field in the Main Toolbar (see Figure 5.1). This search field allows you to type in specific words that will be compared to item titles, returning a list of matches for you to further explore.

When search results are returned—that is, the listing of items that match your query—you'll find this same search field will be available at the top right-hand header of subsequent screens, so you can easily and immediately launch another query for goods.

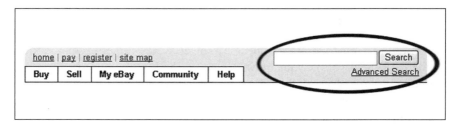

Figure 5.1 The quickest and most basic search tool is found right on eBay's home page in the familiar Main Toolbar.

Just as handy as the main search are the Search Options that are displayed along the left-hand column of a search result listing (see Figure 5.2). The Search Options allow you to immediately refine your current search terms by enabling you to specify particular attributes of the matching items—

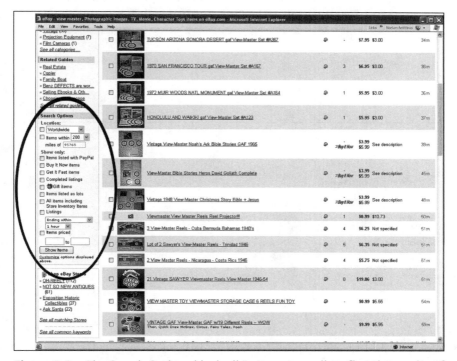

Figure 5.2   The Search Options block allows you to easily refine the results of any active search.

perhaps you only want to see items where the seller accepts PayPal payments or maybe you're only interested in items with Buy-It-Now terms. The list of easy-to-apply options (they're search result *filters,* really) allows you to home in on precisely what you're looking for without having to rekey your search terms.

With a search result list in front of you, simply click on one or more of the search option checkboxes, then click the Show Items button to apply your selections. Beyond this, you can even customize the selections that appear in the Search Options box by clicking the Customize text link at the bottom of the box. From there, you can select which options you want to have fast access to whenever you're signed in to eBay (see Figure 5.3). It's very much *Your eBay,* isn't it?

---

 eBay TIP: Incidentally, the refinements offered in the Search Options box can also be applied in the Advanced Search screen, to be discussed in detail later in this chapter.

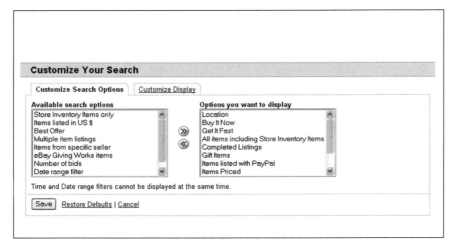

Figure 5.3   Customize the Search Options selections using this customization table.

The Refined Search

Notice that beneath each of the basic search tools there is a subtle colink that reads "Smart Search," "Refine Search," or "Advanced Search." These links, as well as the more prevalent Search button on the main toolbar all lead to the same place: eBay's search screen.

The Advanced Search

In the eBay main search window, recall the text link labeled "Advanced Search"; click on the link and you'll navigate to eBay's dedicated search screen (see Figure 5.4); this is your window to more narrowly defined search criteria. Here, you can precisely define how your search keywords will be used by specifying which additional words to exclude (to restrict close but unwanted title matches), which specific categories to search, which geo-

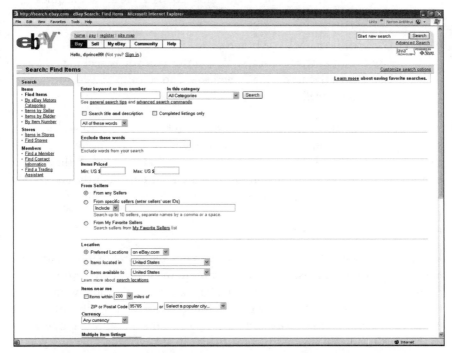

Figure 5.4 The Advanced Search text link navigates you to the search screen, where you can specify, narrow, and filter results to more precisely mine eBay's listings.

graphic locations to consider, and what price range is of interest to you. Additionally, you can sort the results of your search. With the objective of zeroing in on a certain item or type of item, these additional search filters, many of which were also available to you via the Search Options block, help you perform more efficient searches and avoid needlessly wading through "close but no cigar" results.

The Keys Are in the Keywords

Now, perhaps more important than the sorts of filters you may apply to your search results, understand the importance of the keywords you specify when you perform an item search. Keywords are just that: *keys* to unlocking the vault of treasures within eBay. They help you uncover exactly what it is you want so you don't have to laboriously sift through thousands of category pages. Your success here comes from knowing the best keywords to use in searching for items, which you can learn to do by observing how sellers seem to be crafting their item descriptions for these goods. Here are some quick tips for utilizing keywords in your searches:

- Use specific names and brands.
- Use common terms associated with the item you're seeking.
- Use associative terms (i.e., *genre, era,* and so on).
- Use proper spelling.

As you sort through the listings that match your keyword search, take special note of any additional terms that seem to be commonly used with these goods and consider including those (or excluding them if they're not *exactly* what you're looking for) in future searches. Remember the commonly used words later when you are selling your own goods.

Harnessing Search Commands

Besides utilizing good keywords in your searches, recognize that there are several character commands you can incorporate to further refine your search results (it's true). This is an aspect of eBay searching that many new users overlook but which savvy shoppers have found can have a significant impact on search results. *Search commands* allow you to apply additional operators to the way in which eBay interprets your specified keywords, enabling you to wrest exact items from the listings or uncover hidden treasures. Table 5.1 provides the search commands you can apply to your keywords to help you become an expert eBay miner.

Table 5.1   eBay Keyword Search Commands

Search Command	Example	Result
Space (keyboard space)	lunch box	Returns listings whose title includes the separate words "lunch" and "box" (as opposed to "lunchbox," which could be used as an alternate form of this search).
Quotation Marks (" ")	"my mother the car"	Returns listings whose title includes words in a specific order as opposed to listings that may contain one or more of the individual keywords specified.
Minus sign (-)	harry potter -movie	Returns listings that include the keywords specified but *excludes* those that also include the additional word filtered out by the immediately preceding minus sign (the example would not return any Harry Potter listings whose title also included the word "movie").
Minus sign with parentheses -( )	harry potter -(movie, toy)	Allows you to specify multiple words to exclude when filtering search results. The minus sign immediately precedes the open paren and the multiple words to be excluded are separated by a comma with no embedded spaces.

Parentheses ( )	coffee (cup,mug)	Returns listings where one or the other of the keywords within the parentheses is present in the title. The example would return listings including "coffee" and "cup" as well as listings including "coffee" and "mug."
Asterisk (*)	sac* kings	Returns listings that contain the sequence of letters prior to the asterisk and anything else that might follow them (as in "Sac Kings," "Sacto Kings," or "Sacramento Kings")

> **eBay TIP:** Beware expanding search terms. Often when you search by a particular keyword, you will get results that don't even contain a word you specified. Why is this? eBay has implemented what it terms *Keyword Search Category Expansions.* In plain English, this means that eBay will provide listings of other items in a particular product category that contain some listings matching your keyword query. For example, if you search for "action figure," eBay will return all listings from the item category Toys & Hobbies > Action Figures even if the item titles don't contain the keywords "action figures." In eBay's thinking, this is a method to deliver listings that match the *intent* of your search. In my thinking, this is a common practice called *cross-selling,* and it often forces buyers to fend off items they don't actually want.

Searching by Seller, Bidder, and within Stores

Look back to Figure 5.4 to see some additional search options available to you from within eBay's search window. Located in the left-hand box labeled simply "Search," you'll find text links that allow you different ways to uncover items beyond searching by item title keywords. Notice the text link Items by Seller; clicking this link will provide a new window of search conditions, as shown in Figure 5.5. Searching by seller is the quickest way to see what your favorite seller is selling.

When you find a seller who seems to offer the sorts of items that most interest you, this is the easy way to keep up with what the person is offering. A look at past auctions from the seller (check the Included completed listings checkbox) also provides an indication of the volume of sales the seller has been managing, the prices the seller has been getting for goods, and how many of the seller's auctions have been successful.

As Figure 5.5 shows, it's easy to enter the seller's ID, select whether completed items (closed auctions) should be queried, and indicate how the results should be sorted. Another savvy search technique is to search by bidder, achieved by clicking the Items by Bidder text link. When you do this, you'll navigate to a screen similar to that shown in Figure 5.6.

Figure 5.5   Search by seller to find only those goods offered by a single user.

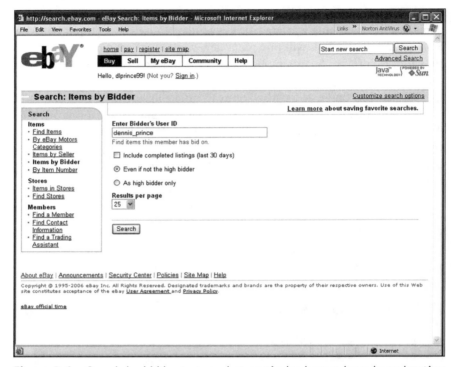

Figure 5.6   Search by bidder to see what particular buyers have been hunting down and bidding on.

Why search by a bidder's ID? Sometimes you'll encounter other bidders who seem to bid on the same items as you. Aren't you curious about the other items they may also be bidding on or have recently won? (Check the Include completed listings checkbox to do so). More to the point, this is a useful way to monitor the bidding practices of particular bidders who seem to have a penchant for consistently outbidding you on items you're hopeful to win (more about a bidding strategy to thwart this later). And perhaps *you're* selling and you're curious what your high bidder is currently vying for within the auction space; with this method, you can quickly and easily find out.

Finally, the last text link worth noting is that labeled Items in Stores (see Figure 5.7). This search screen provides a way to restrict your search results to those items listed for fixed-price sale in eBay. eBay Stores, recall, are direct-sale outlets where sellers can offer items for immediate sale, at a designated price, outside of the usual auction method. No bidding. No waiting. Just find it, buy it, pay for it, and you're done.

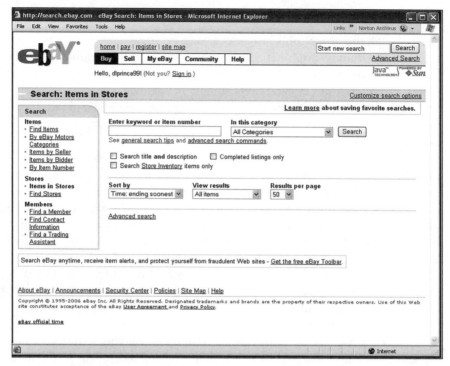

Figure 5.7 Searching by Items in Stores allows you another way to filter to only fixed-price sale items.

Notice how the search fields for eBay Stores behave in a way that is similar to those of the Find Items search options. Naturally, the search results for this smaller division of eBay will be far fewer than if you searched the entire site for both fixed-price and auction items.

eBay TIP: It's often revealing to perform a bidder search using a seller's ID. To get a better feel for whom you're dealing with and what sorts of items these folks are buying as well as selling, take a look at their activity on both sides of the virtual sales counter.

Rooting Out the Hidden Treasures

Even with all the search tools just described, great items can still slip between the cracks. Although you've tried mightily to extract all the goods possible using the various tools, some will still elude you (and other shoppers) and, if found, can often result in great finds at great prices. You can become a bona fide treasure hunter by turning over the virtual stones on the site to find those items that have been mislabeled or misfiled, and, if you're not diligent, will be incredible deals on which you'll miss out.

To begin the treasure hunt, review the results of your usual searches carefully. Identify the categories where these items seem to be referenced and take a bit of time to search through a large number of listings in that category to determine whether there any other terms you've yet to consider. Look to see what other goods appear in the category of listings and whether they're the sorts of things you're seeking and have been titled or described in a way you hadn't considered or expected. More important to the treasure hunt, this is also how you'll determine whether there are any common misspellings used in association with these items (as in "Beanie" versus "Beenie" versus "Beany"), which you'll likewise want to make note of in order to ferret out the mistitled, and thereby passed-over, treasures.

Also, keep an eye open for completed auctions (in your various searching and browsing activities) where the item perhaps didn't sell. If the item never received a bid and essentially slipped by you during its run, it's still possible to query the seller about the item to see if a sale is still possible. Oftentimes, sellers will elect to relist their item and give it another go—yet many are highly motivated to make the quick sale upon receiving your inquiry.

Save Time by Saving Searches

You may have noticed that each search results page has a text link labeled Add to Favorite Searches, located at the upper right-hand corner of a search result screen. Upon clicking the link, you'll capture the search criteria in your My eBay settings under the My Favorite Searches heading (see Figure 5.8), and your searches will be much more efficient.

Rather than try to recall what you've been searching for, the searches you save are readily available for another query just by clicking the Search Now link in the My eBay screen. Better yet is the checkbox labeled "Sign up for Emails" where, when enabled, an e-mail message will be sent to you whenever a new item is listed at eBay that fits your search criteria. Essentially, eBay is now doing the searching for you.

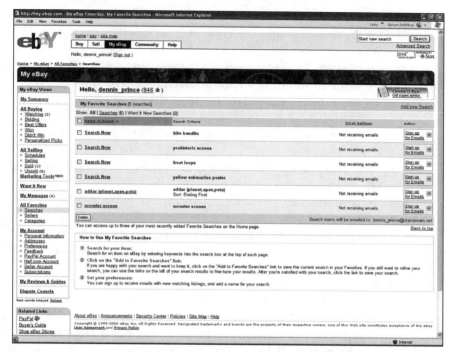

Figure 5.8 Save your searches for easy reuse in the My eBay Favorite Searches area.

THE ABCs OF BIDDING

Sometimes bidding at eBay is as much about gamesmanship as it is about commerce. There are several auction formats in use at eBay, and there are certain tactics and strategies in each format that will yield the best results. Before you can become an expert seller, striving to make your fortune, you'll need to become an expert bidder, understanding the methods used to win auctions and applying that knowledge to your eventual sales strategy. Moreover, there are some great items available on eBay that perhaps you'd simply like to own for yourself. The following section shows you how to approach the exciting world of eBay bidding.

Things to Do before Bidding

We've all been counseled to comparison shop before buying anything, and the same advice is just as applicable—perhaps doubly so—at eBay. Unlike the brick-and-mortar world of commerce where you can hold the item, stroke the finish, or kick the tires, the wares at eBay exist in the ether (during the bidding process, at least), requiring that you take some extra measures to ensure that you won't get cheated. To guarantee that what you bid on is what you really want and is coming to you from a reliable source, you'll need to do a bit of homework up front. *Before* you bid on anything, do the following:

- Carefully review the item description to be certain you know what you may be buying.
- Closely examine the illustration(s) of the item and make sure that what you see matches what is being described.
- Determine the costs of shipping, handling, or other add-ons to your final price.
- If you're unclear about anything, use the link to "Ask the seller a question." A good seller will respond via e-mail to answer all of your questions clearly and completely.
- Using eBay's Items by Seller search option, research other items the seller is currently offering as well as what has been offered in the recent past.
- Review the seller's feedback rating and read the comments others have left regarding their experiences with this seller.
- Compare and contrast the item you're interested in with the same or similar item(s) being offered by other sellers. Look for description consistency, condition, and price.
- Be certain that you understand and agree with the seller's terms including postage and handling costs and options, insurance, accepted payment methods, and refund and return privileges.
- If anything you discover causes you uncertainty or anxiety, best skip this item (or seller) and look for another. eBay considers all bids as "binding contracts to purchase." Should yours be the winning bid, it's critical you are certain about what you'll bid on *before* you bid.

Placing a Bid

It's simple, really, to get into the action. When you find an item you like and that you believe is what it's advertised to be, simply click on the Place Bid > button on the item page (see Figure 5.9 for an example).

Immediately, you're whisked to another area of the screen where you'll enter your maximum bid amount (which must equal at least the current high bid plus the minimum bid increment but can be as high as you'd be willing to

Figure 5.9 Ready to bid? Just click on the Place Bid > button and join in the excitement.

ultimately pay), then click the Continue button to complete the process and see how your bid fares against the previous bidder (see Figure 5.10).

It's as simple as that. If your bid surpasses the current high bidder's maximum bid amount, you'll be declared the new high bidder. Of course, the job now is to withstand any subsequent bids from others who might come along to try to take the item. A dose of good bidding strategy will help you win more auctions; that compelling discussion is coming up next.

Bidding Strategies

Here's where the real fun begins and the point at which the experts distance themselves from the novices. It's perfectly acceptable to place incremental bids on an item, hoping to ultimately get in the last winning bid before the auction ends. Nevertheless, the good news is that winning can be much easier and less time intensive than maintaining an active presence in the virtual auc-

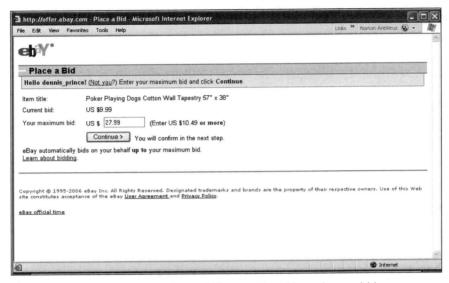

Figure 5.10   Enter your maximum bid amount and launch your bid.

tion parlor. To begin, it's helpful to understand how eBay's *proxy bidding system* works. As previously mentioned, when bidding on an item you're prompted to enter your *maximum bid amount;* this is the most you'd ever be willing to pay for a particular item, your ultimate dropout price. The proxy system will consume only as much of your maximum as is needed to maintain your high-bidder status, incrementing the current bid value for you (bidding on your behalf) when other bidders come along and up the price.

You'll retain your high-bidder standing so long as your maximum bid value isn't eclipsed by another bidder's. Once that happens, you will effectively be outbid and another user will be proclaimed the current high bidder. There's no trick to the proxy bidding system; it all comes down to whoever puts more money on the table. There are a few things you can do, though, to increase your odds of winning.

The Penny Principle

Would you laugh if I said that you could win an auction with a mere penny? Here's how it's done. First, understand that whenever two bidders submit the exact same maximum bid value (say, $100), eBay will recognize the first to have submitted that maximum as the winner of the tie. At this point of incremental bidding, you need to enter another bid that satisfies the minimum bid increment in order to become the new high bidder (in this case, an additional $2.50). However, if the current bid is $50, the high bidder having previously stated a maximum of $100, you can win this auction with a penny by bidding a maximum of $100.01. Your maximum will meet the minimum bid increment (that required while the current value is at $50) and as eBay's proxy bidding system takes over to bid on behalf of you and the current high bidder, your bid will ultimately win out because you succeeded in bidding more than the previous bidder—*just a single penny.*

Since you laid more money on the table, you walk away victorious. This principle works in reverse as well. In other words, your maximum bid of $100.01 will thwart other bidders who might come along after you originally submitted your bid and submit a maximum value of $100. Your single penny will retain your high-bidder status. To this end, it's good to be in the habit of bidding odd values such as $100.01, $25.37, and so on. Those few extra pennies might be all it takes to gain you the win without sending you significantly beyond your intended spending budget.

Snipe Bidding

Perhaps the most maligned bid practice of all is *snipe bidding,* or "sniping." Essentially, you lie in wait for an auction to approach its conclusion, then just seconds before the time expires, you launch a stealth bid in hopes of supplanting the current high bidder while leaving no time for a rebutting bid. It sounds sneaky, but it's perfectly allowable and is widely practiced by many veteran bidders; only those who are sniped are squawking about it.

In essence, it's the same as traditional ascending-price bidding—only the timing is different. In step-by-step fashion, here's how snipe bids are executed:

- Snipe bidding is most effective when using two browser windows, one to load and hold the bid to be placed, another to count down the auction clock (see Figure 5.11).
- If you haven't already signed in at eBay, be sure to do so before proceeding. This saves you the time and inconvenience of signing in as you're preparing to place your snipe bid.
- Refresh the item window to monitor the countdown of the clock.
- *Pay special attention to how responsive eBay and your Internet connection are, noting the number of seconds before the refresh completes.*

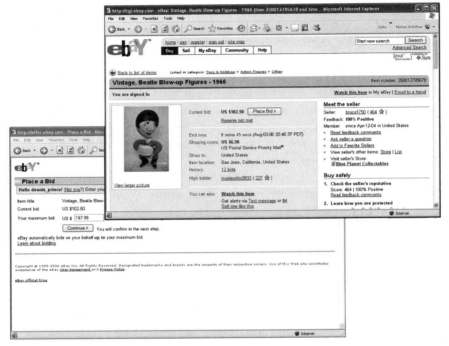

Figure 5.11   Use two item screens when preparing to execute a snipe bid.

- Open a second screen to the same item (CTRL-N on your keyboard will do the trick) and click the Place Bid > button. Enter your maximum bid amount *and wait.*
- About two minutes before the auction ends, click on the Continue button in the Place a Bid window. The site will display a Review and Confirm Bid screen with a button labeled Confirm Bid (see Figure 5.12). *Don't bid yet!*
- Toggle back to the other item page (using your keyboard's ALT-TAB key sequence) to continue refreshing to count down the auction clock. Position the two windows in a staggered arrangement so that you have clear access to the Confirm Bid button on the bidding window.
- Refresh the main item window until the clock counts down to the point where you feel you can just place the bid before the auction closes. Quickly click the Confirm Bid button in the second window.
- If you were successful in placing your snipe bid, eBay will report the results of your bid, either naming you the winner or revealing that you were outbid by the previous high bidder's proxy.

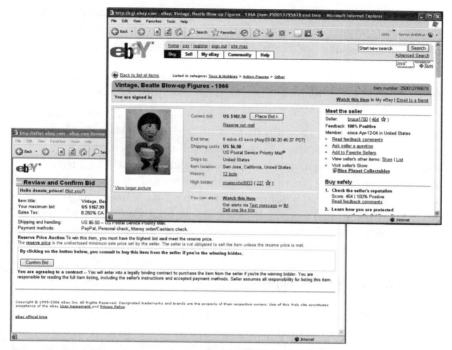

Figure 5.12 At the two-minute mark, the snipe bid lies in wait.

- Recognize that a last-minute bid will *not* ensure a win; the *maximum bid amount* in effect when the auction ends determines who will win. However, a successful snipe bid that does supplant a previous high bid is usually successful in that there is scant time left for another bidder to place a follow-on bid.

Again, there's nothing unfair about snipe bidding (if there was, eBay would prevent its use). In the end, no matter how long you wait to place a bid, if another bidder has offered more by way of a maximum bid amount, that amount will still win out.

As exciting as sitting at attention to launch a snipe bid can be, sometimes you can't be present to monitor the end of an auction; you can still snipe, however. There are several automated snipe programs you can use to place your snipe bids for you. My personal favorite happens to be located at www.esnipe.com. This server-based sniping assistant allows you to enter your snipe bid information long before the auction ends. It will then log on to eBay and place the snipe bid on your behalf. Though you'll pay a fee to use eSnipe, it costs only pennies on the dollar and often delivers big results. Again, no manipulation is going on here, just well-timed last-second bids.

Dutch Auction Bidding

Recall the Dutch auction format discussed in Chapter 1. These are auctions where multiple units of the same item are offered in a single listing (sometimes referred to as a *lot* auction). Each bidder will specify how much he or she wishes to bid, maximum, and *how many* units are desired. The current price remains at the opening bid value set by the seller until all units have been bid on, and then incremental bidding takes over to push the lower-maximum bidders out of the winner's circle. If you bid low on a Dutch auction and are barely clinging to your winning status once all units have been bid for, you're said to be "on the bubble"—you're primed to be bumped off should another bidder come along and outbid you. To increase your chances of winning a Dutch auction, take these steps:

- Unique to Dutch auctions is the ability to review the current bank of bidders and their bid amounts (see Figure 5.13).
- Monitor whether the entire quantity of units has been bid on and track how much time is left in the auction.
- To better ensure a win without needlessly driving up the final price, place a bid that falls in the midrange between the high and low bid amounts. The key to Dutch auctions is that, in the end, each winning bidder will pay only *the price he or she offered;* the auction will entail that the group of bidders will likely be paying different prices for the number of units they've won.

True winning of a Dutch auction, then, is achieved when you successfully win a quantity of units but do so at the lowest possible price among the winning bidders. The Yankee auction is a variation of the Dutch auction whereby each winning bidder pays the exact amount of his or her winning bid.

The Strategy of Not Bidding

It sounds crazy, but it's true—sometimes it's more advantageous *not* to win an auction. Simply put, it's easy to get caught up in the excitement and competition of an auction, losing sight of the price being paid, and winning the item

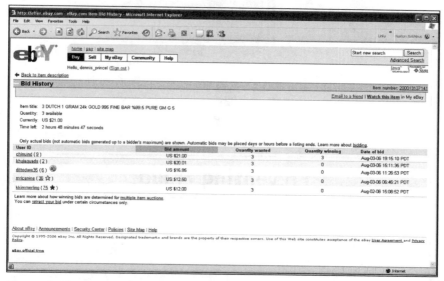

Figure 5.13 In Dutch auctions, you can monitor who has bid and how much they've offered.

but at an undesirable final cost. Always consider the following when you're tempted to get caught up with winning an auction:

- If the item offered has reached a price equal to or higher than what you could pay for it elsewhere, there's no reason to bid.
- If an item isn't in the condition you'd prefer, wait for another, better one to show up.
- If the seller's feedback rating is low or sales policy is suspect, consider skipping this one.
- Consider avoiding an item whose bid history reveals two bidders who have been active in back-and-forth bidding through the course of the auction. This might be a *bidding war* in the works, and you'll likely not fare well between the two impassioned bidders.

Searching, bidding, and winning at eBay is great fun and can result in some wonderful acquisitions along the way. As you constantly consider your potential fortune, utilize the various search and bid strategies noted here to gain the greatest (yet fair) advantage in your find-and-bid-and-win exploits.

6

Preventing Fraud

Although eBay has been effective in implementing new safety programs and local and national government agencies have been prosecuting auction criminals, auction fraud still tops the National Consumers League's list of online scams. From fake paintings to undelivered goods, auction-goers have encountered the sorts of illicit acts that threaten to taint the auction giant's good name. This is not to suggest that your experiences at eBay are destined for trouble, though; the site still accurately reports that 99.9 percent of all transactions are completed successfully by honest eBay users.

Still, part of being successful in a business venture is to understand how the resident scoundrels operate and what manner of sly shenanigans they busy themselves with. Recognize, also, that many of the common aggravating acts that eBay users encounter are just that—aggravating; few are blatantly criminal, and most are simply petty antics. Nevertheless, you need to be aware of the sort of bad business, prolific or paltry, that sometimes goes down at eBay, how you can detect it, and the steps you can take to protect yourself.

THE TOP 10 ONLINE AUCTION OFFENSES

This section describes the most common auction offenses attempted in the auction space, lists their warning signs, and offers some tips for responding to and avoiding them.

Offense No. 1: E-mail Phishing and Site Spoofing

So here's the newest bit of trickery today: attempts to lure online citizens to divulge their logon IDs, account passwords, and personal data. *Phishing* is a method of delivering an e-mail message that appears to be a legitimate communication from a known business or institution (like eBay, PayPal, or various banks and lending institutions). The goal of these messages is to lead you to a bogus Web site that looks identical to a business's actual site—this is known as a *spoof* site—where you'd be able to provide your site ID, password, account numbers, and other sensitive information.

If you receive an e-mail phish—perhaps a message that appears to be from eBay informing you that your account will be canceled if you don't verify your information immediately—*don't respond to it!* These e-mails contain active text links that take you to the spoofed site page to harvest your information for illicit use. The result is that your account can be hijacked and used to host bogus listings, draw money from accounts, and who knows what else.

DETECTING THE SCAM

- Watch for unexpected e-mail notifications alerting you to act quickly to confirm or update your account information.
- Watch for e-mail messages that request personal information such as social security numbers, passwords, and other such unique identifying data about yourself.
- Watch for e-mail messages that include active links that would direct you to Web pages (spoofs of actual company sites).
- Watch for e-mail messages that generally contain poor or inconsistent grammar as well as company logos that appear to be slightly skewed or appear different than they would on an official Web site.

PROTECTING YOURSELF

Now that you know how to detect a phish and spot a spoof, it's easy to avoid falling into their clutches. No matter how authentic an e-mail appears to be (and some legitimate business Web sites actually do send e-mails with actual links—not a good practice these days), never click a link embedded in an e-mail, especially where you're asked to provide sensitive data. Instead, open up a Web browser window and access the business's Web site directly, log in, and review your account status and activity. Chances are, you'll find that your account is just fine and you will have exposed and avoided a phish.

Offense No. 2: Bid Shilling

A dishonest seller will make use of multiple user IDs or will enlist associates to place bogus bids to unfairly and falsely raise the number of bids received and the price of an item. This scam is perpetrated by sellers who are looking to artificially increase the bidding activity and increase their final sales price.

DETECTING THE SCAM

- Watch for recurring user IDs that are used to place bids on several of a particular seller's auctions.
- Watch for a recurring pattern whereby the same bidder or bidders place last-minute bids on a particular seller's auctions.
- Watch for bidders and sellers who regularly bid on one another's auctions (especially if they never appear to actually win).

PROTECTING YOURSELF

If you think you've been the target of a shill bidding operation, report the incident to eBay immediately via the Security & Resolution Center. Provide any supporting evidence such as other auctions where you believe the seller employed shilling. Your best bet for prevention is to block the user ID from your auctions by utilizing eBay's Blocked *Bidder/Buyer List;* the link can be found under the Selling Activities heading within the Site Map page.

Offense No. 3: Fake Photos and Misleading Descriptions

In this sellers' scam, auctioneers falsely embellish or distort the presentation of the items they're auctioning. Borrowed images, ambiguous descriptions, and falsified facts are some of the tactics a seller will employ when lacking confidence, knowledge, or good judgment. The eventual buyer will typically receive an inferior item that doesn't match what was promised and isn't worth the bid price.

DETECTING THE SCAM

- Watch for item descriptions that seem too good to be true.
- Watch for disparities between a written description and an embedded image of the item.
- Watch for ambiguous or incomplete descriptions.
- Watch for seemingly borrowed images (something that appeared in a

previous auction or concurrently, or something that looks as if it was lifted from a commercial advertisement).

- Watch for heavily touched-up photos.

PROTECTING YOURSELF

Be informed about the items you'll bid on. Carefully scrutinize all descriptive information, including images. If you have any questions or hesitations, contact the seller to inquire. If the seller seems evasive, avoid the auction and the seller.

Offense No. 4: Final Price Manipulation

This is another seller's scam in which the final price is not what it should be—perhaps you're asked to pay your *exact* bid for a Dutch auction purchase instead of the lowest winning bid amount, or you are asked to pay your maximum bid if a previous high bidder retracted, even though your winning bid was registered at the site as just enough to beat the bidder below you. Alternatively, there may be superfluous additional charges tacked on—charges that were never previously disclosed and that don't make much sense, such as a transportation fee, a base fee, or any other creative fee a shifty seller might attempt to levy.

DETECTING THE SCAM

Really, price manipulation doesn't give you much advance warning, since the costs requested by the seller come after the auction is over. However, be on the lookout for sales policies that ambiguously refer to odd or potentially excessive costs and end-of-auction prices.

PROTECTING YOURSELF

Your best protection is to quote the seller's policy back by return e-mail. If the seller seems confused about the calculation of a final high bid (as in the case of Dutch auctions), refer the seller to the host site's rules. Do not pay if you believe price manipulation is occurring, and report the seller to eBay immediately. Avoid the seller in the future.

Offense No. 5: Inflated Shipping and Handling Costs

This one is akin to some aspects of final price manipulation, though it can be somewhat more subtle. Perhaps a seller requests $7 for postage, but the item is something small and light that wouldn't cost more than $4.20 (if that) to ship. Sellers sometimes inflate postage and handling costs to garner a few extra dollars for themselves.

DETECTING THE SCAM

- Watch for sellers who charge a handling or supplies fee, especially when they use free packing supplies from the major carriers.
- Watch for sellers who charge flat rates for shipping and handling that seem beyond the acceptable norm (say, more than $6).
- Watch for sellers who charge high flat rates for small items, regardless of the items' size and weight.
- Watch for sellers who are evasive or unwilling to clarify their shipping and handling fees.

PROTECTING YOURSELF

Start by being sure you understand all fees you'll be asked to pay, and question any fees that seem excessive. Politely ask the seller to clarify fees and how those fees were derived. Request specific carriers (such as the U.S. Postal Service) and quote *to the seller* what the cost should be for shipping and any other services (politely, of course). Avoid the seller in the future.

Offense No. 6: Failure to Ship Merchandise

This is probably the most feared and most enraging of all scams: the seller simply never sends the goods. The buyer pays up front in good faith for an item that never arrives. A dishonest seller might claim the item was shipped and has since been lost—but most often the seller fails to respond or communicate at all after having received the buyer's payment.

DETECTING THE SCAM

You typically aren't aware that you're about to be scammed until after you've sent your payment. But here's the modus operandi of most nonshipping sellers (also known as *deadbeat sellers*):

- They are quick to make contact and request payment.
- They don't send confirmation that payment has been received.
- They don't reply, even after repeated attempts to contact them.

- They leave bogus contact information (phone, street address) with the hosting site, so irate buyers can't get through to them by other means.
- They try to auction the same item again at the auction site, at a different auction site, or under a different user ID.

PROTECTING YOURSELF

The bottom line is that this is classic mail fraud and is high on the list at investigative agencies as well as at eBay.

- Keep complete records of all correspondence, including any messages received from the seller when payment was requested.
- Be sure all correspondence you send to the seller is professional and nonthreatening.
- Make a final request to the seller and advise him or her that you will turn the matter over to eBay and/or other agencies.
- When paying for items, try to use a credit card whenever possible: you will be able to dispute the charge and the card issuer will help you sort the matter out. But let justice take its course and be on the lookout for this seller in the future.

Offense No. 7: Selling Knockoffs, Fakes, and Reproductions

It looks like the real thing, it sounds like the real thing, and it might even smell like the real thing, but it's *not* the real thing. Knockoff, reproduced, and copycat goods make their way into the online auction marketplace every day. Sellers might claim an item is real or might hedge a bit about authenticity, but these scammers know they're selling a cheap imitation and are hoping to catch a high-paying buyer who doesn't know how to spot a fake.

DETECTING THE SCAM

- Watch out for truly rare and hard-to-find items suddenly appearing in unbelievably pristine condition.
- Watch out for scarce items that are suddenly plentiful and "like new."
- Watch out for roundabout descriptions in which sellers say they *think* it's the real thing or got it from another source who *said* it has to be authentic—no, it doesn't and it probably isn't.
- Watch out for sellers who can't seem to provide satisfactory information about the origin of an item.

PROTECTING YOURSELF

It's the old rule of caveat emptor ("let the buyer beware") at online auctions, so buyers need to know their stuff. Study up on the items you'll consider bidding on, especially if they have the potential to become quite expensive.

- Ask as many questions as you need to in order to clearly identify the item—and beware of the seller who cops an attitude by saying, "It's real, okay? Just bid on it."
- If you receive an item that is not authentic, contact the seller immediately for a return and a refund. If the seller does not respond, report the incident immediately.

Offense No. 8: Improper Grading Techniques

The seller states that the item is "definitely in excellent condition. A real '10' here." The item the buyer receives is less than perfect, might be flawed or damaged, and could even be incomplete. The seller has painted a rosy picture to bring in the bids, even though the goods aren't of the top quality needed to command a high-end price.

DETECTING THE SCAM

- The seller claims the item is in "100 percent mint condition." Even newly manufactured items usually bear some sort of imperfection.
- The description fails to offer full disclosure of the item's condition or completeness, especially when it's a well-known item and is highly desirable.
- The seller has omitted critical details that are key to accurate grading of the particular item.
- Embedded images seem to show signs of being altered, selectively photographed (only one side is displayed), or unnecessarily cropped where damage might be concealed.

PROTECTING YOURSELF

Your best protection in cases of gratuitous grading is to understand the item well, to be able to spot potential problem areas quickly, and to ask specific questions about an item's condition. Grading can be very subjective depending on the grader's experience, expectations, and methods of comparison.

- If an item is less than stellar when it was billed as exquisite, send it back.

- In fact, if you're concerned about purchasing an item based on its grading, ask if the seller offers return privileges. If not, then it's caveat emptor all over again.

Offense No. 9: Phony Loss and Damage Claims

A buyer contacts a seller to state that an item never arrived or was seriously damaged. The buyer requests a refund and asks the seller to work out the details afterward. The item may have arrived just fine, but the buyer is hoping to ice the cake by getting the bid price back to boot.

DETECTING THE SCAM

- A buyer contacts you weeks or months after the item was shipped to claim loss or damage.
- A buyer demands a refund immediately, before you've had sufficient time to assess the situation or involve the carrier for resolution.
- A buyer offers to throw a damaged item away for you since it won't be worth anything in such bad condition.
- A buyer is on record of having signed for or otherwise received an item that is now claimed to be lost in the mail.

PROTECTING YOURSELF

Again, this is a classic case of mail fraud. The best protection from phony claims is to insure your outgoing goods or use tracking methods for all your packages.

- Be sure the buyer is aware of his or her responsibility for loss and damage if insurance or tracking is declined (remember, the buyer should pay for these services).
- Keep all receipts and tracking numbers until you have confirmed with the buyer that the package arrived safely and the contents are in the same condition as when shipped.

Offense No. 10: Switch and Return

Some buyers will purchase an item, receive it, claim they're dissatisfied, and return it for a refund. The scam: the item they return is *not* the same item originally sent. This is a method whereby unscrupulous buyers attempt to upgrade their items for free, sending back an item of lesser quality or condition.

DETECTING THE SCAM

- A buyer might seem overly interested in your return policy before bidding or winning.
- A buyer is vague about the reason for wanting to return an item.
- A buyer wishes to return an item after a significant lapse of time (weeks or months).

PROTECTING YOURSELF

Unfortunately, this scam is the key reason why many sellers do not offer return privileges.

- You can still accept returns, but indicate that all items must be inspected prior to issuing a refund. Your clear description and good images will serve as proof of intrinsic details of your item, which helps identify a swapped item that was dishonestly returned.
- If the return is an attempt at a switch, notify the buyer that the item is not the same one shipped and return the bogus item to the buyer (accompanied with clarification of points of dissimilarity).
- Block the buyer from bidding in any of your future auctions.

Bonus Scam No. 11: Bid Siphoning

While not a true scam, the unwanted practice known as *bid siphoning* can be quite active at eBay and bears some explanation. Essentially, this is a situation in which you're actively engaged in bidding on an auction item and unexpectedly receive e-mail notification from someone who's offering to sell you the same item elsewhere, either in another listing or offline. By this practice, some sellers are attempting to lure bidders away from an auction, thus potentially devaluing the item in the process. By eBay's rules, this is a prohibited practice.

Further, this could be a roundabout attempt for a scammer to entice bidders where they might be stung by any one or more of the other scams already described. Of course, if you're contacted in this manner, use your own discretion regarding whether you'll entertain the bid siphoning seller. Otherwise, feel comfortable in expressing your disinterest to the seller and possibly notifying eBay's Security & Resolution Center if you feel compelled to do so.

MISDEEDS OR JUST MISUNDERSTANDINGS?

With the exception of the infrequent but heinous frauds described here, recognize that some situations that appear to be scams are not scams at all—they may simply be missteps by inexperienced buyers or sellers. Before jumping to a conclusion, take time to inquire and clarify, and you may end up helping another auction user get a grip on the ways and means of auctioning.

> **eBay TIP:** Here's an example where the seller might be confused rather than dishonest. Recall the rules of the Dutch auction whereby winning bidders are only required to pay their exact winning bid price (plus the seller's shipping fees). Some newer sellers believe that all winning bidders are to pay the *highest* winning bid price, a rule that applies to the auction format known as the Yankee auction. Your knowledge that Dutch auctions require only the winning bid price, not the Yankee pricing format, can be helpful in explaining the difference to the new seller who, again, might just misunderstand the format rules.

You should be cautious, though, if the other party becomes evasive, erratic, or irascible—signs that the person's original intentions were never designed to be honorable. This could be a scam in the works.

ADDITIONAL PROTECTIONS AND PROVISIONS FROM eBAY

Though it's useful to know how to spot, respond to, and avoid the top 10 auction frauds, you're not altogether on your own. eBay is also very interested in keeping everyone happy. In cases where fraud has reared its ugly head, eBay steps forward with specialized policies and programs to help you recover from your loss and get you back in business. Here are the programs eBay provides to offer comfort and recovery in case a deal goes awry.

Auction Insurance

For buyers, eBay has acknowledged the risk involved with prepaying for an item and facing the possibility it may never be received or is received in a condition that is significantly different from (worse than) what was originally described. The site offers a buyer's insurance program that will reimburse dissatisfied customers up to $200 (minus a $25 deductible); this is increased to coverage of up to $1,000 if the buyer used PayPal to pay for the purchase.

eBay does require buyers to first exhaust all avenues in seeking a successful completion of the deal, as detailed in these steps:

- The buyer should request the seller's contact information (address and phone number) to attempt direct communication to resolve the problem.
- If such overtures go unanswered for more than 14 days, eBay encourages buyers to log a dispute via the Dispute Console (accessible from the Site Map page) to initiate an investigation, track, and ultimately resolve the problem. Buyers should also contact credit card issuers (many offer 100 percent protection and charge dispute assistance) as well as package carriers to assist with wayward package claims.
- And if this is a truly heinous fraud, eBay encourages buyers to seek assistance from the National Fraud Information Center, the Internet Fraud Complaint Center, local law enforcement agencies, and the U.S. Postal Inspection Service (when applicable).

Final Value Fee Credits

For sellers who are scammed or otherwise subjected to unreliable bidders, eBay will offer to refund the *final value fee* (the end-of-auction commission) if the winning bidder fails to pay; he or she has become a *deadbeat,* by eBay's own definition. Of course, eBay requires you to take the prescribed steps to try to complete the sale successfully first:

- If payment hasn't been received within seven days of the auction's close (and you had previously notified the bidder of the amount due), open an *Unpaid Item Dispute* record within the Dispute Console. eBay tracks and manages these disputes and will suspend users who consistently ignore their commitments to pay.
- Unfortunately, you cannot recover your insertion and special listing feature fees, but the recovery of the final value fee is a reasonable form of compensation when you encounter a deadbeat bidder.

PREPARE YOURSELF WITH A PLAN FOR ACTION

Being prepared ahead of time will be your best tactic for detecting and responding to problems, be they simple miscommunications or premeditated con jobs. Here are the steps to take as you manage auction encounters, seek mutual resolution, and guard yourself from online trickery:

- **Be informed.** Make sure you understand eBay's auction rules and methods, especially with the particular auction format you're participating in.

- **Investigate.** Research sellers and buyers by investigating their feedback ratings (the community grading system covered in depth in Chapter 15) and comments at the site; those numbers and notes will immediately reveal whether you're engaged with a known troublemaker.

- **Know your rights.** Be sure you understand eBay's rules and recommendations for combating fraud and how to invoke the protections provided.

- **Communicate.** Keep your communication flowing with the other person and be professional at all times, *especially* if you believe a scam is in the works; never resort to threats or other such affronts.

- **Be direct.** If you suspect a scam (or at least a significant disregard for the site rules), indicate that to the other person and state how you intend to complete (or terminate) the transaction, including reporting misdeeds to eBay.

- **Follow through.** If it's a scam, take action by reporting the incident to eBay's Security & Resolution Center administrators, then consider going the next step to report particularly flagrant scams to the proper authorities and organizations.

- **Document and file.** Keep all correspondence of the incident as well as a record of how the events transpired. This is the sort of information that will be needed in the case of any investigation.

- **Keep a positive outlook.** Don't fall into the trap of becoming paranoid or otherwise suspicious about every person you deal with. Recognize that 99.9 percent of the time you'll enjoy simple and straightforward transactions with honest eBay users.

KNOWING WHEN IT'S TIME TO TAKE A LOSS

It's a bitter pill to swallow, but sometimes resolution and recovery just aren't in the cards. Though this should clearly be the exception to the rule, there is a time when it's best to accept a loss and move on. Sometimes a scam can get the better of you and you'll be best served by chalking it up to experience.

Here are the indicators of when it might be best to cut your losses:

- The item you were buying was of low (practically negligible) value.
- The feedback rating of the user indicated potential trouble and you chose to ignore it (never again, though).

- The cost (in time, effort, and money) to pursue the situation is far more than the item is worth, or more than it's worth to you.
- The organizations you've gone to for assistance indicate that your loss will be unrecoverable.

While it's never pleasant to admit that someone has gotten away with an illicit deed, convince yourself to move on and let the situation go if it seems no restitution is in sight. Auction fraud is a rare occurrence, and it's highly unlikely that you'll ever endure such a hardship again. Apply the methods described in this chapter and you'll stand the greatest chance of avoiding and averting those nasty little deeds that someone might be trying to carry out.

7

Becoming an Online Auctioneer

Now that you have a solid understanding of how eBay works, how bidding strategies help you become a better buyer, and how to determine if a deal is on the up-and-up, it's time to take the next step and become an auctioneer yourself. Listing items at eBay is quite easy and the site does a good job of providing guidance along the way. Still, if you're new to listing at eBay, having someone alongside to guide you through the process can be a great help. This chapter will quickly guide you through the simple listing process and help you recognize all the features eBay makes available as you present your item for bid.

FIRST THINGS FIRST: WHAT WILL YOU LIST?

The listing process begins with the question What will you offer for bid? There are probably plenty of items at your feet (figuratively or possibly literally) that you'd like to rid yourself of or cash in on. The best news here is that you can sell practically *anything* at eBay. Provided you've priced the item reasonably, there's generally a buyer out there for everything. Surely, while you were searching the site, you encountered several pieces that likely caused you to muse, "Someone's really trying to sell *that?*" Moreover, you also might have been shocked that those quirky goods actually received bids. It's true—practically everything is worth something to somebody. Therefore, I work by this motto: *Don't throw it away—throw it on eBay!* I can practically guarantee you'll find a bidder for nearly anything you might decide to offer.

To that end, start your listing adventure with some simple items. The

Figure 7.1   A Del Monte California Raisins premium helped me *earn it* through the grapevine.

best items are things you might have seen up for bid that you also have lying around the house. You don't need to necessarily strike it rich on your first sale; your goal is to get acquainted with the listing process. Of course, don't be surprised if you do fare better than you might have originally expected. Look at Figure 7.1; it's a picture of the first item I offered at eBay, long, long ago, in January 1996.

The California Raisins premium consists of three PVC figures that stand atop a musical sandwich stage that plays, "I Heard It Through the Grapevine." I originally offered this novelty for sale within the Usenet (under rec.collecting) and was offered $49. It seemed a great price, but I also considered that this potentially collectible item could garner a higher price at the auction venue. At the close of the auction, those singing raisins sold for $79. Not bad for something that had been packed away in a box in my garage. The point is, there's certainly something of interest that you're sure to sell and that likely isn't near and dear to your heart at this time. So your first task in this exercise is to do some quick rooting around, find an item, and get ready to list it.

USING eBAY'S SINGLE-ITEM LISTING FORMS

To demonstrate how to easily list an item at eBay, I'll be offering a custom set of refrigerator magnets that are quite popular with the nostalgia crowd. Figure 7.2 gives you a peek at these Monster Scenes magnets that I've been selling quite regularly at eBay, a hit with folks interested in the original plastic model kits from 1971 that these magnet designs are based upon. You find

Figure 7.2 These Monster Scenes magnets are going on the auction block.

whatever it is that you want to sell—a piece of china, a cute doggy sweater, a quilt, an old eight-track player, or whatever.

Keywords and Categories

With your item in hand, here's a straightforward review of eBay's single-item listing process. Assuming you had created your Seller's Account at the time you registered with eBay (refer to the discussion in Chapter 4), click on the Sell button from the Main Toolbar to access the Sell page. The process begins with a first screen that asks you to enter keywords for the item you're selling (see Figure 7.3).

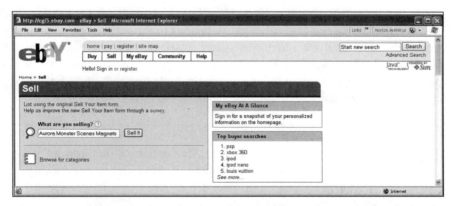

Figure 7.3 Listing an item begins with providing relevant keywords in the "What are you selling?" field.

Remembering the discussion from Chapter 5 regarding the importance of keywords when searching for items, here is where you'll use that insight to identify the keywords that will best suit your item and could guide the highest number of bidders to your listing. This isn't your actual item title; this is just an initial step that will help you determine the best keywords and the proper item category to use, as you'll see in a moment. Enter your keywords and click the Sell It button.

 eBay TIP: The keywords I chose for my listing represent the following:

- "Aurora"—this is the name of the now-defunct company responsible for originally releasing the Monster Scenes products.
- "Monster Scenes"—this is the series or brand name of the original as well as this new product, naturally.
- "Magnets"—this is the *type* of product being offered.

As you can see, each of these keywords serves an important purpose in ensuring that buyers for this type of item can utilize a variety of words to find my listing. These keywords will figure prominently in my eventual item title.

Upon submitting your keywords, eBay displays the Select a Category screen (see Figure 7.4), where you'll appropriately classify your item. Notice how eBay provides weighted recommendations of potential categories based upon the keywords you provided. Here, eBay utilized the keywords and scanned its database to find other active listings that use the same or similar keywords, providing you a listing of category selections and a percentage of instances where the keywords matched a category. In a way, eBay is actively performing research for you to help you easily and effectively choose the best category for your item.

eBay TIP: Notice the Search button that appears to the right of the keywords field. If you like, you can modify your keywords and elect to search again to browse an update listing of matching categories.

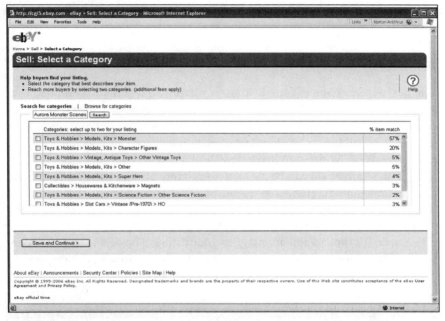

Figure 7.4 eBay uses your chosen keywords to help you select the best category for your listing.

For my listing, I clicked the checkbox to choose Toys & Hobbies > Models, Kits > Monster. But this isn't a model kit, you say? Absolutely correct, although the magnet designs are based on original model kits from 1971 and, therefore, the customers who may be interested in this sort of subject matter would most likely be browsing this category. Remember, too, that most savvy buyers avoid searching for goods via a browse of a category and elect, instead, to browse offerings that appear in a keyword result list. Ah, how it all comes together.

After selecting the category, click the Save and Continue button. Before you can actually move forward to begin crafting your listing, eBay will provide a pop-up window to ask if you want to list your item in a second concurrent category—the single listing could be visible from *two* categories. Immediately, I'd recommend against this because choosing two categories will double your listing fees. Since you know that the majority of items are found via keyword searches and result lists, paying for a second category is of little benefit to you and will needlessly increase your listing costs. In the pop-up window that appears, choose the "No second category" option to progress forward.

Item Titles and Pictures

The next screen, Create Your Listing, is where you'll actually compose your listing (see Figure 7.5). Begin with the Title by using your selected keywords plus any additional words that will provide the best short description of your item. You're limited to 80 characters, including spaces, in your item title, so use them wisely. Notice that just below the Title field is another labeled "Subtitle." This second field can be useful if you simply need to enter more relevant information than 80 characters could provide, but recognize that using the Subtitle field will add another 50¢ to your listing costs (so save the cost and use the best keywords in the Title field).

Next, it's time to add an image to your listing. The best listings will contain quality pictures of the item, allowing the buyer to visually inspect the

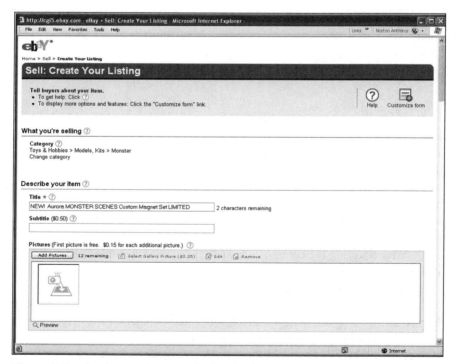

Figure 7.5   Begin creating your listing in this screen.

item being offered. Grab your digital camera or power up your scanner and get a good-quality image of your item to help encourage more bids. (For more discussion about creating the best images, refer to Chapter 17.) Once you have an image of your item, store it on your computer or connect your camera to your computer so it can be transferred to your listing. To begin the image addition process, click the Add Pictures button within the Pictures area of the listing form. When you do, eBay will provide a pop-up window where you'll access your image and upload it to eBay (see Figure 7.6).

From within the pop-up window, click the tab labeled "Basic" and then click the Browse button to search your computer to locate the image you want to include with your listing (just as you use your computer's file manager program to locate any other sort of file you want to view). After you've selected the image from your computer (or camera, if you've attached that), click on the Upload Pictures button at the bottom of the pop-up window. Upon doing this, eBay will access the image in the file location you specified and will make a copy of it to include in your listing (that's right, eBay will store a copy of your image on their computers for the duration of your listing). When the

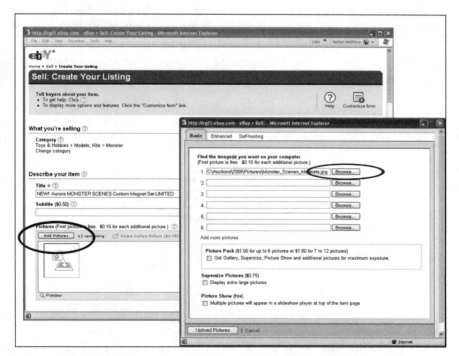

Figure 7.6   Add pictures to your listing with just a few clicks of your mouse.

upload is complete, the image you selected will be displayed on the Create Your Listing page. At this point, click the image once to enable the selections along the top of the Pictures area, giving you the ability to utilize the image for an important second usage (see Figure 7.7).

Click the text link, Select Gallery Picture, as shown in Figure 7.7. When you do, a tiny camera icon will appear at the bottom right-hand corner of the image, also shown in Figure 7.7. What's a Gallery Picture? Recall that when you were searching for goods at eBay, many of the listings in the result list provided small images alongside them; those are Gallery Pictures and they're highly effective at drawing shoppers' attention amid a list of results. This small image can be the persuasive factor that will compel a shopper to investigate your item further rather than pass it over for another item on a result list. Yes, enabling the Gallery Picture will add 35¢ to your listing costs, but it's an investment that definitely pays dividends (and, as I'll show you in Chapter 16, you can even specify a gallery-friendly image that will be best suited for this use).

The first image eBay hosts for your listing is free, and each additional image you include costs 15¢. (There are other image options, such as Picture Packs and Slide Shows, for which there are likewise additional fees.) Your best bet in terms of controlling your listing costs is to use a single image that properly captures the key details of an item. In Chapter 16, I'll explain other ways to manage images that suit your needs, satisfy your customers, and keep your costs down.

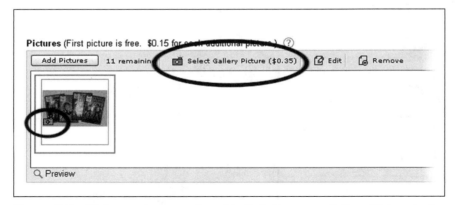

Figure 7.7   Click your image and enable it for use as a Gallery Picture to increase bidder looks.

> **eBay TIP:** I'm quite diligent when it comes to control-
> ling listing costs. Recognize that eBay has nicely provided
> numerous options and additions to spruce up your listings,
> but they typically come at a price. As I am *your* advocate in this venture,
> I know that every cost you incur from eBay deducts from your per-item
> profit. While some of these listing option costs seem to be negligible,
> consider how quickly they'll add up when you list 20, 50, 100, or more
> items. That's your profit—your fortune—being sapped. Therefore, I'll
> continue to point out eBay features that you can skip, providing expla-
> nation or alternatives to their use, to ensure your profit remains as high
> as possible with every listing.

Item Descriptions

Scroll down the Create Your Listing page to reveal the Description area (see
Figure 7.8). This is where you'll write up the text portion of your listing, faithfully and fully describing your item, in a way that suits and supports the image
you've already specified. This is also where you'll include the terms and conditions of how you'll manage the sale after a high bidder or buyer has been
declared (to be discussed in detail in Chapter 9).

You'll notice that you can easily apply text characteristics within the
Description area of your listing. Effects and enhancements such as text font,
color, size, and alignment used to be possible only by employing complex coding methods, but now they are readily available for use here.

> **eBay TIP:** Yes, you can still utilize HTML (HyperText
> Markup Language) coding to deliver a highly specialized
> and stylized item description, as indicated by the tab labeled
> "HTML" (refer to Figure 7.8). Chapter 16 contains a discussion of how
> to easily harness HTML capabilities.

When your description is complete, be sure to indicate the condition of
your item from the pull-down selector box seen in Figure 7.8. Then, choose
your Visitor counter style so you can keep track of how many times your item

Figure 7.8   Your item description should include useful details that completely and honestly represent your item.

was viewed. I recommend skipping over the Listing designer area for reasons that will be covered in Chapter 16.

Listing Type and Payment Methods

Scroll further down the Create Your Item page to establish the type of listing you want to create: Online Auction or Fixed Price. Figure 7.9 shows where you'll make this selection (via the selectable tabs) and the fields you'll need to complete depending on your choice. If listing an online auction format, complete the following fields:

- **Starting price.** This is the minimum opening bid amount.
- **Quantity.** This determines how many items like this you're offering. If you're offering more than one identical item, you're effectively launching a Dutch auction.
- **Duration.** This is where you determine how many days your auction will run before bidding is closed and a high bidder is announced.

Notice in Figure 7.9 that I've entered a Buy-It-Now price to allow a potential bidder to end the auction immediately by offering the price at which I'll sell immediately. Notice how I've skipped over the Reserve price; this field allows me to state a price that will be my minimum selling price, which, if not reached during the course of bidding, relieves me from having to sell the item. I'll discuss both of these fields in greater detail in Chapter 18.

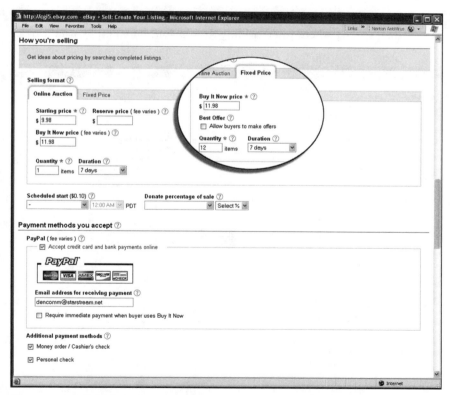

Figure 7.9   Establish your pricing in this area of the listing form.

Now, if you elect to create this listing as a fixed-price offering, you need to complete the following fields (as shown in the inset in Figure 7.9):

- **Buy-It-Now price.** This is the selling price you'll accept for the item.
- **Quantity.** This determines how many items like this you're offering. In a fixed-price listing, multiple items offered indicate this is a "lot" listing.
- **Duration.** This is where you determine how many days your listing will run before it is closed, provided a buyer hasn't already claimed however many items you've offered.

Next, indicate the payment methods you'll accept (to be discussed in Chapter 9).

Shipping Details

Scroll down the page again to access the Shipping area (see Figure 7.10). Here, you'll specify where you're willing to ship your item and by what carrier

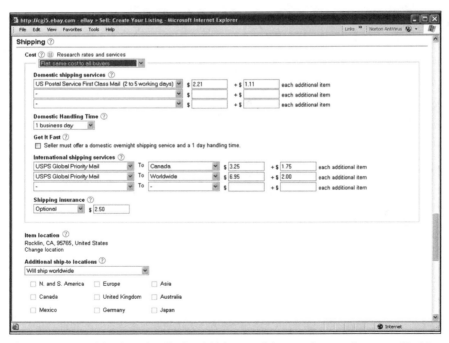

Figure 7.10 Shipping details let bidders and buyers know where you'll ship, how you'll ship, and at what cost.

and method. As you read later in Part III of this book, this is where you can determine options and offer choices that will serve both you and your customers in efficiently managing a sale and delivery. Notice in the example that I've offered delivery worldwide using flat shipping rates.

> **eBay TIP:** Don't forget—it's standard practice that buyers pay shipping costs, just as they would for any other mail-order type of purchase. To this end, specify your shipping costs fairly (don't forget the unwanted effect of Scam No. 5 described in Chapter 6) so bidders and buyers will be prepared for the additional fees you'll be levying within their final payment amount.

Buyer Requirements, Sales Tax, and Returns

Scroll down one last time to access the Additional information area of the Create Your Listing page (see Figure 7.11). Here, you wrap up your listing by establishing any buyer requirements that must be met before allowing a bid or Buy-It-Now purchase (see the inset in Figure 7.11). Then, determine whether if you're required to collect sales tax for your item and, if so, specify the appropriate percentage. Next, indicate whether you'll offer a return policy and specify the conditions appropriately. Last, the Additional checkout instructions box provides you with space to include any other instructions or limitations not already specified elsewhere in the listing form. When finished, click the Save and Continue > button at the bottom of the page.

Review and Submit

With your information entry complete, you'll now navigate to a screen where you can review, adjust (if necessary), and launch your listing. First, though, you'll need to fend off some appeals to add more features to your listing, the sort that eBay assures you will improve your chances for success but which, in my experience, serve largely to increase the site's fee collection. To avoid appearing cynical or paranoid, I recommend skipping over cost-laden enhancements such as picture packs, extra icons, title adornments, and category upgrades for the following reasons:

- Your carefully selected keywords, crafted into your item title, will serve you well in attracting bidders and buyers who will be specifically searching for such goods.

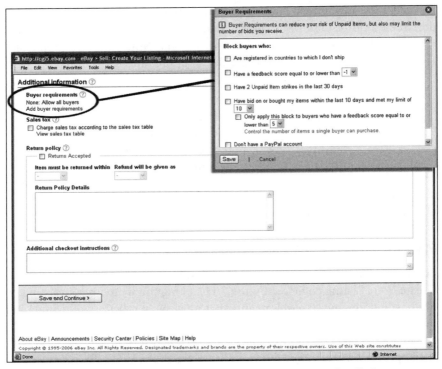

Figure 7.11   Establish buyer requirements, tax, and return details here.

- Your thoughtful selection of the key category that best represents your item will suffice in gaining visibility to those who would browse for this sort of item.
- Your Gallery Picture upgrade will effectively entice bidders and buyers to take a deeper look at your item beyond what any bold or highlighted item title text could achieve.

With that, scroll down the Promote and Review Your Listing page to see how your Gallery Picture will appear in a sample search result list (see Figure 7.12).

Then scroll through the listing preview pane to see how your images, text, and other specifications will appear in a live listing. Scroll further down to review the fees that will be assessed by eBay based upon the following:

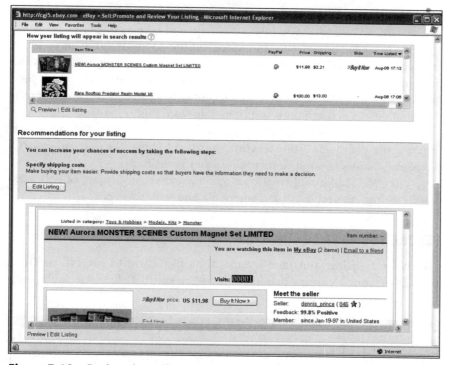

Figure 7.12   Review the gallery image in this preview area for your listing.

- The opening bid price, the Buy-It-Now price, and/or the Reserve price
- The number of items you specified that will be available (if this is to be a Dutch auction or lot listing)
- The listing features and enhancements you selected while crafting your details

---

eBay TIP: For the moment, don't be preoccupied with the listing fees. A complete discussion of how to best control those to maximize your personal profits will be presented in Chapter 26.

Now, before launching your listing, be sure to carefully reread your item description, be sure your item image is correct and is being displayed properly, and double-check your terms and specifications to ensure all is in order. If anything requires adjustment, simply click on the Edit Listing text link at the bottom of the screen. If all looks in order, then click the List Item for Sale button (see Figure 7.13). Upon doing so, eBay will provide you a new screen that contains an active link to your item page (see Figure 7.14).

With your listing submitted, the auction clock is now ticking. Upon selecting the View your listing text link shown in Figure 7.14, you can jump to the page bidders will soon be reviewing (see Figure 7.15).

eBay will send a confirmation e-mail message to notify you of your successful listing. As simple as that, you're off and selling.

BEFORE YOU LIST AGAIN

Chances are, seeing your item listed will motivate you to run off and find another of your treasures to offer—that's the spirit! Before you grab some

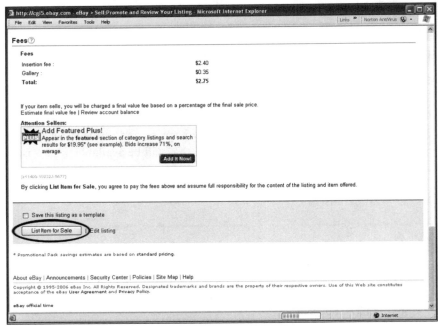

Figure 7.13   When you are satisfied with your listing, click the List Item for Sale button.

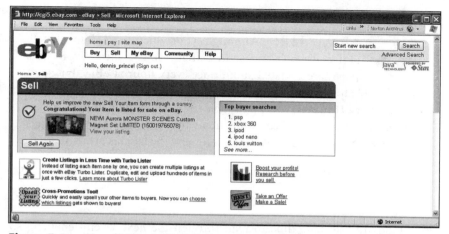

Figure 7.14 Your listing is live! Follow the text link to view the actual listing page.

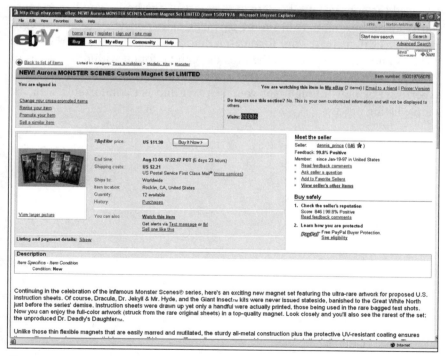

Figure 7.15 Your official item listing page.

> **eBay TIP:** Although your auction is immediately active, it won't appear in search results right away. Results pages are updated about once every hour at eBay, but soon you'll be able to search on a keyword and your item will show up in the search results. However, you will be able to find your item immediately if you (or your customers) search for items by your user ID; that always lists every item you have available the moment the listings are submitted.

more goods to sell, take time to read through the next several chapters so you'll have a greater understanding of how to best present yourself and your items as a seller in the eBay realm.

The goal of this chapter has been to expose you to the listing process and the details you'll manage when you offer items at eBay. After you've reviewed the subsequent chapters in this part of the book, you'll gain more clarity about how matters of online payment, sales policies, and pricing considerations will increase your fortune-making potential. Of course, the subtle nuances and selling strategies the pros use can be found within the pages of Parts III and IV of this book; that's where you'll truly hone your auction expertise. For now, though, get your feet wet and get comfortable with the simple listing process.

PART II

THE FUNDAMENTALS OF SELLING ON eBAY

8

Understanding and Offering Online Payment

When talking about fortunes, you're talking about money. The great prices you earn in your auction exploits are only as good as your ability to take them to the bank—that is, to actually *collect* the cash in the end. Although you've likely considered the venerable payment vehicles—money orders, cashier's checks, personal checks, and cash—dealing in the online realm practically requires you to become adept in these ways of online payment. In this chapter, you'll learn what online payment is, where and how it's managed, and, most important, how using it can help you gain even higher prices as you amass your fortune.

THE FEAR FACTOR: IS ONLINE PAYMENT SAFE?

If registering at eBay gave you reason to pause, uncertain whether it would be safe to provide sensitive credit card and bank account information online, the consideration of sending and receiving actual funds through cyberspace, not to mention having to again surrender personal finance account information, often causes folks great concern. However, take comfort in the fact that online payment has definitely matured into a secure and preferred method for managing payment transactions. In fact, many bidders and buyers at eBay today insist that they be able to pay electronically and will shop only with sellers who allow them to do so.

For sellers, online payment accounts have matured to the point where they're highly secure and adept at providing protections against unauthorized or illicit account tampering. As you'll read later in this chapter, this level of maturity has gained one online payment site the status of being the de facto standard—with scant competition—in the online payment sector.

Coupled with the payment site securities, your financial institution probably has also matured in matters of online payment and has responded to your needs (and anxieties) for managing account-funded cyberpurchases. Today, most reputable credit card issuers and personal bank account managers offer protections to their customers should something go amiss in an online transaction. Here again, check with your issuer and other financial institution to be clear about their safeguards and your responsibilities as an account owner (just as you did when you established your eBay account). The bottom line, though, is that millions of online transactions are completed every day, managed as easily as those at your local department store. So fear not.

THE HOWS AND WHYS OF ONLINE PAYMENT

Experienced bidders and other online buyers have found online payment to be the fastest and arguably the easiest method to quickly pay for a variety of goods, at eBay and other venues. As easy as sending an e-mail message, online payments can be made in a few simple steps:

1. The buyer establishes an account with an online payment provider.
2. The seller, also with an active online payment account, indicates the user ID to which payment is to be forwarded (separate from an eBay user ID).
3. The buyer posts the agreed-upon payment amount via the specified online payment site and is provided verification of the seller's account that will receive funds.
4. Payment is posted to the seller's account and deducted from the buyer's account, and a notification of the transaction is provided via e-mail to both parties.

Thanks to online payment services, an auction transaction can be completed in a matter of minutes. Many buyers and sellers indicate they've been able to close the postauction deal in less than 30 minutes' time.

But is time *really* of such importance in completing an online transaction? Can't the sending of a traditional snail-mail payment still suffice?

Actually, traditional payment methods, as previously mentioned, are just as viable today as ever. Nevertheless, going hand in hand with the speed of the Internet and the access to vast goods and services at the click of a mouse, fast online payment simply makes sense and offers a truly integrated approach to selecting, purchasing, and paying for goods, all made possible from the same computer.

> **eBay TIP:** When dealing online, a speedy transaction is usually the best. The seller is able to quickly receive payment, thus developing trust in the buyer, via online payment. The buyer is likewise able to receive goods more quickly, thereby gaining confidence in the seller and the entire online bidding and buying experience. Both parties are able to complete the transaction quickly, which spells success for all involved.

Most compelling, though, is that the use of online payment services enables buyers and sellers to transact via credit card. Without the cost and complexity of establishing a traditional merchant account, sellers—even first-timers—can advertise acceptance of credit card purchases via an online payment venue. Likewise, buyers can manage their purchases via use of a credit card, no longer limited to funds in their checking or saving accounts alone. For both parties, online payment serves as another convenient option in managing online business transactions.

WHO'S WHO IN ONLINE PAYMENT SERVICES?

Where do you go when you want to sign up to utilize online payment? Today there are just a couple of sites that regularly manage online payment transactions, and chances are, you've heard of—and perhaps have already used—the reigning leader. I'll give you a peek at these two sites that you'll likely encounter.

PayPal (www.paypal.com)

By and large, PayPal.com is at the top of the mountain in the online payment arena. Like eBay itself, PayPal arrived on the scene early (October 1999) and gained fast brand and service recognition (originally launched under the inauspicious name of X.com). Many other contenders have come and gone, but PayPal has stood fast. The site, boasting a registered user base of more than 100 million accounts, was so successful it even supplanted eBay's former Billpoint payment site. In an about-face, eBay acquired PayPal for $1.5 billion in October 2002, making it a truly integrated tool in the eBay experience. Pay-Pal is free for buyers and charges a sales commission to sellers (see Table 8.1), deducted from the amount of payment received.

Account activation can be accomplished in a matter of minutes. Business and Premiere accounts are available to sellers, at a monthly fee, that give access to automated e-mail tools, an invoicing system, inventory management, and more. PayPal also enables transactions to 55 different countries and allows payment for auction goods and non-auction-related goods and services. (See Figure 8.1.)

BidPay (www.bidpay.com)

BidPay came along in 1999, and its original goal was to allow buyers to purchase and forward actual money orders to sellers. Originally backed by Western Union (a subsidiary of First Data), the long-recognized name in fund transfers, BidPay allowed buyers to purchase money orders online using a credit or debit card (brick-and-mortar institutions typically accept only debit cards or cash). That has changed now, since the BidPay money order forwarding service has been discontinued. In March 2006, BidPay was acquired by CyberSource Corporation and the service was temporarily interrupted to rework its processes and infrastructure. In June 2006, the site reopened to

Table 8.1 PayPal Sales Commission Rate Table

	Standard Rate	Merchant Rate (Qualification Required)*		
Monthly Received Payment (USD)	$0.00 USD– $3,000.00 USD	$3,000.01 USD– $10,000.00 USD	$10,000.01 USD– $100,000.00 USD	>$100,000.00 USD
Fees per transaction (USD)	2.9% + $0.30 USD	2.5% + $0.30 USD	2.2% + $0.30 USD	1.9% + $0.30 USD

*Merchant rates require sustained receipt of at least $3,000.00 each month.

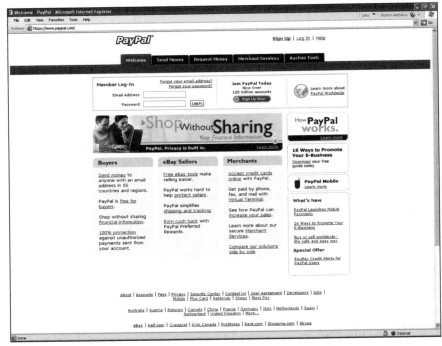

Figure 8.1   PayPal is the front-runner in the online payment race.

provide a PayPal-like method allowing buyers to pay sellers via debit or credit card.

Sellers (payment recipients) must be registered with BidPay to receive payment. Eliminating the delay of awaiting receipt of the money order, Bid-Pay now provides immediate payment notification to sellers, allowing them to immediately ship goods to their buyers. (See Figure 8.2.)

Escrow Services (www.escrow.com)

Because of some of the high-price items being sold on eBay, a *third* service worth noting is escrow services. This site doesn't manage electronic transactions in quite the same way as PayPal or BidPay, but instead, like a traditional escrow account, online escrow accounts serve to confirm and hold a buyer's payment, prompting a seller to send the item purchased. The buyer,

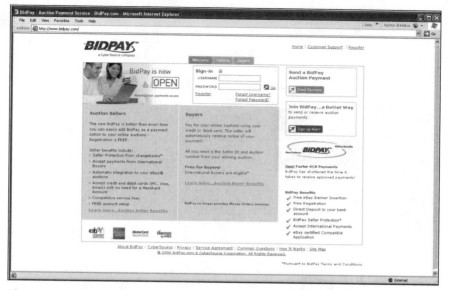

Figure 8.2 BidPay is a second option in online tools that facilitate payment for auction goods.

upon receipt of the item, confirms delivery and satisfaction, thus prompting release of funds to the seller. If the buyer is dissatisfied, the funds in escrow are held until the seller confirms receipt of the returned item. If the buyer fails to even confirm item receipt, funds will be released to the seller within three days of the tracked delivery confirmation (per the package carrier's records).

Escrow is typically expensive, as it's generally used for high-value purchases (usually greater than $500). Buyers and sellers can negotiate who will pay the escrow fees or can agree to split the cost. Escrow.com (www.escrow

 eBay TIP: Interestingly enough, you'll find you can utilize your PayPal account as a source of funds to manage an escrow.com transaction.

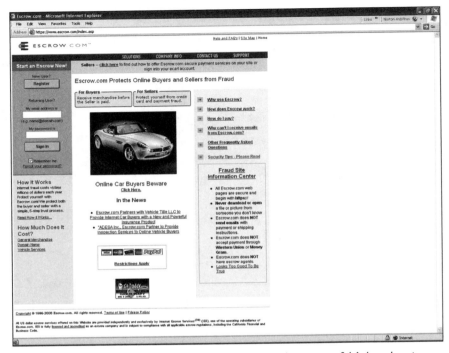

Figure 8.3   Online escrow services take the anxiety out of high-value transactions.

.com) is recommended for use with eBay. The site also lists several other escrow sites for use outside of the United States. (See Figure 8.3.)

Online Merchant Accounts

Though initially you have your sights set on eBay activities alone, there may come a time when you endeavor to go beyond the auction space to further bolster your fortune-making opportunities. If you decide to create an online store or other such commercial Web site, you'll be glad to know that traditional merchant accounts are available online as well. If you keep your business restricted to the virtual storefront, you needn't bother with a credit card terminal or clunky charge plate. Instead, online merchant accounts are usually accompanied with online shopping cart solutions, enabling shoppers to select items from your inventory, carry them in a virtual cart, and check out by paying via a credit or debit card. Again, this is probably a consideration to entertain a bit later. For now, just be aware that the option is available if and when you decide to expand your online horizons.

THE FORTUNE FACTOR: IF YOU OFFER IT, THEY WILL PAY (*MORE!*)

The original question persists: if checks and money orders are still suitable and acceptable, why bother with online payment? It's a good question that evokes several good answers. Consider these reasons why online payment is something you should embrace, especially when you're the seller:

- **It fits the bill.** In the early days of online auctions and cybershopping, it seemed clumsy to utilize the speed and convenience of online buying only to be relegated to the comparatively ancient process of actually *mailing* payment and waiting for checks to clear. Integration is what it's all about, and online payment fits seamlessly in this new way of doing business.

- **More options draw more customers.** As you learn in Chapter 9, when it comes time to create a sales policy, bidders and buyers crave options and alternatives. Specifically, the more choices you offer regarding terms of payment (especially the cutting edge of online payment), the better your ability to encourage more business toward your online offerings. Buyers love choices.

- **Buyer profiling has concluded that consumers tend to spend more money when they can shop on credit.** Since online payment services enable you to accept credit card payment, you stand a greater chance of earning higher prices for your goods. The best part of all: online payment services make the whole transaction transparent to you, ridding you of the cost and coordination of maintaining an actual merchant account of your own.

- **Online payment services are adaptable to your business.** As they service all manner of transactions, auction or otherwise, online payment can support all of your business transactions no matter where or when you sell goods or services.

As you can see, online payment offers plenty of benefits to your business and to your customers, too. As easy as it is to establish an online payment account and immediately begin to accept credit card payments, you'll be operating like those other merchants in just minutes. And if you're eager to do volume business at eBay while managing payment transactions in an efficient manner, online payment is the best method to set you up for success.

9

Developing a Professional
Sales Policy

At eBay, a seller's policies serve as the road map for the transaction to come. The sales *terms* and *conditions* you establish drive your customers' expectations and enable a smooth and successful transaction. Bidders and buyers typically look for clear and comprehensive sales policies when they consider bidding on items, in essence seeking out sellers who demonstrate their good business sense through sound and satisfactory transaction guidelines. Before jumping too deeply into selling, ensure that you have a comprehensive and well-represented sales policy to help guide you and your sellers through the actual exchanges to come.

THE RULES TO THE RICHES

Start by understanding the terms and conditions you want stated up front, keeping in mind that these are the guidelines buyers use to decide whether they'll bid or buy your goods; that is, the sales policy not only serves your needs but also communicates to customers how *their* needs will be met. To this end, your listing should have clear and complete coverage of the different aspects of a sales policy to encourage more business at your virtual doorstep. This chapter discusses which policies will bring you the best success and make your transactions easy for both you and the buyer.

Defining Payment Methods

It all starts with the money, and your buyers will be looking for the most secure yet convenient ways to settle up (as are you). Remember, the more options you can provide, the better chance you stand to attract buyers of all dispositions. At a minimum, consider offering the following payment methods:

- **Online payment.** Based on the discussion in Chapter 8, this should be first and foremost in your policy. Not only do you enable buyers to pay with their credit cards, you also offer the ability to pay quickly; they get their goods faster and you get your cash more quickly. And as this is the fastest way to collect payment from a buyer, it's common that sellers will *encourage* this method above all others; offer immediate shipping to customers who pay this way.
- **Money orders and cashier's checks.** A close second to online payment, these allow buyers quicker receipt of their goods, since, once received, the seller knows this is as good as cash. If you accept money orders and cashier's checks, offer to ship immediately on receipt of payment.

---

eBay TIP: Hey! What about the rash of counterfeit postal money orders that appeared in 2005? Yes, this enduring form of secure payment was recently besmirched by the illicit efforts of some very clever offshore crooks. Postal money orders are still as good as cash, provided you recognize the real thing when you see it. Here are the distinguishing characteristics of the bona fide article (see Figure 9.1):

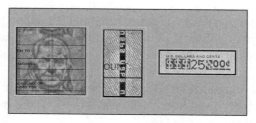

Figure 9.1 Study these distinguishing characteristics to determine if a money order you received is the real deal. From left to right: Benjamin Franklin watermark, security thread, dollar amount coloring.

Continued

- When held to the light, a watermark of Benjamin Franklin is repeated from top to bottom on the left side.
- When held to the light, a dark line (security thread) runs from top to bottom with the abbreviation "USPS" repeated.
- There should be no discoloration around the dollar amounts, which might indicate the amounts were changed.
- Domestic postal money orders may not exceed $1,000, and international postal money orders may not exceed $700.

If you're uncertain about the genuine nature of a received money order, determine that you'll delay shipment until you can have it verified at your bank or local post office.

- **Personal checks.** Some buyers still prefer to whip out their checkbooks and scribble their payment. Cheerfully accept personal checks, but make it obvious that the check will need to clear your bank before goods will be shipped. If you have a repeat customer who has successfully paid via personal check in the past, consider waiving the waiting period (a nice touch that promotes trust and entices follow-up transactions).
- **Escrow.** Again, this is one of the costliest methods and should typically be reserved for high-value transactions (at least greater than $500), and the buyer and seller need to agree on who will pay the fees. It's a good idea to be open to utilizing online escrow if the buyer seems especially intent on it; the seller has the option to require that the buyer pay the entire escrow fee if, in the seller's estimation, the exchange could be managed simply and securely via a lower-cost alternative.

Don't expect to utilize COD (cash on delivery) much, if at all, and try to steer your customers away from cash transactions, as the money cannot be tracked or otherwise accounted for.

Payment Remittance Policies

You've been good to offer a variety of payment methods, but don't forget to likewise establish *when* you expect to receive the funds. Some buyers will dally a bit or outright forget to pay unless they're prodded up front. There's nothing clever or mysterious about this condition: state that payment must be received within seven days from the close of the auction—period. Unless you intend to offer some sort of layaway service, you have every right to expect payment quickly. Typically this isn't an issue, as the majority of buyers are eager to collect their winnings. Since prepayment is the norm in online auctioning, the sooner they pay, the sooner you can ship their item. Just proactively state the deadline for when you expect to be compensated and explain that their high-bidder status could rightfully be revoked and the item offered to the next-highest bidder or relisted for another go-round.

Shipping and Handling Costs

Knowing that these additional costs are sometimes the source of price-hiking attempts, buyers can be skittish about the fees they'll be expected to pay to get their item from your hands and into their own. Be clear and *honest* in quoting these charges, making absolutely sure you've stated your shipping and handling policy before bids are placed.

You actually have a few choices to make:

- **Charge the exact shipping fee.** This is generally the most desirable method from the buyer's perspective, yet it can be cumbersome to the seller, who might not know the fee until the package is sent on its way. By that time, the buyer was charged either too little or too much for shipping costs. Of course, if you're selling a similar item on a consistent basis, you'll likely anticipate the exact postage amount, or you can employ the use of a postal scale to help you in times of doubt.
- **Charge a flat fee.** Many volume sellers have fairly and effectively employed this method. The key to being successful in levying a flat fee is to charge a cost that's within 50¢ (high or low) of the actual shipping costs. Remember, it's considered a scam if the seller charges $6 for an item that cost $3 or less to actually ship.
- **Offer various shipping methods.** Options entice, and your buyers should be given a couple of alternatives when it comes to shipping, too. It's fine to state that your default method is USPS Priority Mail or UPS Ground, but also offer faster shipping to anxious buyers or those who need their items fast. Both carriers just mentioned have express delivery services available, and if overnight delivery is critical, consider providing FedEx or DHL delivery. Of course, you'll want to pass these costs on to the buyer.

There is a sensitive area in the realm of shipping costs: *handling* fees. There's an ongoing debate over whether sellers should charge for their time to prepare, pack, and ship items. This is purely a personal choice; however, if you decide you will charge handling fees, be sure to clearly state those costs in your sales policy. If not, you risk being accused of the infamous Scam No. 5 (see Chapter 6).

> **eBay TIP:** To avoid controversy when starting out, I suggest you forgo the handling fees, considering that time and effort as part of the cost of doing business. Instead of charging for this time spent, look for ways to make your end-of-auction routine faster and more efficient.

Insurance and Tracking

If you're shipping UPS or USPS Express Mail, tracking and insurance are usually covered in the cost of delivery. However, for basic delivery, insurance and package tracking involve additional cost. Always offer your buyer the option to purchase these services, yet be clear that if such insurance and tracking are declined, the *buyer* will bear the risk if something goes awry in transit. Most packages arrive at their final destinations just fine, but in that odd instance when something does go wrong, be certain you and your buyer are clear about who absorbs the unfortunate fallout.

Delivery Expectations

Buyers need to be shown that the onus is not all on them in terms of package delivery. A good policy will include information regarding when items will be shipped. If you can ship immediately upon payment confirmation, say as much in your policy. If you can ship only on Mondays and Thursdays, be clear about that. Understand that buyers are taking the initial risk of prepaying for their purchases; ease their concerns by including shipment and delivery expectations within the body of your sales policy.

Refunds and Guarantees

There's not much debate here: either you support a policy of 100 percent satisfaction guaranteed with no questions asked or you don't. Actually, there is some middle ground to be found when it comes to refunds and guar-antees, but your first challenge is to decide whether you're willing to take back an item after it's been sold. If you're completely confident about your items and believe it is best to offer total satisfaction (which includes absorb-ing the cost of buyer flubs and fibs), then proudly state you'll honor all returns.

You can, however, be just as successful if you provide *conditional* refunds. You can state that if the item received is not as advertised, you'll gladly accept a return. It's okay to stipulate that all returns are subject to inspection and verification (recalling Scam No. 10 from Chapter 6). It's like-wise your prerogative to state that all sales are final (which is especially appli-cable for the sale of easily duplicated items, such as music and video). You may need to experiment with this portion of your policy, but it's most prudent to begin with the conditional return at the outset.

SUMMING IT ALL UP

To wrap it all up, consider these examples of a sales policy you might include in your item descriptions:

> High Bidder will please prepay plus shipping costs (calculated at close of auction). Payment by PayPal is preferred and will result in immedi-ate shipment payment posted to my account. Payment by money order or cashier's check will gain immediate shipment of item upon receipt and verification. Personal checks gladly accepted but will need to clear (approximately 10 days) before item can be shipped. All items shipped via USPS Priority Mail or Express Mail. Insurance and delivery confir-mation available at additional cost. If insurance is declined, buyer assumes responsibility for damage or loss. All items guaranteed to arrive as described with refunds cheerfully granted if item received is materially different than as listed. Items must be returned within 10 days of original delivery and are subject to inspection prior to refund being issued. If there are any questions regarding these terms and con-ditions, please contact me via e-mail before bidding. Thank you for your interest in my auctions.

If you'd prefer to post an "as is" policy, consider this:

> High bidder to prepay plus $5.85 fixed shipping/insurance cost. Payment must be received within 10 days of auction close. Payment by PayPal is preferred and will result in immediate shipment payment posted to my account. Payment by money order or cashier's check will gain immediate

shipment of item upon receipt and verification. Personal checks gladly accepted but will need to clear (approximately 10 days) before item can be shipped. All items shipped via USPS Priority Mail or Express Mail. All items guaranteed to be as described and are offered on an "as is" basis with no warranty or refund implied. If you have questions, please contact me via e-mail before bidding. Thanks!

Of course, you're free to adjust the terms shown in these examples to best suit your needs; these are merely templates (though actively in use) to help get you started. Note the intangibles, though: the success of your sales policy is just as dependent on tone and style as it is on terms and conditions. As you craft your own policy, take these considerations to heart:

- **Be exhaustive but not exhausting.** Be certain you've covered all pertinent aspects of your policy, but avoid laying down so many rules that your sales policy winds up feeling more like an iron-clad contract than a transaction guideline. If your policy comes off as too rigid or dictatorial, you might unwittingly drive away bidders.
- **Be customer oriented.** The goal of your policy is not only to establish a road map for your transactions but also to encourage customers to buy from you. Therefore, remember to offer as many options and alternatives as is practical. Offer services that clearly protect your customers as well as yourself.
- **Say it with a smile.** Some sellers become tone-deaf when presenting their policies, appearing stolid or overbearing. Read your policy back to yourself (or read it to a friend) and determine whether it sounds relatively friendly in its delivery.

POSTING YOUR POLICY

With your policy ready to go, make sure to post it plainly for all bidders and future buyers to see. The easiest method of posting your policy is to include it in the body of your item descriptions. If, later, you decide you want to improve the visual appearance of your policy, consider utilizing HTML code in your item descriptions (see Chapter 16) to offset the text, present it in a different (slightly smaller) font, or enable an off-site link to your own Web page. However you decide to present it, be sure it's always available and easy to find. Go the extra step by encouraging potential customers to contact you directly *before* bidding if they have any questions, concerns, or doubts.

WHAT TO DO IF YOUR POLICY COMES UNDER FIRE

Whether truly sincere or sincerely belligerent, bidders and buyers sometimes question your sales policy and may seek to coerce you to bend the rules. Being flexible is always a good idea, but if you simply cannot alter your methods or you take offense at a customer's *extreme* requests, here are some of the best ways to respond:

- Refer to and restate your sales policy as it appeared in your item listing; the bidder essentially agreed to these terms upon placing a bid, provided no other agreements were made with you in advance.
- Explain that your volume of business doesn't lend itself to making special arrangements of the sort requested and that your policy is constructed to offer a reasonable range of terms. Be comfortable in standing by your policy as stated.
- Ask the customer *why* special arrangements outside of your stated policy are necessary.
- If the customer remains insistent or proclaims dissatisfaction, offer to cancel the high bid and offer the item to the next bidder or relist it; the customer will be faced with deciding whether the need for special treatment is more important than acquiring the item won.
- Give the special request thoughtful consideration. This might be a legitimate and reasonable request and could well be an area where your policy could stand refining.

This final point is key in determining the effectiveness of your policy and its ability to encourage business. Always look for ways to improve how your business will operate and how you can best serve your customers. Remember that your sales policy exists to *enable* easy transactions, not hinder them. Keep an open mind about refinement, and you'll be on track to continually improve the potential to acquire your fortune faster.

10

Determining What Your Goods Are Worth

One of your greatest challenges as a seller is determining, with confidence, the value of the items you intend to offer. These days, everyone is looking for a deal, a steal, and items with unparalleled appeal. Sure, you've been told to "buy low, sell high," but is it really possible to sustain an existence in such a merchandising Nirvana? While it's true that once or twice you can haul in a mint on a well-timed (or downright fortuitous) listing, the fact of the matter is that you're not likely to find your auction fortune overnight because not everything you have that glitters will become gold. The task, then, is to determine how to run the marathon—not the short-lived sprint—on the track to your auction fortune. The method by which you determine the value of the items you intend to sell will poise you for either a glorious finish or a quick exit. It's all in how you price and present your goods.

REALITY CHECK: HAS THE FEVER SUBSIDED?

If you knew anyone who was vigorously selling at eBay between 1996 and 1998, you likely envied their good fortune as they secured astounding prices for the strangest of goods. The emerging opportunity of selling online, fueled largely by the astronomical success of eBay, created enough buzz to coax people to get online for the first time for the sole intention of bidding and winning. The novelty of online auctioning, coupled with the fact that previously elusive items were springing out of closets, attics, and local thrift stores and onto the global online market, fed the overnight success of online merchandising. As if intoxicated by the allure of the online treasure trove, buyers feverishly and often capriciously paid above-market prices for the goods they found.

Whether relieved to simply find a sought-after artifact or entranced by the bid-and-win allure, buyers were happily *overpaying* for items in the fresh new auction place. Sellers savvy enough to jump on this gravy train early were delighted to see their profits soar like never before. Of course, once word gets out about such an oasis, it's only a matter of time before it becomes an overcrowded tourist trap that sees its once lofty status reduced to that of a commonplace attraction.

That's what happened at eBay; once the novelty wore off a bit and the die-hard buyers and collectors had scooped up their cherished acquisitions, the market cooled—and so did prices. The reality check today is to come to eBay with a level head and a well-grounded education about the prices this "perfect market" will now bear.

---

eBay TIP: Don't misunderstand me—there are plenty of opportunities to strike it rich quick, yet the staying power of such an income influx is difficult to predict or prolong. When the national and global economies sputter, prices fall; expect that. Interestingly, though, prices have never truly bottomed out at eBay, especially in the realm of collectibles and pop culture curiosities; the "boomer" and "tweener" generations hold such items in high regard and are willing to continue paying well for those items that rekindle memories of simpler days gone by. In other words, there's plenty of water left in this well.

FINDING THE RIGHT STUFF TO SELL

Before you can consider the value of the goods you'll sell, you need to determine which goods will bear the sort of value that propels your profit potential. For starters, you'll need to identify those sorts of goods that will sell at the profit margins that will support your income goals. As this book's title promises, you *can* sell practically anything at eBay these days (and, of course, make a fortune doing it). So what sells? Here's a high-level list of the sorts of items that consistently sell well in the virtual auction space:

- **Antiques.** The most venerable goods are those that have been around for some time. These trade hands daily—furniture, artwork, tools, simple appliances, statuary, and more. While the official definition of an antique is "something that's at least 100 years old," there are plenty of "vintage" goods that are as young as 20 or 30 years old and that command good prices day in and day out. If you have this sort of stock—plenty of it—or have access to such goods, you're on the fast path to fortune.
- **China, silverware, and glassware.** Check your buffet, china cabinet, and anywhere that dishes, glass, and serving utensils may be stored. Perhaps you aren't particularly thrilled with the looks of this outdated tableware but the auction market would likely break down your door if they knew you had it.
- **Advertising, premium, and promotional items.** Whether you saved up trading stamps or clipped box tops, those items you sent away for or were given as courtesy samples are real gold in today's nostalgic culture. Gas station giveaways, fast-food toys, and more, continue to stay high on buyer's lists of most wanted items.
- **Old product packaging.** It's no longer Prince Albert in a can that draws the attention of collectors worldwide. Collectors and speculators are paying handsomely for just about anything we once called garbage. Vintage milk cartons, cereal boxes, even TV dinner trays and peanut butter jars (see Figure 10.1) are hot commodities if they've been around 30 years or more. The trick to the big dollars here is to have the stuff in stellar condition.
- **Anything in Grandma's attic or the kids' room.** That stuff that's been sitting in boxes since the late 1960s and early '70s is pure treasure in today's retro market. While Grandma's stuff that dates back 50 years or more could be worth significantly more, the youth of the Nixon and Ford years are eagerly seeking out reminders of the old days—good, bad, or otherwise.

Don't limit yourself to just these sorts of items, though. It's true that practically everything and anything is desirable to someone, somewhere. If you're not certain about that whatever-it-is you're ready to throw away, run a quick search on eBay's current and recently closed auctions to see if people are bidding for this stuff. More often than not, you'll find your goods are in demand and you'll quickly discover which items you'll want to focus your attention on as you discover their value.

Figure 10.1 Who in their right mind would pay $100 for an empty peanut butter jar? Me, that's who. ("Koogle" jar, mint condition, dated 1976.)

SO WHAT'S IT WORTH?

The old adage applies: nothing is worth anything until at least two people want it. Your task is to determine the price that will cause at least two bidders to tussle over ownership of your item. After reviewing current and past auctions, you should be developing an idea of the prices certain items command, indicating whether such goods will help you realize your fortune goals. Here are important additional considerations to ponder as you determine a value for your goods that, by and large, will be shared by your potential customers:

- **Supply and demand.** Always, the value of your goods is determined at the time they sell by these two inescapable economic drivers. If supply is high, the value might be lower than you'd like unless demand is likewise high. If supply is low, the value can quickly climb unless there's simply little demand for what you're offering. Remember, supply and demand are the two factors that enable an accurate *current market value* for any item.

- **Condition and completeness.** No matter how rare the item, no matter how many folks are clamoring for it, the condition of your goods will play a key role in determining its value. Your job here is to assess your item as compared to others like it that have recently sold. If your item is in lesser condition or is incomplete when compared to another similar item, expect the value to be less as well. However, if your item is in better condition than those that have been sold before yours, expect the value to increase, sometimes markedly, especially if yours is in a condition rarely found in the marketplace.

- **Time sensitivity and seasonal appeal.** This is an aspect you'll later consider in your selling strategies. For now, just know that certain items that have strong appeal during specific times of the year are not likely to gain maximum price potential if you attempt to sell them off season.

- **Presentation and positioning.** Again, this is an aspect to be discussed more fully when we examine applying a sales strategy, but understand at this point that *when* and *how* you present an item can directly influence its moneymaking potential. As you research other, similar items that have sold (and those that haven't), look for differentiators that may have affected the item's value and see how those factors could play in your item's favor or against it as you assess its price potential. No, timing isn't *everything*, but it certainly influences a lot of things—namely, price.

WHERE ELSE CAN YOU TURN FOR VALUATION ADVICE?

If you're still somewhat stumped about the potential value of an item you have, here are some other resources you can tap to better determine whether what you have is trash or treasure:

- **Talk with other sellers.** Most merchants you'll encounter at eBay are generally quite friendly and forthcoming. The days of closely guarded sales secrets are pretty much gone, with so many of the millions of eBay users having summarily "seen that, done that, sold that item." Politely inquire of other sellers their opinions about what you might offer, especially if it seems particularly obscure. I've yet to meet a seller who *didn't* have an opinion on the value of some item.

- **Consult price guides.** Most items, especially collectible fare, have been well catalogued and documented in one sort of price guide or another. Take heed, though, that price guides are just that: guides. Carefully read the guide's grading policy (the assessment of an item's condition and how that is factored into the suggested value) to make sure you're clear about how the value was derived. Make value adjustments as appropriate based on, again, the condition and completeness of the item you have to sell. Also take note of the date of publication of the guide; the market has definitely changed—largely due to eBay—and the value of the items described is certain to have been adjusted in relation to guides that are even a year or two old. Remember the bobblehead craze of 2002—and where are *they* now? (See Figure 10.2.)
- **Investigate the value of related items.** If you're having trouble finding another item just like yours, look for a close cousin to that obscure artifact in front of you. Search for items of the same time period, of the same manufacturer, and of the same or similar style. Much the way anthropologists assess the origin of their latest diggings, you might need to do a bit of digging to identify what you have and what it might be worth.

Figure 10.2 Bobbleheads: once, they were hot, hot, hot. For the moment, they're not, not, not.

WHAT IS IT WORTH TO YOU?

The ultimate value of any item is always determined by its current owner. Some sellers will hold out for months and years, insistent that their goods are worth far more than any of the uneducated would-be buyers have yet offered. Others turn treasures over for a pittance, happy to simply rid themselves of the burden of ownership. At this point, you'll need to do a bit of soul-searching yourself to decide what *you* feel the item is worth and what *you* consider a reasonable minimum selling price. To help you with this effort of personal valuation, think about the following:

- **Are you in distress or disillusionment?** If you simply need to get rid of an item or items quickly (emptying a storage unit, emerging from a divorce, or whatever), you'll probably be glad to get a few bucks and get the items out of your sight. You'll probably be satisfied with less in price and should consider this as you determine what it's worth to be rid of the stuff.
- **How much do you have invested in the item?** If you paid through the nose hoping the value of an item would appreciate, you'll need to consider whether you can recover your investment and how much opportunity you have to garner a profit in the current market. If prices are down, you might need to hold onto the item until the market rebounds. If, however, you need to cut your losses and recoup at least a portion of your investment, you'll want to take that into consideration as you look to get what you can.
- **How badly do you need the income today?** If you need quick cash, you'll be better served to collect a fast nickel than wait for a slow dime. This is the key reason some sellers "blow out" their merchandise. Whether they're getting out of the business or need quick cash to invest elsewhere, the need for funds has a direct impact on how an item is valued by the seller.
- **How realistic are your expectations?** This goes back to the reality check and requires you to make an honest and well-informed assessment about what your item is truly worth and not what you *wish* it was worth. Yesterday's gone and tomorrow's promise hasn't yet arrived; don't dream about the prices that once were or those that you're sure are just around the corner. If you can afford to wait, by all means do so, but make sure you're reasonable in your aspirations.

Take heart from the fact that even lesser-valued items can pay off quite handsomely. Think of it this way: if ever you've seen those seemingly insignificant ATM purchases—a mere $14, $22, and such—add up to a bundle before you realized it, recognize that income from eBay can add up just as quickly. Suddenly, the comparative nickels and dimes you could earn in volume sales can accumulate quite quickly and deliver some tidy sums. Sure, you'll hit a home run from time to time, but few make their fortunes overnight. It's an endurance race, and if you value your items accurately and reasonably, you'll be in perfect position to bring in a steady stream of sales. Add a bit of sales strategy to the mix (covered in depth in Chapter 18), and you'll see that you don't necessarily need gold to cash in at eBay.

11

Completing the Sale

When the auction ends, it's time for you to leap into action. Some new sellers harbor a certain anxiety over making contact with and collecting payment from virtual strangers while others jump in too forcefully to extract their due. In reality, collecting payment and closing an auction deal need not be worrisome nor does it require a brash affront to ensure the transaction comes to fruition. A well-thought-out and skillfully executed end-of-auction routine is all that's needed to bring the sale to a close professionally, peacefully, and pleasantly.

PROMPT ACTION PROMPTS BUYERS TO ACT

Your first task is to set the stage for a fast, efficient, and satisfactory transaction. Your buyer, whether a seasoned user or a newbie to eBay, will look to you for guidance and direction. When you snap to attention as your auction closes, you'll establish the mood for the deal and can instill immediate confidence and responsiveness in the winning bidder. Most important, your fast action will encourage receipt of a fast payment.

At the close of your auction or when a Buy-It-Now item has been purchased, eBay will send an automated e-mail message to both you and your buyer (see Figure 11.1). The message not only serves as notification that a successful transaction has occurred but also indicates that it's time for the buyer and seller to make arrangements for the exchange.

While it's perfectly acceptable to await eBay's official notification of the listing's close, it's likewise just as acceptable to initiate contact with the high

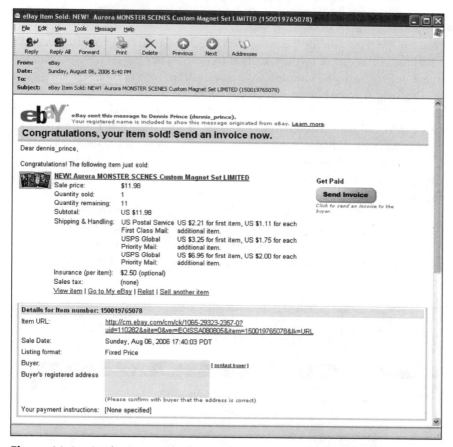

Figure 11.1 At the transaction's completion, eBay will forward a notification like this one.

bidder before eBay's automated message arrives, which sometimes takes several hours to a day to be received. Again, a fast transaction is the best course for a smooth exchange. Here's why:

- Your quick action shows your buyer that you're well organized and ready to complete the deal.
- You catch the buyers or high bidders while they are still high on the win and motivated to receive the item they've just won or purchased.
- You'll typically be paid more quickly.
- Your fast and customer-oriented action will likely gain you praise in the form of positive feedback in eBay's Feedback Forum.

INITIATING THE INVOICE

Now, rather than wait for the buyer to contact you to arrange remittance, take advantage of the easy invoice method to notify your buyers that payment is due. Look again at the sample e-mail notification from Figure 11.1 and you'll see the Send Invoice button contained within the message. Click that to begin the invoice transmission. The alternative method to launch an invoice is to visit the My eBay area and manage your items sold there (see Figure 11.2). To achieve the same invoice launch from My eBay as from the e-mail notification, click on the Send Invoice text link associated with the item sold. Either way, you'll navigate to the invoice creation and transmission page as shown in Figure 11.3.

Notice that the invoice eBay generates includes the buyer's user ID, the item title, the cost, and the shipping fees previously designated in the original listing. If you need to collect sales tax, make that specification here (perhaps you overlooked that during the listing creation). Also, it's a good move to

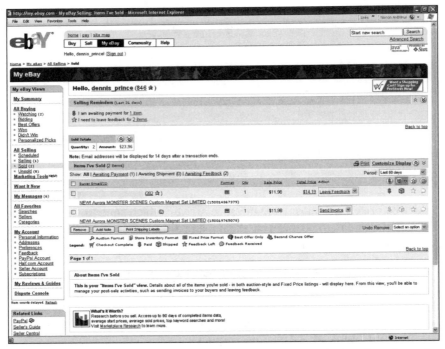

Figure 11.2 Visit the My eBay page as an alternate method to launch an invoice for an item sold.

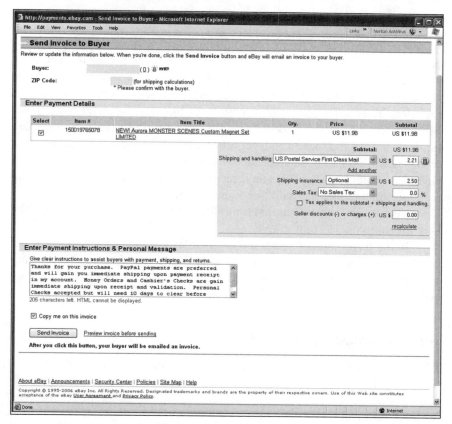

Figure 11.3 The eBay invoice is a fast and easy way to get a transaction under way.

restate your accepted payment methods and again encourage your preferred method, if any. When the details are complete, simply click the Send Invoice button at the bottom of the form.

> **eBay TIP:** What if you get a newbie? Here's where that fast action and well-thought-out business process allows you the opportunity to guide a newcomer through the transaction. Every time you meet a newbie, welcome it as a new opportunity to establish a return customer.

COLLECTING THE MONEY

At this point, collecting payment should be relatively simple. Thanks to your original listing terms and conditions followed by your timely and complete invoice, the buyer should have no questions about how payment should be made, when it should be remitted, and what sort of delivery service can be expected. You've done your job for now; it's time for the buyer to respond. Most buyers will respond to your invoice by remitting immediate payment (most *do* use PayPal these days), yet others may reply with an e-mail message of their own indicating whether they'll utilize a different form of acceptable payment. If paid via PayPal, you'll receive an e-mail notification indicating that your high bidder has paid (see Figure 11.4).

Visit PayPal to confirm that funds are in your account, then prepare the item for shipping. It's that simple.

If the buyer elects to send a money order, cashier's check, or personal check, keep a keen eye open for arrival of payment and be sure to send e-mail confirmation to the buyer when the payment arrives. At that point, indicate how and when you will be shipping the item.

TRANSACTIONAL TROUBLES?

What happens if the money's *not* good? Well, once in a while some transactions will hit a snag and might require a bit of extra effort. In your quest to make a fortune, expect the occasional slow payment or bad debt; it's just part of doing business.

Of course, your sales policy will have filtered out most payment problems before they occur, having clearly stated your acceptance of the safest and most reliable forms of remittance. But if a problem does arise despite your proactive efforts, you'll need a plan of action to rectify the situation.

Slow Payment

For whatever reasons, legitimate or otherwise, some buyers and winning bidders are slow to pay. Your prompt action at the close of the listing and easy payment methods will usually get most bidders to pay quickly (and some are downright impressive in their shared commitment to a fast transaction), a few are less motivated than you'd hope. If you've stated that payment must be received within 10 days and it's been 8 days with no cash in hand, send the buyer a reminder of the win and his or her commitment to complete the deal, such as:

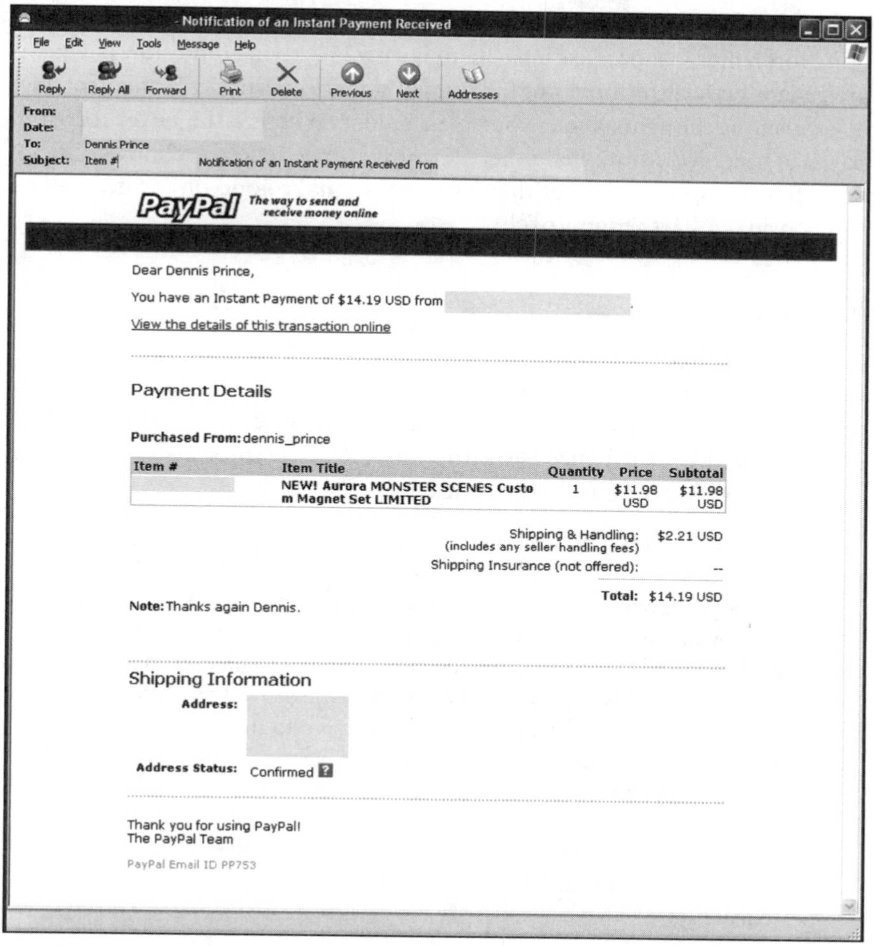

- Notification of an Instant Payment Received

File Edit View Tools Message Help

Reply | Reply All | Forward | Print | Delete | Previous | Next | Addresses

From:
Date:
To: Dennis Prince
Subject: Item #   Notification of an Instant Payment Received from

PayPal *The way to send and receive money online*

Dear Dennis Prince,

You have an Instant Payment of $14.19 USD from

View the details of this transaction online

Payment Details

Purchased From: dennis_prince

Item #	Item Title	Quantity	Price	Subtotal
	NEW! Aurora MONSTER SCENES Custom Magnet Set LIMITED	1	$11.98 USD	$11.98 USD

Shipping & Handling: (includes any seller handling fees)	$2.21 USD
Shipping Insurance (not offered):	--
Total:	$14.19 USD

Note: Thanks again Dennis.

Shipping Information

Address:

Address Status: Confirmed ⬚

Thank you for using PayPal!
The PayPal Team

PayPal Email ID PP753

Figure 11.4   PayPal sends e-mail notification of the good news: you've got cash!

Hello,

I haven't heard from you nor have I received payment for the item you have purchased from me at eBay. Please confirm you have received my original invoice dated 8/6/06 and let me know when I can expect to receive payment. I'm sure this was a simple oversight or unforeseen delay; I look forward to delivering this item to you. Please refer to the original invoice transmission for all pertinent details for payment and delivery.

Best,
Dennis
eBay ID: dennis_prince

Notice that the reminder message is never threatening and is actually quite forgiving. Just because a payment is slow in arriving (and slow payments are generally the exception, not the rule), it's not necessary to form all manner of suspicious thoughts about your high bidder. Whether the buyer forgot to pay, has been away from his or her PC, or has experienced technical difficulties, offer the opportunity for that customer to make good on the deal before you consider a harsher approach.

No Payment

If your listing has been visited by that .001 percent of the eBay population who just won't pay up, you'll need to take a firmer stance in your attempt to collect your due. If your messages have gone unanswered, your payment clock is ticking, and your patience is wearing thin, it's time to escalate a bit. Begin with a final notice message such as this:

> RE: FINAL NOTICE—Purchase of eBay Item
> Hello,
> I haven't received response from you following my original invoice and my follow-up reminder. As my sales policy stated in the original eBay listing, all payments are to be remitted within 10 days of purchase; that time has now passed. I will consider, then, you have chosen not to pay for your purchase and, therefore, are forfeiting your claim to the item. I consider this transaction null and void at this time.
> At this time, I will submit a dispute claim at eBay to report this as a nonpaid item.
> If you have questions about my course of action, please contact me immediately. Otherwise, I'll consider our business complete.
> Sincerely,
> Dennis
> eBay ID: dennis_prince

The "final notice" message is direct and to the point. It remains professional, though it could evoke any number of responses from the negligent buyer (or none at all). The key to the message is that it does not leave the situation open-ended ("our business is complete") and indicates your response to the buyer's inaction ("submit a dispute claim"). It's still possible, of course, that the buyer will make good on the deal, and you're wise to keep the door opened, if just a crack, to allow the transaction to be completed successfully. However, when you start managing multiple auctions on an ongoing basis, there simply isn't time to deal with a drawn-out exchange or engage in a personal battle.

Bad Debt

What if the money's no good? Usually, you'll run into this problem only if the buyer has sent a personal check (those do still bounce from time to time). In this situation, take these steps to sort out the problem:

- Contact the buyer immediately via e-mail to explain that the check has been refused.
- Avoid accusations, as this may be as much a surprise to the buyer as it is to you.
- Politely but firmly request repayment via online payment, money order, or cashier's check plus reimbursement for the returned check charge your bank may have imposed.
- When the payment is finally received and verified, confirm to the buyer, issue the appropriate thanks, and prepare to ship the item.
- If the buyer fails to make good on the payment, consider canceling the transaction.

THE KEY IS COMMUNICATION

To enable the smoothest transaction and highest level of satisfaction for your buyer as well as yourself, keep the lines of communication open at all times. From the point of invoice transmission through the receipt of payment, ensure you and your buyer can communicate freely and appropriately to instill confidence in the exchange. When the money's in the bank and you're ready to ship, keep communicating to set the buyer's expectations and demonstrate you're committed to providing exceptional service. Since your next step in the process is to pack and ship the item, turn now to Chapter 12 and learn how to pack like a pro.

12

Packing and Shipping Like a Pro

When the auction ended, you leaped into action to make contact with the high bidder and collect your earnings. But your job isn't finished yet. Once that payment arrives, you have to do a little more work. The excitement of selling at eBay often overshadows what's really going on: a seller is offering to sell and ship an item to a buyer. After the auction ended and the buyer paid, the onus is on the seller to bring the deal to a successful close by getting the item delivered quickly and safely.

Packing and shipping are something of an art and nothing to be underestimated or taken lightly (although "light is right" when it comes to controlling shipping costs). This is the point of the transaction where you, the seller, will establish your reputation in the buyer's mind. Take this step seriously and you'll be recognized as a stellar seller. If you're new to packing and shipping, don't fret over the hows and whys of the process; this chapter will help you determine the best supplies to have on hand, the best way to use them, and the best methods to use to ensure that item gets from Point A to Point B safely, to your buyer's delight.

SETTING UP YOUR SHIP SHOP

Believe it or not, many sellers overlook a key element in their packing process: *where* they will pack up their items. You might think you can grab a box, bubble wrap, and packing peanuts, and do your packing anywhere at anytime. Certainly, you can take that approach, but it's not the most efficient way to work, and besides, a transient "ship shop" could result in loss or damage to the items you'll pack.

If you'll be managing a significant amount of auctions (and therefore will be packing a lot of goods), you're best advised to establish a designated area for your packing activities. Choose a clean, well-lit environment that is dry and reasonably free from excessive foot traffic (in other words, avoid folks who may share the same living or working space with you and might tend to move items or abscond with the packing tape). A good ship shop lends itself to easy staging of items; it features a sizable flat work area (like a large table or workbench) that keeps the items free from damage and dirt, it provides easy access to all your shipping supplies, and it helps you develop a packing flow or routine that will save you time while ensuring your customers' ultimate satisfaction.

TOOLS OF THE TRADE

Efficiency begins with a well-stocked supply of the packing goods you'll need to ship items. Before that buyer's payment ever arrives, make sure you have the following supplies:

- Sturdy shipping boxes, reinforced envelopes, mailing tubes, and any other containers that will safely transport the items you sell
- Box fill, bubble pack, shredded paper, or other such cushioning materials that will protect the item inside the package
- Shipping tape
- Shipping labels
- Shipping forms such as insurance tags and international disclaimers
- Shipping tools: permanent markers, tape dispensers, utility knives, and so on

SOURCE OF SUPPLIES

Though you'd be right to consider the cost required to stock a ship shop, you'll be happy to learn that the bulk of the materials and supplies can be had for free. For starters, begin with the U.S. Postal Service (USPS) to stock up on all manner of boxes, envelopes, tubes, labels, and more, to handle the majority of your shipping needs. Besides these supplies being free, they're easy to order right from your PC. Simply go to shop.usps.com in your favorite Web browser and navigate to the Shipping Supplies area (see Figure 12.1). Order

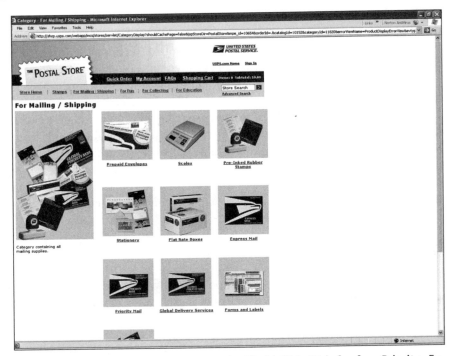

Figure 12.1 Visit shop.usps.com on the World Wide Web for free Priority, Express, and Global Mail supplies.

the items and amounts you need to stock your ship shop, then use the simple checkout screen to have the items sent to you. As with the regular mail you receive every day, the USPS will deliver these supplies right to your doorstep.

> **eBay TIP:** If you prefer to use post-paid packaging, the USPS supplies site also offers such items in the form of flat envelopes, boxes, and tubes for sale. If you use this sort of packaging, determine that you'd charge that same per-package flat rate to your customers.

If you'll be using United Parcel Service (UPS), Federal Express, DHL, or another carrier, look them up on the Internet, as they, too, offer free shipping supplies for packages you ship using their services. Of course, you can also get these same supplies at your local carrier's offices or designated partner stations.

Some packing supplies, though, are not free. When it comes to box fill, specialized cartons, and the like, you may actually need to purchase these items. Visit your nearest wholesale or club warehouse for better prices on packing tape or specialized envelopes not readily available from the carriers. Visit your local office supply store or shipping office for large bags of styrofoam peanuts and rolls of bubblepack.

---

eBay TIP: Don't be bashful about picking up such supplies free from time to time. Offices, liquor stores, and even grocery stores routinely throw out reusable packing supplies. Ask around if you see those materials ready for the dumpster, and if they're clean and seem suitable for your packing task, ask whether you can take those supplies for yourself.

And don't forget eBay itself: it's full of merchants selling these sorts of packing supplies, and usually at better prices than you'd pay at retail office supply stores. Also, if you're actively buying while selling, be sure to recycle the packing materials that protected the items you received. Most interior packing material can be used over and over again without any significant degradation.

PACKING PROTOCOL

Although packing is something of a profession, it's a skill easily acquired if you have the right supplies and know how to use them properly. Here are some things to consider as you approach your packing job:

- Think "lightweight" to save on shipping costs but not at the expense of safe delivery.
- Pack items snugly in boxes, but don't overdo it lest you damage the item through the crush of cushioning.
- For fragile items, use the "box within a box" method to ensure extra cushion and protection (still mindful of total package weight).
- Use rigid mailers or padded envelopes, or insert cardboard stiffeners to protect flat items.
- Be considerate of the recipient and don't overtape or otherwise excessively seal a package; the item could be damaged as the buyer tries to wrest it free.

With the item ready to ship, send it on its way at the nearest carrier's office or authorized forwarding station. Be sure to retain your receipts, insurance forms, delivery confirmation numbers, and so on; not only will you want to have these important documents when verifying shipment and ultimate delivery, but many such expenses might be suitable as a business tax deduction (see Chapter 25 for more details). Once the package is en route, send another message to the buyer to indicate the item is on the way and provide tracking numbers (if available) so the buyer may monitor the package's journey (another free service available from most carrier's Web sites—see Figure 12.2). In your message to the buyer, request a confirmation response to indicate when the item has arrived and if all is satisfactory.

eBay TIP: If packing supplies are costing you money on a regular basis, you can consider recovering that cost in your shipping and handling fees. If you're maintaining a high volume of sales, those costs can likely be recovered by adding as little as 25¢ to your shipping fee. Be careful, though, as any cost much higher than that could be construed as a form of final price manipulation.

GETTING SPECIFIC: WHAT ARE YOU SHIPPING?

For added guidance, here are a few rules of thumb that experts use when they approach a particular packing job:

- **Photos or other nonbreakable flat items:** Use a suitably sized envelope with a same-size piece of cardboard for stiffening. For particularly old or delicate flat merchandise, consider putting the item in a plastic sleeve, then sandwiching it between two pieces of cardboard. Don't just lick that envelope flap; use a strip of packing tape to seal it shut. If it's a particularly large item, consider rolling it (if that won't cause damage) and send it in a sturdy (repeat, *sturdy*) mailing tube with both end-caps taped securely in place.
- **Glassware, pottery, and other fragile items:** Wrap the item in light tissue paper first, then wrap it again with bubble wrap. Put it in an appropriate-sized box with a cushion of packing peanuts around the item. Next, place this box inside another box, again using a cushion

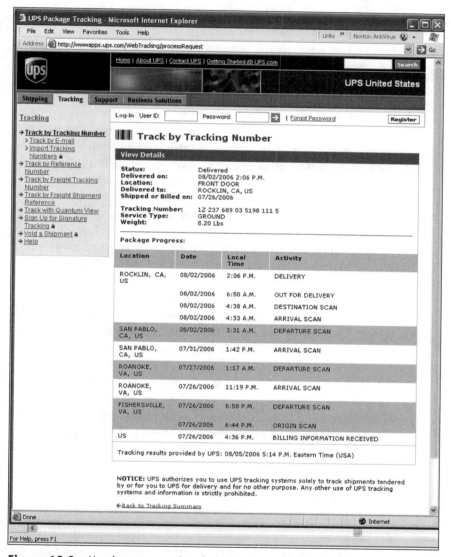

Figure 12.2 Here's an example of the UPS online package tracking service, helping you and your buyer monitor a package's journey.

of packing peanuts around the box within a box. Styrofoam sheets also work great as outer box siding material.

- **Framed items:** Size matters here, and you'll need to size up the task to see whether it's within your potential to do a good job and whether you'll be able to work with the supplies you have. For starters, if the item is behind glass, it's best to disassemble the piece and pack the elements separately (see the preceding tips on flat items). Bubble pack and foam sheets are a must here, and you should wrap frame corners with sheet foam to prevent them from puncturing the packing box or causing damage to the piece itself (be it a litho, photograph, or whatever). Although you can find special packing boxes just for framed items, if the piece is too valuable or too unwieldy for your comfort, take it to a professional packing and shipping service.

- **Oversized items:** If it's too big to handle, if you think you'll have to improvise a patchwork of packaging, or if you just don't think you'll be able to get it in and out of your car when you're all done, then by all means, hand the job over to a pro.

- **The little things:** Whether a small piece of jewelry, a stamp, or any other small collectible or item that could have big value, be sure it doesn't get lost in the mail. First, protect it: put the item in an appropriate-sized box with the right amount of packing peanuts or foam sheets to cushion it. Next, make it visible: Put that little box into a medium-sized box with appropriate interior cushioning. The second box might add more protection than required, but the goal is to be sure that little darling doesn't fall into some crevice, crack, or piece of mail-sorting machinery, after which it might never be seen again.

ADDITIONAL PACKING CONSIDERATIONS

You may have never thought there could be so much to simply packing an item. This discussion isn't intended to overcomplicate the process but does recognize how important it is—to you and your customers—that items are shipped and received in satisfactory, undamaged condition. To that end, here are a few more considerations to take into account.

Shake and Break?

One USPS employee imparted this bit of wisdom: "If you can shake it, we can break it." With that in mind, all items you ship should be given the *shake and rattle* test: before sealing an outer box, hold the flaps closed and give the item a few shakes. Do you hear any movement inside? If so, you might want to add a bit more interior padding until it's whisper-quiet in there. Movement could be the opportunity for items to shift and become damaged during their journey to their new home. For some items, even the tiniest scratch incurred can significantly affect the value of the item and pose a significant difference between the condition received and the condition described during the auction's run.

Help Fight Wetness

Other postal and shipping employees tell of water hazards. Somehow, even if there's not a cloud in the sky, items can get wet during transit. Expect that most water damage is irreversible, so take a simple step to ward it off: put the item in a plastic bag whenever possible. It typically doesn't have to be hermetically sealed, but a simple ziplock bag or a larger poly bag sealed with packing tape is usually enough to keep the wet weather out. Also, experienced handlers recommend that clear tape be used to seal the address label on the package's outside. If that gets wet and smeared, your package might end up in the dead mail vault for all eternity.

Don't Overpack It

Okay. If a little cushion is good, a lot should be dynamite, right? Not really. Too much interior packing can literally cause an explosion. Remember that boxes will get bumped, stacked, kicked, and tossed about on their sometimes perilous journeys. Use enough interior packaging to keep the item safe and secure, but if the box bulges like an overpacked suitcase, the item that's inside will probably get damaged the moment you seal it shut.

Sealing the Deal

Not only will too much interior packing lead to potential damage, but an overzealous packer might likewise present buyers with something of a challenge as they try to extract their treasure from a practically impenetrable tape-and-cardboard sarcophagus. Seal the item enough to ensure it won't accidentally open in transit, but don't feel you have to extinguish an entire supply of tape, staples, and whatever else to guarantee the item's safety. Many buyers tell of accidentally damaging an item themselves as they struggle to free it from it's packaging. And don't forget, excessive packaging adds excessive weight—which results in unnecessarily increased shipping costs.

Little Extras Make a Big Difference

If the item is particularly fragile and would fare best if unpacked by a certain method, include special unpacking instructions inside the box, positioned so they can be found the moment the recipient opens the package (write "Open This End First" on the shipping box to ensure this). Also, be sure to include an extra shipping label *inside* the package; often labels will come loose or become unreadable during the journey or they might get wet. In some instances, packages are opened by the carrier in the hope that he or she will find an extra label to get the item on its way again.

KEEPING IT REAL

Be sure to make use of the rate calculators that the different carriers make available on their Web sites (see Figure 12.3); these will help you be more accurate when quoting shipping costs to your buyers. However, if you accidentally overcharged the buyer by a dollar or more for shipping costs (perhaps the package didn't end up weighing as much as you anticipated), put a refund in an envelope and seal it up with the item. That sort of honest service speaks volumes to buyers, and you'll feel better knowing you did the right thing.

POSTAGE AS CLOSE AS YOUR PRINTER

Perhaps one of the best developments in saving time with shipping (next to all the free supplies mentioned previously) is the advent of online postage purchase and printing. As you're working to make your postauction process as smooth and efficient as possible, be sure to harness the time-saving value of printing preposted shipping labels from your home office, whenever you need to. Here's a look at how it's done and how easy it is to say goodbye to stamps and long lines at the postal station and say hello to postage on demand.

Who Offers Online Postage

Both USPS and UPS postage purchase are already integrated with eBay itself, the site having previously recognized the value to sellers who want to squeeze out every bit of inefficiency from their selling activities.

When one of your listings has concluded, you can collect your payment from your buyer and click a link (from within the actual item listing page or from within your My eBay page) and purchase and print the shipping label (see Figure 12.4).

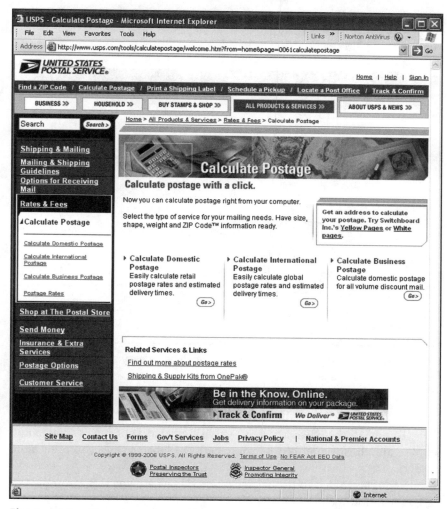

Figure 12.3 At www.usps.com, the postage calculator helps you determine the cost to ship your package.

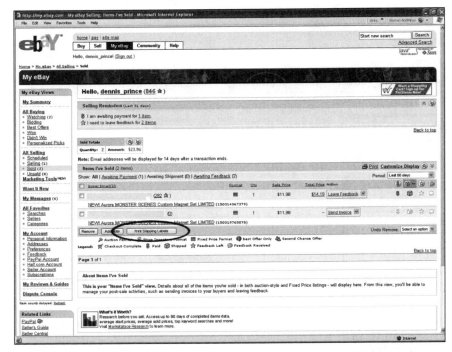

Figure 12.4 Creating post-paid shipping labels is as easy as clicking a button from the My eBay page.

To add to the efficiency gain, you'll find that your buyer's name and address are already prefilled as you create the label, saving you even more time.

You'll be guided to the carrier's Web site, where you'll be prompted to verify the following:

- Shipping method (standard, priority, overnight)
- Package type (envelope, package, oversize package)
- Package weight (in pounds and ounces)
- Insurance option (specify the value of the package contents)

Once that information has been entered, the site will process your input and provide you a cost to deliver the package as you have specified it. At this point, you simply purchase and print the shipping label (you will need to create an account and provide a valid credit card for charging the shipping costs).

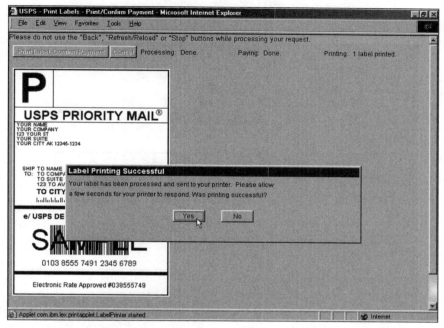

Figure 12.5 Your shipping costs and applied effort just got slashed again thanks to online postage purchase and printing.

> **eBay TIP:** If you've received a PayPal payment and complete the postage purchase through the PayPal site, you can elect to have the shipping label costs deducted directly from your PayPal account balance.

Now it's just a matter of printing the label on an attached or network-accessed printer, and you're done (see Figure 12.5). Oh, and don't forget to select the Economy Printing mode from your printer properties menu to save on ink consumption, too. Now you're packing *and* shipping like a pro!

13

Dealing with Difficult Customers

The customer is always right.

How many times have you heard that? Well, it's a great mantra to utter when you're a customer deserving (maybe demanding?) total satisfaction. How about when you're the seller, though? Sure, most auction sellers work hard to satisfy their high bidders, but there are times when that bidder-cum-customer turns out to be . . . well . . . difficult. In the interests of good business and good customer relations, this chapter provides some sage advice and useful tips for the time when you might find yourself dealing with a buyer who requires more hands-on treatment than you had originally expected.

FIX THE PROBLEM, NOT THE BLAME

To be successful with your customers, you're going to have to get to know them—and have them get to know you—quickly. Recall the discussion of the anxiety some buyers and sellers encounter at the end of the auction. While buyers are taking the leap of faith, so to speak, in paying up front, sellers sometimes feel even more vulnerable, fearing the possibly undesirable whims and moods of potentially impatient or irrational buyers. If this sort of situation rears its head, fall back on your clear and concise communication and your straightforward sales policy to help you navigate these choppy waters.

Be attentive, though, to the cause of the difficulty you're engaged in with the buyer and determine whether it's a response to something potentially troublesome or otherwise ambiguous in your policy. If you encounter the same difficulty with more than one customer, it could be an indication that your policy requires some revision. To that end, try to determine why the customer is dissatisfied and otherwise disgruntled with the way in which you're conducting the transaction. Whenever possible, seek to be collaborative and sensitive to the customer's needs; make an ally out of the buyer, and you'll stand the greatest chance of steering the deal in a cooperative direction and winding up with a win-win situation in the end.

PERSONALITY PARADE

Of course, you never know how a deal might go until you're in the thick of it. As stated before, most buyers will honor the auction agreement without much complication, but there are some who have more peculiar and problematic styles. A difficult deal doesn't necessarily mean a bad deal, nor does it always involve a creep on the other end. Nonetheless, to help you best prepare for the sort of personality that might lie behind the difficult deal, keep an eye open for bidder types like these:

- **The newbie.** Newcomers don't necessarily intend to be difficult to deal with—they're often just a bit uncertain or overanxious when conducting business online. Unless they manifest the behaviors noted in some of the following profiles, simply welcome them to the auction space and show them some extra consideration. Help them learn the ways of online auctioning and you'll help yourself to a smoother exchange. You'll be an ambassador to the new cybermarket they've found, plus you might gain yourself a repeat customer—someone who will come back and buy your items again—in response to your patient efforts. (I'll discuss the dynamics of dealing with newbies in greater detail in Chapter 14.)

- **The antsy buyer.** This is the one who wants the item fast, fast, *fast.* You might receive pestering e-mails that continually ask, *"When will it arrive?"* Of course, until you have a buyer's payment, there can be no progress. However, communicate frequently with this person and clearly state when payment was received, when an item has shipped, and when the person might expect to receive it. Acknowledge the anticipation of impatient buyers by encouraging them to pay for a shipping method that provides online tracking; they can monitor the progress of their packages themselves while you move on to your other business.

- **The paranoid buyer.** Trust is the key to these individuals and, truth be told, they might not trust you. Regardless of your fair policy, your engaging communication, or your professional style, paranoid buyers find it outright difficult to deal with strangers. Quickly, but completely, lay out how the deal will take place and offer them additional services—insurance, package tracking, escrow, or whatever—to help them feel more secure (of course, this will be at *their* cost, not yours). Keep the communication flowing and work to bring the deal to a quick and happy close. Once you've earned their trust, you might have earned a faithful customer in the process.

- **The postauction haggler.** Believe it or not, some buyers think there's still opportunity to negotiate a better deal *after* they've won one of your auctions (this is especially true of multiple-item winners). "How about if I just send you such-and-such dollars for the three items I won?" Sure, offer to combine items in a single shipment to save on carrier costs, but don't go beyond that. Politely thank the buyer for the offer but, just as nicely, state that the person needs to honor the high bid in accordance with auction rules. If a particular buyer becomes obstinate, stick to your price and policy (this could be a test of your resolve). If the buyer becomes irascible, consider cutting off the deal and also consider opening a dispute within eBay's Dispute Console, noting this one as a nonpaying bidder (refer to the discussion in Chapter 11).

- **Unhappy Harvey.** Some people just can't be pleased. Whether it's complaining about your sales policy, griping about your shipping charges, or whining about the item they ultimately receive, some folks seem born to be dissatisfied. If you sense this early in the transaction, you might consider letting the bidder off the hook right away and avoiding the whole deal at the outset (the person in question would, of course, have to agree with this move without repercussion). If you've already received payment and are preparing to send the item, be painstakingly clear about your shipping method, guarantees, and return policy. Carefully file all correspondence in this sort of situation; you're blazing a paper trail here (physical and virtual) and you might need to recall it if the buyer simply cannot be pleased no matter what you do. In the case of a return, it's sometimes best to take the item back (in the *same* condition sent), refund the money, and avoid any further encounter with the individual. Check the buyer's feedback rating—he or she might have a history of this sort of thing. It's okay to cancel bids from any bidder with a spotted past or overall negative feedback rating. Bottom line: if you can't please 'em, avoid 'em.

- **The deadbeat.** This is the same personality introduced to you in Chapter 11—the one who, for whatever reason, isn't talking and isn't paying. Simply restated, it's best to establish a time frame for payment receipt within your sales policy. If the time elapses, directly communicate your option to negate the sale. When you get into volume selling, you'll have little patience and even less time for this unreliable renegade.

> **eBay TIP:** Though their intentions aren't necessarily to be considered suspect, some buyers simply have difficulty following instructions. Whether they live by a more casual credo or simply don't understand why making a timely payment is important ("What's the big deal?"), you'll likely encounter a buyer or two who just won't move very quickly. Exercise patience to the best of your ability, but if this buyer might frequent your auctions in the future, gently but firmly explain your policy in one-on-one correspondence, or if that proves fruitless, consider blocking the bidder from your future auctions. Use your best judgment in these cases.

Naturally, there are some buyers who will embody two or more of the personality types mentioned here. Don't forget, also, that difficult buyers generally constitute a very small percentage of the eBay community. The point of exploring the nature of these more difficult types, though, is to understand what might be driving their behavior and strive to meet on common ground. Be honest in asking whether the problem could be *your* policies and engagement style. With just a bit of effort, you'll find you can usually resolve problems quite quickly.

SHARE THE OWNERSHIP

Remember, it takes two to transact—a deal can be successful only when both parties are committed. As a seller, you state your policies and methods up front—no surprises. If there is concern or disagreement on the buyer's part, the two of you have the option to negotiate a *mutually agreeable* solution (you can also stick to your original policy if you choose). Whatever agreement you reach, though, is ultimately a deal that's owned by both parties in the transaction. So long as you, the seller, hold up your end of the bargain, there's no room for the buyer to contest the agreement.

DIFFUSE THE SITUATION

One of the basic tenets of customer service is to kill 'em with kindness. While you should never completely yield to anyone—neither your core policy nor your principles—you can head off caustic situations by showing understanding and a willingness to make the deal work. If a buyer becomes irritated, quickly ask what the problem is. Often, it's nothing but a simple misunderstanding. If the buyer won't settle down and seems bent on arguing with you, it might be best to respond by saying, "Perhaps it would be better if we cancelled this deal." Whether the buyer just doesn't like you or is trying a harsh tactic to weasel out of a commitment, you're probably better off to cancel the deal and sell to someone else.

A WORD ABOUT LEAVING NEGATIVE FEEDBACK

When things get ugly, most everyone throws out this threat: "I'm posting negative feedback on you!" Long-time eBayers know the value of their feedback rating (Chapter 15 will show you how to get the most from yours) and many will go to great lengths to maintain a spotless record—and some bothersome buyers know this. As a seller, threatening a difficult buyer with negative feedback isn't necessarily an effective way to coerce compliance. As demonstrated in the "final notice" e-mail shown in Chapter 11, communicate your option to post negative feedback, but expect that you could receive the same in return. Though you shouldn't feel unjust in speaking your mind in the public forum (that's why Pierre created it), take a moment to ask what the negative feedback might truly achieve. Give it some thought first, then do whatever you think will serve you best, both now and in the future.

RISING ABOVE IT ALL

Finally, if you have been through somewhat of a bumpy experience with a buyer but the deal comes off smoothly in the end, recognize that fact and thank the buyer for working with you. Though we often would like to lash out at that hard-to-please so-and-so, a professional manner always leaves you standing in the best light. Chalk it up to the further development of your customer management skills.

14

Satisfaction Guaranteed: Keeping the Customers Happy

You were introduced to many of the auction-going personalities in Chapter 13. This chapter discusses another personality type that will pose a different set of challenges as well as afford you interesting opportunities. Now that *you're* the seasoned seller, it becomes your duty to usher in newcomers to the auction experience and, for some, it poses a sort of dilemma for the new age. On the one hand, sellers like you want to actively attract the interest and patronage of online newcomers, while on the other hand, you must anticipate the possibility that you'll need to work harder with these uninitiated buyers in the cybermarket.

Although not all newbies are problematic, many sellers agree that working a sale with a first-time auction-goer or online buyer can require some extra effort, extra explanation, and occasionally extra patience. However, if you're prepared to assist a neophyte through the sometimes perplexing world of e-commerce, you'll find yourself in prime position to acquire a long-term customer for your efforts.

Get to Know Your Newbie

When you encounter someone who's "new in town," put your best foot forward while mentally preparing yourself to help the person through a process that could seem quite foreign and even intimidating.

For starters, be prompt in all of your communication and be prepared to answer additional questions regarding your terms, methods, and policies. Then, remember that some of these new shoppers might find conducting long-distance business with complete strangers a daunting and uncertain undertaking. Your punctual responses and polite answers to their questions will assure them you are there to assist with their purchase.

Of course, be on the lookout for the occasional dark cloud—you know, the buyer or bidder who's looking to scam and scamper. The undesirable elements are out there, and if your newbie turns out to be this sort of charlatan, be sure your terms and conditions clearly outline your expectations of timely payment and so on. If the newbie is trying to be clever, cut that one loose and move on.

> **eBay TIP:** Most of all, when sizing up and making first contact with newbie shoppers, remember that you're going to make an early impression on them about how the online marketplace works. Guide them through the transaction, guard against shenanigans, and encourage them to come back again.

Newbie Shopping Habits: Under Control or Out of Hand?

Of most interest to sellers should be the shopping habits of a new bidder. Though it's difficult to evaluate a newcomer's activity in fixed-price venues (outside of your own), if you're meeting them in the online auction spaces, a seller quickly can ascertain whether the new shopper is adopting one of two common buying styles:

- **The supercautious.** Some new shoppers won't buy much at all (either in dollar amount or in the number of items concurrently bid on) until they can gain a certain level of comfort and familiarity with the online process. If they have good first encounters and believe the cybermarket to be a venue of success for them, they'll typically loosen up and get a bit more active in future pursuits.
- **The supershopper.** Other new shoppers, however, find online shopping to be a veritable feeding frenzy. Although their enthusiasm is appreciated, a quick check of their virtual shopping cart or auction bid history might reveal they're committing to a hefty tally. So what? So you'll want to act fast to ensure the item they purchase from you

will be quickly and fully paid for, lest your new customer turns out to have overcommitted his or her present bankroll.

Of course, these are pretty much the two extremes and you can expect a good many newbies to fall somewhere in between.

> **eBay TIP:** Although some might argue it's not a seller's business to know about how, when, and how much a newcomer bids or buys, those who've been selling for years now understand that it's worth noting how newbies are shopping and how to actively engage them to ensure the deal comes to a successful close to both parties' ultimate satisfaction.

A Satisfying Opportunity

It's wise to recognize the special opportunity to aid and build rapport with new shoppers. There's certainly little time for intense hand-holding of new-comers (a seller *must* attend to other customers, after all), but consider these methods of engagement and approach—some of which have already been touched on earlier in this book—that can be especially helpful to ensure a win-win transaction with a newbie:

- **Set the tempo.** Many new buyers aren't exactly savvy about the pro-tocol of online buying—they might be overanxious; they might be undercommitted. Working with good e-mail communication and an even better sales policy of terms and conditions, promptly get the exchange in motion once a sale has been decided. Demonstrate your tried-and-true professional business process, and newbies will know they're working with a real pro—someone who'll reliably orchestrate a smooth transaction.
- **Be their guide.** It's also good practice to help newcomers (*your* new customers) better understand how online fixed-price and auction sales work. Remember, if you're there to assist them, chances are they'll remember you, your products, and your good business style. That's usually the recipe for earning repeat business.

Embrace the New Attitude

At the end of the day, a seller's bottom line is determined by the amount of care extended to customers. Though it's certainly not just newbies who frequently require additional attention, lending a hand to a wide-eyed newcomer is an opportunity to form a lasting customer relationship. Take the time to understand and assist newbies, and you'll likely become their seller of choice.

KEEPING YOUR BUYERS INFORMED

An informed buyer is generally a happy buyer. As an online seller, strive to do your best to keep your buyers in the know throughout the entire transaction process. From sending out timely end-of-auction (EOA) invoices to informing them about an item's shipping status, the more buyers know about the deal in process, the better they'll feel about doing business with you.

Service with a Smile

Some sellers say they get too bogged down by sending e-mail updates to their customers, and some even make it a policy to provide minimal or no e-mail contact (feedback is enough, they contend). However, sellers who forgo this kind of helpful customer service risk causing unnecessary concern for buyers, especially newbies, who might panic if they don't hear from sellers once their payment has been sent.

If you can't ship immediately, which would prompt an automated shipment notification, sending a brief status update via e-mail can be very reassuring. Take the appropriate steps to let your buyers know how the transaction is progressing. Remember: a lack of communication and "virtual" silence can scare off potentially repeat buyers.

Key Interaction Points

The first step in keeping your buyers informed is to send an EOA invoice after the auction ends. Once the auction finishes, make the contact as soon as possible—this will reassure nervous buyers. Beyond the customary EOA step, you also should consider sending these customer-satisfying status updates:

- When the payment has been received
- When the payment has cleared (if applicable)
- When the item is shipped

Additional Considerations

Here are two additional considerations to help buyers stay informed: be sure to update your item descriptions with any additional information or photos, and respond quickly and thoroughly to all user queries and e-mails. Just as you scoped sellers when you were buying, you might be similarly under review by a prospective bidder. In short, keeping the buyer abreast of an auction's progression will make you a standout seller. How far you want to take it depends on your own personal sales philosophy as well as the time you are able to devote to supplemental e-mail contact. But let's face it: the more comfortable the buyer feels with you as a seller, the smoother the transaction will be, and the greater the likelihood that this same buyer will bid on one of your auctions again.

> **eBay TIP:** If you can manage your payment receipts and shipments via PayPal, e-mail notifications are automatically generated and forwarded as you complete the transaction. Here is another reason to encourage use of online payment, freeing yourself from the time needed to craft an e-mail communication.

DEALING WITH DAMAGED GOODS

Sometimes there's a bit of postsale trouble that creeps up on sellers in the form of damage claims. Sooner or later, one of your buyers will probably receive a broken item or—worse yet—might not receive the item at all. The reality is that sometimes items are damaged in transit despite your best efforts. If such a claim comes your way, don't fret—*act!* Here's what you can do if there's a disgruntled buyer out there who demands satisfaction for a good transaction gone awry.

Exercising Damage Prevention

Before deciding what you'll do if an item you've sold at auction is received damaged (or isn't received at all), examine the things you can do to prevent damage and protect both yourself and your buyers ahead of time.

First, consider the value and/or rarity of the item you're selling. If its price rivals your monthly mortgage payment, consider using an online escrow service. Not only will escrow ensure payment has been made before you ship the goods, it also demonstrates your willingness to ensure the customer is satisfied before you ultimately collect your funds.

Of course, be very clear in your sales policy about how you manage returns and refunds. In the case of damage claims, be sure your policy is

explicit regarding how you and the buyer will work *together* in the unfortunate event that an item becomes lost or damaged in transit (often dictated
by the chosen carrier's damage claims process). By making your policy
clear before the bidders bid, you'll provide yourself a sturdy foundation to
stand on if trouble arises, one that the buyer shouldn't claim ignorance
about.

Cover Your Assets

Since it's ultimately the carrier that will be involved if an in-transit problem
arises, make sure you and your buyers agree to the shipping method, tracking,
and insurance services you'll use. Encourage speedy shipment methods, online
tracking, and adequate insurance protection for valuable items. If the buyer
elects to save a buck and opts out of such protections, be sure you're clear who
will bear the loss if the package is damaged or unrecoverable. (Some sellers will
cover such situations in an effort to provide 100 percent guaranteed satisfaction—you need to decide if that will be your policy as well.)

A Broken Item, Not a Broken Relationship

This point can't be emphasized enough: in the event of damage, focus on the
situation at hand, not on debasing one another. Your up-front stipulations of
how the transaction will work, the special payment and shipping services
you'll use, and what sort of guarantee or recourse you'll offer in the event of
trouble are the true matter at hand. Through collaboration, you and your
buyer can resolve the problem and, ideally, retain the ability to transact again
in the future.

TRANSFORMING CUSTOMERS INTO REPEAT BUYERS

Not long ago, a good variety of merchandise was the only hook needed to
attract eager consumers to online sales and auction venues. Those days, however, are over. Today, more and more online retailers have recognized the
equal importance of the customer experience: how well the customer is
served, how comfortable the customer feels, and how often the customer
returns. It's no longer a matter of goods alone—serving your customers well
and gaining their loyal and repeat patronage is critical to the long-term health
of your business.

The Staggering Statistics

Today, online shoppers are interested in not only *what* they will be served but equally *how* they will be served. If you invest your efforts only in the particular merchandise you offer, ignoring your responsibility for the customer's shopping experience, you'll soon find you're lagging behind your competitors. Don't believe it? Here are some revealing statistics presented by Vicki Henry, CEO of Feedback Plus, Inc., on why customers *don't* return:

- 68 percent leave because of rudeness or indifference.
- 14 percent judge by first encounter.
- 9 percent prefer competitors.
- 5 percent buy from friends.
- 3 percent move away.
- 1 percent die.

Remember, with the millions of items up for sale or bid online on any given day, it's highly likely that another seller will be offering the same sort of thing that you have on the block. If other sellers greet customers with a friendlier manner and a more attentive policy than you, they may well win the customers that you just ignored.

Setting the Stage for Follow-on Business

A second sale is dependent on how well the first went. With competition running high at eBay and elsewhere online, sellers who are in this business for the long haul need to be sure that when they serve a new customer, that customer will be compelled to return for more.

In most business scenarios, repeat customers are cheaper and easier to serve in subsequent transactions because they've developed trust in you; concurrently, you've managed to establish an awareness of how they manage themselves and their commitments. It's in your best interest to delight your customers at every turn, persuading them that you're the seller of choice. Initially, this may take some extra effort, but in the long run your effort will certainly benefit your business.

So what sorts of things can you do to keep your customers coming back? Consider these core customer-satisfying techniques.

Say "Thank You" Repeatedly

For starters, understand that good customer service is all about attitude. If you truly value your customers and their contribution to your bottom line, you can't help but be thankful. So go ahead and thank the customers who come to shop for your wares, even before they've purchased anything. If you're forthcoming in your desire to answer their questions, allay their concerns, and treat them with respect, they'll likely see you're committed to your business as well as to their satisfaction.

Tell them, "Thank you for your interest in my merchandise," "Thank you for your bid," "Thank you for your fast payment," and "Thank you for your business." This is the first step in building good and long-lasting customer relationships. Too many merchants and businesses take their customers for granted these days, and your grateful attitude will quickly identify you as a bright spot in a sometimes cold, impersonal, and occasionally unfriendly marketplace.

Overdeliver on What You Promise Every Time

Keep in mind that any seller who merely *meets* customer expectations can be easily matched and replaced by another seller offering the same level of service. But when you *exceed* your customers' expectations, you're more likely to be remembered and sought out when customers come back looking for more. How can you overdeliver? Recall these simple methods:

- **Toss in a trinket with an item.** Simple baubles like thank-you cards, small toys, candy, bows, or even a cleverly designed business card will add a special touch and show you care about your customers beyond their purchases. Also, think about including a little extra that relates to the item purchased. For instance, one seller of DVDs always sends along a free mini-packet of microwave popcorn—nice touch.
- **Upgrade the shipping or offer free shipping.** When those bidding wars ensue and you make out much better than you expected on an item, consider surprising the high bidder with upgraded or free shipping service. *That's* definitely an extra that's always remembered.
- **Ensure your items will always be considered "better than expected."** Remember to be careful in grading and consider slightly undergrading your items so your buyer is pleasantly surprised at how much better the item appears upon receipt.

- **If ever there's a problem, don't delay in resolving it.** Though many sellers fear being abused or exploited by unsavory buyers, it's not worth risking your reputation by being hard-nosed. Take care of the customer quickly, whether it is by way of replacement or refund, and keep a smile on your face throughout the process.

Always Sweat the Small Stuff

If you're looking to pull well ahead of the pack, you'll need to do more than everyone else. Of course, there's not much to listing items, providing basic communication, and shipping merchandise—all of which is pretty much the modus operandi of the industry. But your customers' delight is in the details, and when you take note and take action on the oft-overlooked minutiae of method, you begin to surpass customers' basic expectations, leaving them delighted while leaving much of your competition in the dust.

For example:

- **Choices and voices.** Give your customers more options (e.g., shipping, payment methods) and they'll see you're customer focused. Hear them out when they have comments or concerns about your methods and they'll know you care.
- **Rapid response.** Don't keep them waiting, especially when the auction clock is ticking. If you're typically unavailable to respond, they'll typically be unavailable do business with you again.
- **Don't be satisfied until they are.** Though you shouldn't relegate yourself to doormat status, you should remain at their service until you're sure they are satisfied. Only then can *you* feel satisfied that you're doing exceptional business.
- **Emotional rescue.** Sometimes your customers have a thing or three to say to you—hear 'em out. Whether they're angry, confused, or whatever, you need to interact closely to determine what you did (or didn't do) that left them feeling out of sorts. Consider an informal survey ("Please let me know whether you had any concerns or suggestions about doing business with me") after the transaction, then listen closely if and when they take you up on the invitation.
- **Uncompromising ethics.** Honesty, sincerity, and compassion will take you and your business a long way. Ask yourself how you'd like to be treated in a similar transaction, and then go above and beyond that benchmark when you serve your customers.

Be Consistent . . . Consistently

The key to retaining your customers is to first sustain your own performance (in their eyes). That is, conduct yourself and your business in such a way that you're able to exceed expectations and overdeliver on promises with *every* transaction. While it's great to hear your customers praise you on an initial transaction, it's disappointing to both of you if they consider a follow-up transaction to be of lesser quality. It's up to you to be sure you can fold in premium customer service methods without it costing you consistency in execution.

And so when all is said and done, your efforts here will work to gain you what every serious merchant covets: customer loyalty. Understand that *loyalty* is not the same as *satisfaction*. Though satisfied with some purchases, most bidders and shoppers continue to seek out the best deals, exercising their purchasing options. However, through the building of a relationship with a seller who exhibits exemplary attitude and business behavior, buyers often forgo the hunt for a cheaper deal, realizing they're getting the *best* deal from you, the stellar seller. That's loyalty and that's the big payoff for your extra efforts.

CUSTOMER SATISFACTION: THEIR WORDS, NOT YOURS

"Sure my customers are satisfied—just ask me and I'll tell you."

Though that may sound comical at first blush, there's more truth in that seller-centric sentiment than many would want to admit. It's a trap that's easy to fall into: believing your *own* praises. Experts often remark that to truly excel in customer satisfaction, a seller needs to have a passion to serve customers, leaving it to them to decide when they've been satisfied.

"Real customer service comes from the heart," notes one veteran seller. "If you don't truly and deeply value what the customer means to your business's health, you may as well not bother." These comments underscore the need to let the customer—not yourself—determine what's satisfactory. It's one way to ensure that you remain totally customer focused. For better or worse, you don't give out the grades here; the customer does. The wise seller keeps a pulse on his or her customer's satisfaction as a way to understand which direction the business is going.

And at the end of the day, it's an undeniable truth that customer service should become and remain a seller's top priority in the effort to develop lasting customer relations and further your potential to find your online fortune.

15

Establishing a Stellar
Online Reputation

There was a time when a good variety of merchandise was the only hook needed to attract the eager bidders at eBay. Today, however, bidders are equally interested in *how* they will be served in addition to *what* they will be served. The past several chapters have offered advice and insight into how to stay on top of your auction matters, how to best engage your bidders and buyers, and how to keep the transaction on track for a successful close.

These efforts enable you to present yourself as a committed seller intent on providing good products and great service—through it all, establishing a name for yourself within the eBay community. Your good name, then, is among your greatest assets at eBay—keep it polished, keep it prominent, and promote it with pride. This chapter illuminates the importance of your eBay reputation, helps you get off to a good start in building an excellent eBay feedback rating, and brings to light the additional elements that can make you a stellar seller, attracting and holding customers while creating loyalty in the virtual marketplace.

UNDERSTANDING eBAY'S FEEDBACK FORUM

Next to inventing the online auction to begin with, Pierre Omidyar likewise possessed the vision to recognize the value and importance of a good online reputation. In 1995, the Internet was a flurry of online personalities—computer-savvy users and Net surfers who effectively adopted virtual personae (or *aliases*) used in communicating with fellow Netizens. When it came to trading in the virtual space, Omidyar anticipated the hesitations of those who would feel less than confident in dealing with strangers, especially since any and all could don a digital disguise of sorts; he saw the value of putting a real and reputable face with a virtual name. The result: eBay's Feedback Forum.

The Origin of the Feedback Forum

Simply enough, the Feedback Forum is a virtual public notice board where buyers and sellers share their comments, good and bad, about their transactions with one another. From the beginning, those serious about advancing their auction opportunities were conscientious in their dealings to better ensure they would receive good marks from others. Those less than sincere in their auction exploits were quickly exposed to the rest of the community. That's what it became—a community. Thanks to the Feedback Forum and the community's eagerness to utilize it, eBay for the most part developed as a safe venue for online trading.

How to View a User's Feedback

Anywhere you encounter another user's ID at eBay, most often on item listing pages in the form of either seller or high bidder, you'll find a parenthetical number to the right of that ID; that's the person's numeric *feedback rating*. Click on that number and you'll be able to view the details of that user's feedback (see Figure 15.1).

As shown in Figure 15.1, a Feedback Summary is provided to aggregate the results of feedback posted for the user from other users (this happens to be a current picture of my feedback rating). Near the top of the screen, a quick tally is presented on the left highlighting the number of positive, neutral, and negative feedback comments posted to the user's ID. A positive comment gains one point; a neutral comment gains no points; a negative comment subtracts one point.

Understand that feedback can be posted only between registered users who have been recorded by eBay as buyer and seller in a successfully closed auction; no anonymous or non-auction-related comments can be posted. Also, a single user who might post numerous comments, positive or negative, will be counted as only one numeric rating (positive or negative) to be tallied in the recipient user's feedback rating; this prevents feedback padding—you know, when you ply your mother or your best friend into posting hundreds of

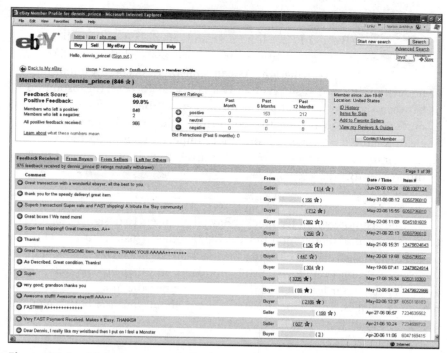

Figure 15.1 Click on any user's feedback rating to view the person's Feedback Summary.

nice comments about you or when an irate adversary attempts to drop many detracting comments. Each unique user's comments, good or bad, are aggregated into a single point to contribute your overall rating.

The right side of the top area shows the eBay *ID card* that summarizes the tally of feedback received within the past 1, 6, and 12 months. This is particularly useful in determining the most recent trends in a user's actions and behavior as reported by other users who have dealt with the individual. Feedback left at eBay is permanent, and though follow-up comments or feedback responses can be posted by the recipient, the original mark will stand. This can be something of a disappointment if you receive a negative comment accidentally (I got one that way) or get one from an incensed ingrate who is later banned from the site (I got another one that way, too). Don't let that fact deter you, though, since your overall record will prevail beyond a couple unfortunate incidents.

> **eBay TIP:** If a buyer and seller get into a conflict that results in a negative comment being posted, there's still room for reconciliation. As can sometimes occur, an initial misunderstanding and rash reaction can still lead to peaceful resolution between the two transactors. In this instance, eBay has allowed for a mutual retraction of negative comments, effectively wiping the slate clean for the users involved and, more important, showing the rest of the community that these two collaboratively found a way to mend their differences. Bravo!

One last note about feedback: eBay allows users to designate their feedback as "private," rendering it unviewable by other registered users. This is a mistake, obviously, since blocking feedback from other users' view implies there's something to hide. To instill confidence in other bidders and sellers, avoid flagging your feedback as private. Remember, the more the other eBay members (that is, your *customers*) can learn about you, the better inclined they'll be to buy from you.

How to Post Feedback at eBay

If you've just completed a transaction, revisit the my eBay page and click on the text link Feedback. (See Figure 15.2.)

Looking at Figure 15.3, you can see the form that will be displayed for inputting and posting feedback. Simply enter your comment, select the type of feedback you intend (positive, negative, neutral), and click the Leave Feedback button at the bottom of the screen. Notice that eBay issues an advisement on this page that states "you are solely responsible for the content," cautioning you against posting libelous comments and encouraging you to seek resolution if there is a dispute. Your comment and its cumulative numeric result will be added to the user's feedback rating. The actual comments posted for a user can be reviewed by any other registered user by scrolling down and clicking through the successive pages of the feedback screen (refer again to Figure 15.1).

BUY FIRST TO ESTABLISH YOUR GOOD REPUTATION

New sellers face something of a dilemma: how can they present themselves as reputable community members if they haven't yet done much, if any, business

Figure 15.2 Visit the My eBay page to easily access the transactions awaiting you to leave feedback.

that would establish a positive feedback rating? It's true that buyers may be hesitant to bid on your auction if your feedback rating is zero; newbies to the site are clearly identified as such by the blank feedback rating and "new member" icon to the right of their user ID (see Figure 15.4).

It's a classic chicken-and-egg predicament, but there is a solution. Your best approach to establishing an initial reputation is to become a good buyer first. Positive feedback, being relevant for both buyers and sellers, can be accumulated if you bid and buy first to earn those initial feedback points. Be certain to post positive feedback for the sellers with whom you've successfully transacted in anticipation that they will respond in kind. Once you've earned an aggregate value of 10 positive points, eBay will award you your first feedback star, visible alongside your feedback rating number. Though the actual feedback comments will indicate that you've only been buying, their effect will successfully indicate that you are committed and conscientious in your dealings.

http://feedback.ebay.com - Feedback Forum: Leave Feedback - Microsoft Internet Explorer

File   Edit   View   Favorites   Tools   Help   Links   »   Norton AntiVirus

ebaY®

home | pay | site map

| Buy | Sell | My eBay | Community | Help |

Start new search   Search
                          Advanced Search

Java™ POWERED BY ◆Sun

Hello, dennis_prince! (Sign out.)

Home > Community > Feedback Forum > Leave Feedback

Feedback Forum: Leave Feedback   help

[   ]   Find Feedback

Enter a User ID or Item Number

Rating other members by leaving feedback is a very important part of transactions on eBay.

Please note:
- Once left, you cannot edit or retract feedback; you are solely responsible for the content.
- It's always best to keep your feedback factual; avoid making personal remarks.
- Feedback can be left for at least 90 days following a transaction.
- If you have a dispute, contact your trading partner to try and resolve the dispute before leaving feedback.

You have 6 transactions for which to leave feedback. Showing 1 - 6 below.

Buyer: (156 ☆)   Single Transaction Form

Item: NEW! Aurora MONSTER SCENES 35th Anniversary Wristband (6056796810) Ended: May-08-
                 06 06:40:58 PDT

Rating: ⦿ Positive   ○ Neutral   ○ Negative   ○ I will leave feedback later

Comment: [Excellent buyer. Great communication and fast payment. Recommen]   11 characters left.

Buyer: (447 ☆)

Item: NEW! Aurora MONSTER SCENES Custom Magnet Set LIMITED (6056796927) Ended: May-08-
                 06 19:57:06 PDT

Rating: ○ Positive   ○ Neutral   ○ Negative   ⦿ I will leave feedback later

Comment: [   ]   80 characters left.

Buyer: (256 ☆)

Item: NEW! Aurora MONSTER SCENES 35th Anniversary Wristband (6056796810) Ended: May-13-
                 06 22:28:26 PDT

Rating: ○ Positive   ○ Neutral   ○ Negative   ⦿ I will leave feedback later

Comment: [   ]   80 characters left.

                                                                              Internet

Figure 15.3   Enter a feedback comment on the Feedback Forum page.

Hello, <u>dlprince99</u> (<u>0</u>) 🔒 me

Figure 15.4 When you're newly registered at eBay, your user ID will bear the new member icon and the zero feedback rating.

MORE ABOUT YOU AT ABOUT ME

If you haven't already created an About Me page at eBay, this is the time. When you're new to selling and are eager to share your intent and aspirations to offer great items bolstered by great service, an About Me page allows you space to tell prospective shoppers a little more about you. Consider including a picture of yourself (there's no need for an eBay transaction to be a faceless encounter), and offer some information about the sorts of goods you'll specialize in. Tell as much about yourself as relates to your envisioned auction activity, and you'll give bidders a better feel for who you are.

REPRESENT YOUR MERCHANDISE, REPRESENT YOURSELF

The manner in which you offer your items often speaks volumes about you. That said, it's important to always present clear and accurate item descriptions to best represent yourself. Here's how your item descriptions reveal more about *you* than you may have first thought:

- Complete item details will show that you understand the items you're offering and you recognize the relevant information bidders will need to consider, both serving as signs of your thorough approach to presenting items for sale.
- Accurate item details likewise indicate that either you're an expert in what you're offering or you are conscientious enough to properly research each item you present.
- Inclusion of thorough item condition details shows you're forthcoming, honest, and committed to helping the bidder make a well-informed decision when bidding on your goods.

- Good grammar still counts and by demonstrating good communication skills you represent yourself as a professional who's attentive to details.

Making the Grade

Experienced sellers know how important accurate item representation can be, not only for the sake of an immediate sale but also for their long-term reputation. *Item grading,* however, remains a gray area in online selling, a subjective assessment that, if not properly understood and communicated, could lead to a contentious matter between buyer and seller. Unfortunately, there are no universally accepted grading definitions for all sorts of merchandise; different terms are used to describe the condition of different items (such as furniture, stamps, glassware, or trading cards).

If this multitude of terms isn't enough cause for concern (and it is), similar terms are used to describe a variety of items but they don't represent the same state of being for each commodity. Therefore, accurate and responsible use of grading terms becomes something of a *learned* discipline, whereby application of a stated grade often depends on the experience of the seller.

The bottom line, though, is that bidders are looking for high-quality items, especially vintage goods. As they're willing to pay top dollar for high-quality merchandise, they're looking for sellers who are accurate and dependable in their grading techniques. So when it comes time to advertise your goods (and ultimately represent *yourself*), consider these guidelines in communicating the condition:

- Use the recognized grading terms for the item. Steer clear of off-the-cuff descriptions like "super condition," "really nice," and "great specimen." Failing to use widely adopted terms suitable to the item type will make you appear inexperienced or potentially dishonest.
- Accompany the grade stipulation with a full disclosure of the item's details. Help the customer decide if your assessment of the item seems reasonable.
- Consider using half grades (Very Fine +, Near Mint −) if you're on the fence about how the item truly grades out.
- Consider skillfully *under*grading your item. Without taking too much away from the item, let buyers know you're using a strict grading system, then grade down a half step. This usually results in feedback from buyers proclaiming that your items arrive "better than described"—exactly the sort of good PR you want.

- Be sure to apply a suitable offering price (if using a reserve or stating a Buy-It-Now price) to the grade you select. A noticeable mismatch between price and condition will not sit well with bidders.

Bidders are seeking out new sellers of desirable goods and will make note of those merchants who seem to be most dependable in terms of item grading. By properly representing your items, you'll develop a reputation for being honest and reliable in all sales.

Your Expertise on Display

When you present yourself as an expert in or authority on the items you sell, you further embellish your online reputation as a seller who can be trusted and consulted. Bidders and buyers at eBay are looking for experts when they search through the auction listings, hoping to find a seller who knows what's what and sells items that are properly described and accurately represented. Being regarded as an expert helps you and your reputation in the following ways:

- Being an expert in what you sell will give you confidence in *how* you'll sell and at what prices you'll offer your items.
- Being an expert helps you find the appropriate customer pool—those actively searching for and buying certain items—and provides you with a better understanding of those customers' wants and needs.
- Being an expert helps you write better item titles and descriptions as well as provide better images that astutely present the critical views to your buyers.
- Being an expert helps you anticipate changes in demand, supply, and your customers' expectations.
- Being an expert helps you answer your customers' questions quickly and accurately.
- Being an expert helps you fend off dishonest buyers (as well as dishonest sellers)—you're forearmed with the facts and knowledge and can best avoid a scam.
- Being an expert gains you the respect of your customers, who realize you know your stuff and can be fully trusted.

If you're already an expert in a certain sort of item or commodity, you're ahead of the game. If not, take extra time to research the items you'll sell, research items like them that have already sold, and turn to other sellers and seller's guides to fortify your knowledge. Soon, you'll find you've developed your own expertise and can confidently present knowledge to your potential customers—and earn the highest price for your various goods.

THE ART OF FEEDBACK AT eBAY

To bring this discussion full circle, return to the foundation of your online reputation: the eBay Feedback Forum. The key to making feedback work at eBay is participation; it's the only way you can build and buoy your auction reputation. If you've had a good experience with a buyer or seller, you'll want to reward that person with positive feedback. If you're had a bad experience, you might consider levying a negative comment. If you're less than tickled but not quite tickled, opt for the neutral comment. Regardless, be sure to leave feedback. Serious users who covet a stellar reputation will work hard to do right in every deal, hoping to build a chart-topping rating.

But *why* does feedback matter? If it's just the opinions of average people on the Net, what noticeable impact can it really have? The answer springs from the need to feel safe and confident in a trading environment. How safe do you feel sending money to an absolute stranger? How safe does that stranger feel sending one of his or her valuable treasures to an unknown buyer? Wouldn't you feel better if you could learn a bit more about the people you'll be dealing with? Granted, feedback can't *make* anyone behave a certain way, but it can help others make decisions about whom they'll deal with and whom they won't. Your stellar reputation will definitely ease your efforts at eBay and will position you to stand out in a positive light.

PART III

SUREFIRE WAYS TO INCREASE YOUR SALES

16

Keys to Better Auction Listings

Now that you have a foundation for the hows and the whys of auctioning at eBay, it's time to turn your attention to the true matter at hand: *selling anything and making your fortune.* It's true that every item has its buyer and every seller can command his or her price, especially at the expansive market known as eBay. Nevertheless, the fruits of your labors will be much more bountiful if you apply deliberate tactics and methods to your activities. Beginning with this chapter, you'll learn the keys to better auctioning and gain the insights that will differentiate you from an average seller. This advanced discussion begins with matters of improving your auction listings using a couple of very simple yet highly effective methods.

KEYS TO USING KEYWORDS

Recall the discussion in Chapter 5 about effectively searching for and finding items based on keywords? Here's where you, the seller, craft the best title possible to draw in the most bidders. As you can imagine, when it comes to the titles of the items you post for sale or bid, your eventual success often depends on how carefully you choose the words in your item title. Since you're limited to only 80 characters (that includes spaces) in your eBay item title, it's up to you to make optimum use of the precious verbal real estate to literally make every word count.

Getting the Most Hits

Your first task is to ensure your items can be found easily. Since you're competing with millions of other active items on any given day, your immediate challenge is to ensure your item has the best chance of showing up on bidders' search result lists. Therefore, begin by including as many pertinent keywords as shoppers are likely to search for (perhaps those words that *you* specified when you were researching). Identify the words and terms that are commonly used in searches for your item, including the most effective word combinations.

As a rule, you'll want to include brand name, origin, year (or time period), and manufacturer of the goods you're offering. Depending on what you sell, color, size, and other such attributes might also be elemental information to include in your listing titles. When in doubt, search eBay yourself to determine how items like yours are being listed and which listing titles tend to attract more bidders and better prices.

Check Your Spelling

Buyers and sellers continually lament lost sales and missed purchasing opportunities due to misspelled keywords. Be sure to spell correctly, especially when items like yours feature intentional spelling variations or are identified by words that are commonly misspelled. Many sellers go so far as to include common misspellings in their item titles to better ensure their listings will be included in a greater number of search results (recall how this serves as a savvy method to root out hidden treasure at eBay). Astute buyers search for these commonly misspelled words to ensure that desirable—albeit misspelled—goods don't get away.

Perfunctory Punctuation

Did you know that punctuation marks such as hyphens, parentheses, and exclamation marks can actually sabotage your sales? Depending on the search tool being used, a keyword search for "Jadite" might actually ignore titles that include punctuated variations like "Jadite!" or "(Jadite)." Some eBay searches will associate punctuation as part of a word and, in the literal sense, will not recognize the keyword match. It's never safe to assume bidders will universally utilize eBay's specialized search commands, and the onus is on you to ensure that simple searches will retrieve your item. Whenever possible, avoid tacking punctuation onto an item title keyword, or you run the risk of having your goods inadvertently passed over.

> **eBay TIP:** When listing an item, you'll see that eBay warns that asterisks, quotation marks, and special HTML tags are not allowed in item titles. If included, these elements could be misinterpreted by eBay's listing process program and result in an item title that could be virtually unreadable.

Stick to the Facts

Don't waste your valuable title space on words that do little to describe the item or properly identify it to the discriminating buyer. Words like "cute," "adorable," and "desirable" do little to attract, let alone convince a buyer. And words like "rare" and "hard to find" are not only superfluous (especially when buyers are already aware of the scarcity of an item) but sometimes have the effect of exposing a seller's attempt to justify a higher price. Subjective words like "awesome," "unbelievable," and "must see" could seem to be enticing but usually just succeed in wasting space. Visual come-ons like "L@@K" and its ilk are nothing short of obnoxious and should definitely be avoided.

Abbreviated Profits

Abbreviations may make sense to you—may even be recognized among purveyors of certain products—but they could cost you a sale if they fail to show up on keyword search result lists. Unless the abbreviations you employ are commonly used by your buyers, it's best to avoid spontaneous contractions or concatenations whenever possible.

> **eBay TIP:** If you have title space to spare, it is a good idea to include the full name of the item along with any recognized and well-used abbreviations; in this way you could find more potential bidders regardless of which naming convention they use in their searches.

SO HOW ABOUT AN EXAMPLE?

To sum it all up, a good item title is specific enough to capture the attention of your potential bidders but also is general enough to attract the curiosity of folks who happened to stumble across your listing (either in a related search result or while browsing the categories). To that end, recall the item I offered from Chapter 7, bearing this title: NEW! Aurora MONSTER SCENES Custom Magnet Set LIMITED

This title is 78 characters in length (spaces count!), and while it may appear simple, it effectively captures the following important search keywords:

- The company name, "Aurora."
- The infamous and sought-after product series, "MONSTER SCENES," presented here in capital letters to improve visibility and readability.
- The precise description of the sort of item (a magnet "Set").
- Indicators of the item's provenance, "NEW!," and availability, "LIMITED." The exclamation point after "NEW" is okay in this instance—I've added it for marketing impact since "new" is not a highly used search keyword, and "LIMITED" is added to immediately indicate the temporary availability of the item.

You'll be tasked with providing similar information in your item titles and may need to try different variations of information until you lock into the most effective keywords. You'll know you've created a successful title when you start to receive a larger number of hits.

WRITING BETTER DESCRIPTIONS

Once you've attracted bidders with your well-crafted item titles, you need to convince them your item is the one they simply must bid on. Your bidders need all the right information, and your item description is where they'll look to determine whether they can bid confidently. While an item description shouldn't become a book-length dissertation, it likewise shouldn't be a scant offering of ambiguous facts. In reality, the item description is where the seller makes the pitch, so to speak, in an effort to encourage bids. The information presented should be as well researched and carefully thought out as was the item title. Staying with the magnet set example, consider this description I provided:

The 35th Anniversary Celebration continues!

Continuing in the celebration of the infamous Monster Scenes® series, here's an exciting new magnet set featuring the ultra-rare artwork for proposed U.S. instruction sheets. Of course, Dracula, Dr. Jekyll & Mr. Hyde, and the Giant Insect™ kits were never issued stateside, banished to the Great White North just before the series' demise. Instruction sheets were drawn up yet only a handful were actually printed, those being used in the rare bagged test shots. Now you can enjoy the full-color artwork (struck from the rare original sheets) in a top-quality magnet. Look closely and you'll also see the rarest of the set: the unproduced Dr. Deadly's Daughter™.

Unlike those thin flexible magnets that are easily marred and mutilated, the sturdy all-metal construction plus the protective UV-resistant coating ensures these will endure wherever you stick 'em—on your fridge, your office wall, or even on your big-zap generator in the depths of your dank dungeon. These measure a large 3.125 inches high by 2.125 inches wide. These magnets are sold by the set—four incredible designs for one low price—so buy one set, two sets, or more now. They're available in a very limited quantity so don't delay. Just click the Buy It Now button for fast shipment today!

High bidder to prepay plus $3.75 fixed shipping cost. Payment must be received within 10 days of auction close. Payment by PayPal is preferred and will result in immediate shipment upon payment posted to my account. Payment by money order, or cashier's check will gain immediate shipment of item upon receipt and verification. Personal checks gladly accepted but will need to clear (approx. 10 days) before item can be shipped. All items shipped via USPS First-Class Mail. All items guaranteed to arrive as described with refunds cheerfully granted if an item received is materially different than as listed. Items must be returned within 10 days of original delivery and are subject to inspection prior to refund being issued. If there are any questions regarding these terms, please contact me via e-mail before bidding.

Thank you for your interest in my auctions!

After reading a description like that, hopefully you, too, are ready to bid. Although this description may seem rather exhaustive, recognize that it answers virtually all questions a discriminating collector/bidder might have. Consider what this description achieves:

- It indicates the origin of the item—new and in relation to the 35th anniversary of the series.
- It offers information on the origin of the artwork used in the designs.

- It provides details regarding the original intent of the Aurora company's use for these designs.
- It indicates the design and construction details of the magnets.
- It explains the limited nature of the offering.
- It provides sales terms and conditions.

Although images will be included in this particular listing, the description alone could paint a very compelling and reassuring picture of the item, sight unseen. See also how the information provided imparts the seller's expertise—mine, in this case—in regard to this sort of item, reinforcing the discussion from Chapter 15.

HOW TO USE SIMPLE HTML FOR SPECTACULAR RESULTS

As mentioned briefly in Chapter 7, HTML (HyperText Markup Language) is the lingo of the Internet and is responsible for the majority of fancy Web pages you see and use online. Although most commercial pages are quite complex in their construction, it's possible for you to harness some of the eye-catching effects for use in your eBay listings. Don't think you need to be a seasoned computer programmer to use HTML. If you can type simple text, you can insert the obscure little keys that will enable your listing to spring to life.

HTML Tags Anyone Can Use

HTML commands that enable text and image effects are referred to as *tags* and are simple notations that are inserted into a regular text listing or document. These tags are simple alphabetic characters embedded between the "< >" signs. Appearing before and after portions of text, these tags will enhance the look or positioning of that text beyond the simple typeset you'd otherwise see. A tag (e.g.,) precedes the text to be enhanced, and then a closing tag that contains the forward slash (e.g.) will ensure the effect is not continued to the rest of the text that follows. Here are the most common tags you can use to achieve professional-looking results.

FONT TAGS
- boldresults in **bold.**
- <i>italics</i>results in *italics.*
- <u>underline</u>results in underline

- <font size=12 color=black face="comic sans">results in text that **LOOKS LIKE THIS**. This font will remain in use until you insert the </font> tag or specify another, similar font equation with different settings.

PARAGRAPHS, LINE BREAKS, AND LISTS
- <p> will produce a paragraph break.
-
will produce a line break (similar to a carriage return).
- <li> will generate a bullet mark before the text, as in a bulleted list.

INSERTING IMAGE URLS AND OTHER WEB LINKS
- <img src=http://www.geocities.com:80/Hollywood/Boulevard/Magnet _Set.jpg"> will insert the specified image into the text.
- <a href="http://cgi.ebay.com/aw-cgi/eBayISAPI.dll?ViewFeedback& userid=dennis_prince">My Feedback</a> provides an active (clickable) link labeled "My Feedback" to direct you to my eBay feedback page.
- <a href="mailto:dlprince@bigfoot.com">eMail Me</a> provides an active link, labeled "eMail Me," to immediately create an e-mail message to my address.

There are a good many more tags available for use in HTML, and if you want to gain a better understanding of the language, grab just about any book that discusses introductory or intermediate HTML coding. For the purposes of your eBay listings, though, these are the essential tags that will make your listing more visually pleasing and useful to potential bidders.

HTML in Action

Turning our attention back to the Monster Scenes magnet set, Figure 16.1 shows how I utilized the HTML tab when specifying my item description to insert HTML-enhanced text and accompanying images into my listing.

> **eBay TIP:** Immediately below the description block on the listing form, you'll find a Preview text link that allows you to preview the results of your HTLM exploits. If the text or tags require minor modifications, close the preview window and make the necessary adjustments.

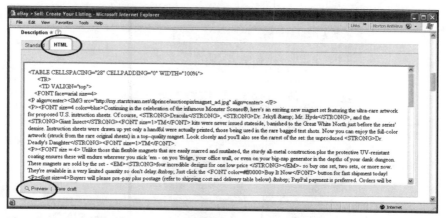

Figure 16.1 Use the item description field to directly enter HTML-enhanced text and images.

When posted, the results of this particular listing can be seen in Figure 16.2. Yes, the result makes for a rather lengthy listing and it may even seem overwhelming as you look at it. There are a few simple tricks at work here, though, as well as a few nifty ways to deliver important information that makes it more compelling than if it were spelled out in simple text. This particular auction makes use of many of the HTML tags previously described, plus a few additional enhancements. So, first look at the actual HTML coding that made this listing possible.

```
<HTML>
<FONT face=arial size=4>
<P align=center>
<IMG src="http://my.web.net/dlprince/auctionpix/magnet_ad.jpg"
align=center> </P>
<P>
<FONT size=4 color=blue>
```
Continuing in the celebration of the infamous Monster Scenes®, here's an exciting new magnet set featuring the ultrarare artwork for proposed U.S. instruction sheets. Of course, `<STRONG>Dracula</STRONG>`, `<STRONG>Dr. Jekyll &amp; Mr. Hyde</STRONG>`, and the `<STRONG>Giant Insect</STRONG><FONT size=1>TM</FONT>` kits were never issued stateside, banished to the Great White North just before the series' demise. Instruction sheets were drawn up yet only a handful were

THIS IS A SINGLE IMAGE FILE

Continuing in the celebration of the infamous Monster Scenes®, here's an exciting new magnet set featuring the ultra-rare artwork for proposed U.S. instruction sheets. Of course, **Dracula**, **Dr. Jekyll & Mr. Hyde**, and the **Giant Insect**™ kits were never issued stateside, banished to the Great White North just before the series' demise. Instruction sheets were drawn up yet only a handful were actually printed, those being used in the rare bagged test shots. Now you can enjoy the full-color artwork (struck from the rare original sheets) in a top-quality magnet. Look closely and you'll also see the rarest of the set: the unproduced **Dr. Deadly's Daughter**™.

Unlike those thin flexible magnets that are easily marred and mutilated, the sturdy all-metal construction plus the protective UV-resistant coating ensures these will endure wherever you stick 'em - on you 'fridge, your office wall, or even on your big-zap generator in the depths of your dank dungeon. These magnets are sold by the set - **four incredible designs for one low price** - so buy one set, two sets, or more now. They're available in a very limited quantity so don't delay. Just click the Buy It Now button for fast shipment today!

Buyers will please pre-pay plus postage (refer to shipping cost and delivery table below). PayPal payment is preferred. Orders will be processed and shipped direct within two days after payment is received.

Method	Transit Time	First Set	Ea. Add'tl Set
U.S. First Class	1-5 business days (from shipping date)	$2.21	$1.11
Canada	8-10 business days (from shipping date)	$3.25	$1.75
International	8-10 business days (from shipping date)	$6.95	$2.00

** California residents please add 7.25% sales tax.

If you have any questions, please ask. And, watch for even more new Monster Scenes products coming soon. It's a 35th Anniversary *Scare-abration!!*

(*Monster Scenes* and the Monster Scenes logo are registered trademarks of Dencomm. Layout and design © 2006. All rights reserved.)

THIS IS TEXT USING HTML

Figure 16.2

actually printed, those being used in the rare bagged test shots. Now you can enjoy the full-color artwork (struck from the rare original sheets) in a top-quality magnet. Look closely and you'll also see the rarest of the set: the unproduced <STRONG>Dr. Deadly's Daughter</STRONG><FONT size=1>TM</FONT>.
<P>
<FONT size=4>
Unlike those thin flexible magnets that are easily marred and mutilated, the sturdy all-metal construction plus the protective UV-resistant coating ensures these will endure wherever you stick 'em - on you 'fridge, your office wall, or even on your big-zap generator in the depths of your dank dungeon. These magnets are sold by the set - <STRONG>four incredible designs for one low price</STRONG> - so buy one set, two sets, or more now. They're available in a very limited quantity so don't delay. Just click the <FONT color=red>Buy It Now</FONT> button for fast shipment today!
<P>
<FONT size=4>
Buyers will please prepay plus postage (refer to shipping cost and delivery table below). PayPal payment is preferred. Orders will be processed and shipped direct within two days after payment is received. <P></FONT>
<FONT color=black>
<TABLE cellSpacing=1 cellPadding=4 border=0>
<TR>
<TD class=tableheaderbg><STRONG>Method</STRONG></TD>
<TD class=tableheaderbg><STRONG>Transit Time</STRONG></TD>
<TD class=tableheaderbg align=middle><STRONG>First Set</STRONG></TD>
<TD class=tableheaderbg align=middle><STRONG>Ea. Add'tl Set</STRONG>
</TD>
</TR>
<TR>
<TD class=tablebg2><STRONG>U.S. First Class</STRONG></TD>
<TD class=tablebg>1–5 business days
<SPAN class=xsmallText>(from shipping date)</SPAN></TD>
<TD class=tablebg align=right>$2.21</TD>
<TD class=tablebg align=right>$1.11</TD>
</TR>
<TR>
<TD class=tablebg2><STRONG>Canada</STRONG></TD>

```
<TD class=tablebg>8–10 business days<BR><SPAN class=xsmallText>(from
shipping date)</SPAN></TD>
<TD class=tablebg align=right>$3.25</TD>
<TD class=tablebg align=right>$1.75</TD>
</TR>
<TR>
<TD class=tablebg2><STRONG>International</STRONG></TD>
<TD class=tablebg>8–10 business days<BR><SPAN class=xsmallText>(from
shipping date)</SPAN></TD>
<TD class=tablebg align=right>$6.95</TD>
<TD class=tablebg align=right>$2.00</TD>
</TR>
</TABLE>
<P class=xsmallText>** California residents please add 7.25% sales tax.</P>
</FONT>
<FONT color=blue>
<P>
<FONT size=4>If you have any questions, please ask. And, watch for even
more new Monster Scenes products coming soon.<B>
<FONT color=red>
It's a 35th Anniversary<I>Scare</I>-abration!!</B></FONT>
<P>
<FONT color=black size=1>
("Monster Scenes" and the Monster Scenes logo are registered trademarks of
Dencomm. Layout and design © 2006. All rights reserved.)</FONT></P>
</FONT></FONT>
</HTML>
```

At first glance, this looks like quite a bit of work, but the real work resides in the first HTML listing you create. Once that's perfected, you can save the document for reuse and modification to be applied to future listings.

In other words, you can create an HTML template that's ready on demand.

So what's really happening in the code? Well, first notice that what seems like a lot of complex combining, tilting, and labeling of different images and text is actually just a single image file. To avoid working harder than necessary, I chose to assemble the large, multi-image area into a single image, created with a simple graphics program.

Once I had all of that content exactly the way I wanted, I saved it to an image file—"magnet_ad.jpg"—and simply included the entire file in my ad with a single "img" tag. Within the image, notice how I conveyed the item images, the anniversary splash, the fun text, and the magnet dimension and construction inset. This makes for a more enjoyable-to-read ad than simply spelling out all this information in mere sentences.

After inserting the large image, I entered my text using HTML tags to alter the font style, size, color, and placement. I also used HTML to create an easy-to-read shipping rate table. Although it looks complicated, you could copy this exact HTML code and immediately replicate the result (of course, you'll need to offer your own images and your own product). But with just a bit of well-applied HTML, you can elevate your listings from appropriately informative to absolutely enjoyable, entertaining your visitors on their way to bid or buy.

Does HTML Really Make a Difference?

While simple listings can be undeniably effective, a touch of well-placed style can certainly enhance your item's presence as well as the bidders' shopping experience. Utilize some simple HTML coding to add special fonts, colors, simple backgrounds, and interspersed images in a way that complements your items and entices visitors to stop, look, and bid. It's the same subtle tactic used by marketing professionals, and it works. When used in moderation, your custom-designed listings can convert otherwise apathetic shoppers from disinterested drop-bys into motivated buyers.

HTML Gone Bad

Of course, too much of a good thing can backfire in your face. Sooner or later, every seller bows to the temptation of outlandishly jazzing up the sales listings to the point of excess. Whether you've just learned HTML, found a great bunch of animated images (dancing hamsters or what have you), or simply feel you have to have the nicest display in the cybermarket, it's not uncommon to get somewhat carried away. If you become obsessed with painting too grand a picture in your item listings, here are the risks you'll run:

- You could detract from the actual item you're offering. All the special HTML effects can upstage the very item you hope to sell.
- Your listing could take too long to load. All the extra features eventually pile up and require a certain amount of download time (especially animated images). Bidders are generally disinclined to wait

more than 10 or 15 seconds before leaving your slow-loading listing. (The example shown earlier fully displays in about 1.5 seconds.)

- Excessive design could unwittingly communicate that you're eager to distract a bidder from the actual details of the item. For best results, utilize HTML sparingly. When used properly, HTML can effectively break up large blocks of text, improving the readability of your item. With a discreet amount of design and appropriate embedded images, it can work in your favor to entice auction-goers to cast a bid for the item that, in plain format, might have lacked the sort of visual excitement and hook to positively sway bidders.

WHAT ABOUT eBAY'S LISTING FEATURES?

Arguably, there's an alternate path to visual enhancement for your items: using eBay's listing features and themes. Granted, with just the click of a mouse, you can employ eBay's canned designs and templates to brighten up your items. However, I tend to avoid these features for one simple reason: they incur additional fees. It may seem trivial to worry about an extra dime, quarter, or dollar when listing an item, yet when extrapolated to tens or hundreds of items, this becomes profit prohibitive and fortune foolish. While I encourage all users to test and try the different eBay offerings, in my opinion, some elements are simply fluff. Look ahead to Chapter 26 for a full discussion of controlling auction costs and improving your fortune potential.

17

Boost Your Profits with Stellar Photos

In the earliest days of eBay, finding an actual image to accompany an item up for auction was a real treat; today, it's an absolute necessity. In order to attract more bidders and buyers and earn higher prices, you need to serve up quality images *every time*. Bidders aren't as prone to take risks on poorly presented items, and with the vast number of items to choose from at eBay every day, they won't settle for items sporting low-quality pictures.

In this chapter, you'll learn how easy it has become to take better pictures and how unnecessary it is to have your auctions summarily dismissed as apparent halfhearted attempts. Even if you're not a professional photographer, taking good photos is easier than you might expect, and the higher bids and increased volume of purchases those photos will attract is like picking money off the low branches of a tree.

IMAGING EQUIPMENT

First things first: good images are the product of good equipment. Before you concern yourself with *how* to take better photos, focus on how well equipped you are for the task.

Digital Cameras

Digital cameras are definitely the tool of choice these days, thanks to their portability and versatility. When shopping for a digital camera, pay close attention to the following features that contribute to better images:

- **Image resolution.** This is the most important factor in determining which camera you should purchase and how much you can expect to pay. Those lowest-priced VGA cameras (offering only 640 by 480 pixels) are all but antiquated in today's high-tech culture. Sure, you can still find them and can likely pick them up second-hand for a steal, but they won't deliver the detail and clarity your bidders are looking for; as a result, they will make you look flatly amateurish.

  No worries, though, because today you can buy a 4.1-megapixel camera (1,600 by 1,200 pixels) for a fraction of what those VGA models cost only a few years ago. For less than $125, you can snap off high-quality images that will provide the right amount of detail your shoppers are looking for. And if you really want to excel here and can lay down just over $200, you can step up to 6.1-megapixel cameras that are easy to use and deliver top-notch pictures every time. When selecting your camera, look to the pixel count to guide you and understand that anything at 4.1 megapixels or higher will deliver outstanding images.

- **Lenses and focus mechanics.** Look for a camera that offers both auto and manual focusing, with a real bonus being zoom capability for illuminating tiny details with crystal clarity. In addition, when it comes to close-up photos, look to a camera's built-in photo modes including *macro,* which is specially developed to deliver details of up-close images.

- **Ease of use.** The simpler the controls, the better. Fighting and fumbling with a camera will not only be frustrating but usually results in less-than-stellar images.

- **Tripod mount.** Most cameras have these by default, but make sure, just the same. Mounting your camera on a tripod reduces blurring caused by shaky hands. Standard tripods can be found every day for around $20.

Digital camera prices will vary depending on the extras you might desire as well as the method of image storage and retrieval (internal memory sticks or disks). Try several different models before you decide to purchase one.

Scanners

Digital scanners are generally the second-best choice for making auction images unless you deal strictly with flat items (postcards, paper memorabilia,

> **eBay TIP:** Although the topic will be covered fully in Chapter 25, understand that some of the equipment purchases you make to support an eBay business might qualify as tax write-offs. If you are serious about conducting a business for profit, the equipment and other necessities to support that profitable venture are often expenses that can be deducted from your annual taxable income. Perhaps that will help take some of the sting out of purchasing the imaging equipment discussed in this chapter.

collectible currency, and the like) where the scanner actually becomes the preferred imaging equipment for its ability to deliver even sharper detail than a camera. Scanners are becoming better and better and their prices keep dropping lower and lower. As with cameras, use image resolution as your guide to which models will deliver the best results (2,400 dpi is the lowest dot-per-inch resolution you should settle for today). The bonus of scanners is that they serve multiple uses. Many scan directly from 35-mm slides or negatives, allowing you to easily digitize that old family album when you're not listing auction items. As for prices, scanners are a great value, with the midrange models priced at less than $100.

Traditional Cameras

And don't forget conventional 35-mm cameras. Although they lack the convenience of photographing directly to a digital source, many film processors (online and off) will still develop your 35-mm pictures directly to downloadable online files or to an easy-to-use CD-ROM. If you've photographed several auction items using a 35-mm film camera, it's now easy to convert those to digital images ready for auction use.

SETTING UP A SIMPLE PHOTO STUDIO

Don't just plop an item on your desk or drop it on the garage floor and start snapping photos—you'll likely end up doing it a disservice by introducing background elements that will detract from the item's overall appearance, not to mention exposing it to all manner of dirt or damage. Rather, find a spot in your home or apartment (or wherever else you'll be working) to create your own designated photo studio.

Setting the Stage

You don't have to commandeer the spare bedroom or begin renovating the garage to establish your private atelier. All you really need is a few feet of dedicated working space. Purchase one or two Parsons tables (the inexpensive kind you find in the bed-and-bath stores) and situate them side by side. If you'll be photographing larger items, get a piece of half-inch plywood that can straddle the tables; it doesn't have to be a fancy setup to be effective—just stable and sturdy.

Dolling Up with a Simple Backdrop

Now, with your studio surface in place, establish a background that will best complement your items and provide a professional appearance. A good choice for establishing a background is a length of inexpensive material in a

Figure 17.1 An inexpensive Parsons table, some dark velvet, and an available corner make for a simple but stellar photo studio.

solid color (with off-white, black, or dark blue offering the best contrast results). Tack the material to a wall or in a corner to form a backdrop, then drape it over your work surface (see Figure 17.1). You now have a consistent background color that will show off the item without showing it up.

Light Source

A key consideration in any photography is lighting. While it's not terribly difficult to establish good lighting, it's almost certain death for an image (and an auction) if the lighting is terrible. Here are few lighting tricks the professionals employ to get high-quality images on a low-cost budget:

- **Go natural.** Photos taken in natural sunlight usually produce the best results in terms of reproducing details and true colors. If the sun is shining, photograph outdoors.
- **If it must be artificial.** Use incandescent bulbs (60 watts or less) for best results. Higher-wattage bulbs tend to oversaturate the item with light, giving it a washed-out look. Also, stay away from fluorescent lighting; it gives your images a yellow-green tint and usually misrepresents the coloring of the item.
- **Control the light.** Aim the light where you need it to get the best results. If you're working outdoors, use a reflector (something as simple as white poster board or a Mylar auto sunshade) to direct sunlight at your item. If working indoors, purchase three automobile work lights and suspend them above and on either side of the item (again, being careful not to blast too high a wattage at it).

As simple as that, you have a professional-quality photo studio at a cut-rate cost. Experiment with the different elements and with your camera's settings until you have the perfect balance to gain consistently superlative results.

TOUCHING UP YOUR ITEM IMAGES

Although you're now equipped to properly light, accentuate, and photograph your items, it still may be necessary to do a bit of postphotography touching up. Whether you need to crop, color-correct, or just sharpen up some fuzzy edges, here are some tips to help you decide when and how to polish up your pictures.

Determining When Touch-ups Are Necessary

Try as you might, the images you shoot sometimes need just a bit of tweaking to properly represent your items. These should be minor adjustments, though, not wholesale reworking. If the image you're working with seems to require significant modification, you're better off rephotographing the item. However, barring a complete restart, here are the sorts of attributes of an image that can be easily adjusted without scrapping the whole shoot:

- Images that are excessively bright, overly dark, or oversaturated with color (see Figure 17.2)
- Images that do not properly represent the actual appearance of the item (problems usually related to coloring and brightness)
- Images that include unnecessary or distracting background elements that should be cropped out (see Figure 17.3)
- Images that are simply too large and should be resized prior to using in an auction

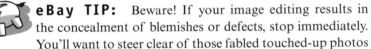

eBay TIP: Beware! If your image editing results in the concealment of blemishes or defects, stop immediately. You'll want to steer clear of those fabled touched-up photos that mask an item's true appearance, serving only to mislead bidders into believing they'll be receiving something significantly different from what you'll ultimately deliver. This is not to say that altering item images is an exercise in deception. However, many sellers have unintentionally misrepresented their items in their honest effort to provide customers with a clearer and more colorful picture. To avoid this accidental occurrence, always compare your final image to the actual piece and ask yourself if the image looks *better* than the item itself; if it does, you've edited too much.

Editing Tools

Photo editing software comes in a wide variety of prices and accompanying features. If you want the Cadillac of applications, look no further than Adobe's Photoshop. It's the application that the pros use (and commands a professional's price of around $600). If a more economically priced application suits you better, look at Jasc Software's Paint Shop Pro, Microsoft's Pic-

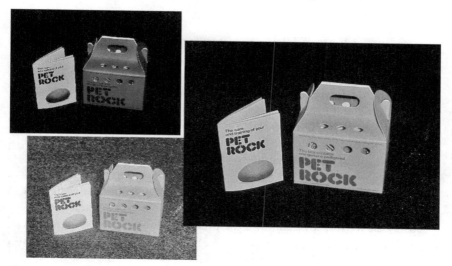

Figure 17.2 Too dark, too light, just right (on the right!).

ture It! or MGI's PhotoSuite—each is generally available for $100 or less and can deliver the fundamental photo editing features you'll need. The truly frugal among us have found many shareware and freeware versions of these applications and others ready to be downloaded from the Internet right into your computer.

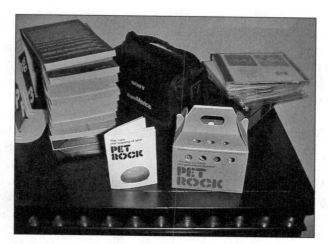

Figure 17.3 Too much clutter around your item is distracting and unprofessional.

> **eBay TIP:** In case *shareware* and *freeware* are new terms to you, they're functional computer programs or applications that are free—that's right, free—for you to download from the Internet onto your PC. By definition, shareware programs are the sort you can download and try for free to decide whether or not you like them. For a nominal fee, you can then download the full-featured version to use (the shareware version of the program usually is missing some features of the fee-based version).
>
> Freeware is free to use and typically has all of the features the programmer intended to provide. To find out more about shareware and freeware, as well as to find lots of programs you can try or have free of cost, visit www.tucows.com; it's the preferred download destination on the Web that features safe (virus-free) applications that are easy to transfer to your PC.

Though these free products might have a limited use period or are equally limited in their capabilities, free downloads are a great way to test-drive an application before you invest in it. And don't overlook any decent image editors that may have actually come preloaded on your computer or in a CD-ROM accompanying the digital camera you purchased.

Fine-Tuning the Fine Details

So what exactly can you hope to correct if your image doesn't represent your item just right? By using one of the image editors previously mentioned, you can make these common image enhancements with just a few clicks and drags of your computer's mouse:

- **Brightness and contrast.** If your image is too dark, washed out, or rather murky, work with the brightness and contrast controls to draw out details and brighten the color tones (see Figure 17.4).
- **Color saturation and hue.** If the lighting you used cast an odd tint on your item's natural coloring, this control will allow you to independently adjust the red, green, and blue levels. With only minor adjustment, you can restore the actual coloring of the item that was otherwise misrepresented in your un-retouched photo.

Figure 17.4 The washed-out image on the left was easily corrected, utilizing brightness and contrast adjustments, to become the image on the right.

- **Sharpen/edge enhance/smooth.** After making other adjustments, you might find the need to add crispness to your image, or conversely, soften what might have emerged as harsh edges. Using these controls, you can bring out blurred detail or smooth out jagged edges. Be careful, though, as this adjustment can often result in giving your image that dreaded touched-up look (you'll know it when you see it).

Size Matters

Finally, don't overlook the importance of being equally attentive to the size of your photos. Online shoppers can be an impatient lot and few are inclined to wait around while a "fat" image creeps onto their computer display.

Rather than risk losing a sale, be sure your images load fast by keeping the file sizes at or near the 30-KB mark. Start with your camera: work image adjustments down from ultra fine detail to medium quality (which still renders a nice photo). You can also use image editing applications to resize larger images (but watch out for image degradation). And you can find image compression software (programs that essentially squeeze large files down to a manageable size without sacrificing picture quality), such as WinSoftMagic's Advanced JPEG Compressor, that can get those files down to size and speedier to display.

More Help—Free!

Naturally, the different image editors use different terminology and manage their features uniquely from product to product. If you're looking to become a real expert with the editor you've selected, hit the Internet and search for Web sites that offer free help. A search on the name of your image editor will typically reveal multiple sites that offer simple tips and even some impressively thorough tutorials.

PICTURE IMPERFECT: EIGHT COMMON IMAGING MISTAKES TO AVOID

While there's no denying that quality images will boost bidding rates and potentially increase your sales prices, it's equally true that poor photos can quickly undercut your best efforts, alienating and even angering potential bidders.

To make sure you steer clear of this digital minefield, here are the eight most common blunders that tend to afflict sellers' online images:

1. **Poor lighting.** If the lighting is dim, the image detail can be grossly underrepresented. Equally, an item too brightly lit will result in a severely overexposed image. Refer to the lighting tips presented earlier to avoid this problem.
2. **Blurry images.** Fuzzy images are an annoyance and indicate lack of attention on the seller's part. Always check the focus before you shoot, and if you have a jittery hand, use a tripod for a true still-life image.
3. **Excessive glare.** A close cousin to poor lighting, excessive glare can be the result of an overlit item but is usually caused by improper flash usage. Shoot items from an angle (left, right, over, or under) or wait until you can photograph outdoors.
4. **Lack of cropping.** Few bidders are interested in scouring an image of your messy desk in search of the item you purport to be selling. Crop your images to cut out anything that distracts from the item—that includes the kids or the kitten, no matter how cute they may be.
5. **Reflective surfaces.** An infamous image that once made the rounds on the Internet shows a chrome tea kettle reflecting a full view of its immodest proprietor. If you've seen this picture, then you know why you need to take care when photographing reflective items that might reveal distracting or even embarrassing elements opposite them. Shoot these at an angle and across from a neutral background.

Figure 17.5 Lost somewhere in this terrific photo studio is a little item begging for a much-deserved close-up.

6. **Bad backgrounds.** Forgo overly fancy backdrops or garish colors—they only distract from your item. Choose neutral or complementary background colors to really make your item stand out.

7. **Confounding combo shots.** Some sellers think it a good idea to photograph multiple items in a single image; they should think again. Other items adjacent to the one you're selling will likewise distract the potential buyer from what you're really offering for sale.

8. **Lack of close-up.** Ever looked at images of jewelry or small collectibles in which the item is too tiny to clearly discern? Avoid this frustration by getting closer to the item (watch the focus) or by taking full advantage of your camera's zoom function (see Figure 17.5).

Certainly, none of these are truly *fatal offenses,* and many can be forgiven by tolerant buyers. Still, take the opportunity to learn from past mistakes of others to further improve your item images and give your auctions the best profit potential.

IS ALL THIS EFFORT REALLY WORTH IT?

If ever you doubt the value of taking and providing good images of your auction items, consider this sentiment shared by longtime auction enthusiast and friend Gretchen Hakala: "I'm annoyed by sellers who post bad images—it's sloppy and shows the seller must not be too concerned with quality." It's a pointed testimony that shows how image quality has a direct reflection on the seller's perceived style. Hakala continues, offering this sobering insight about the effect of poor images in an auction: "I might take a chance [and bid] on an item that has a poor image simply because I'm pretty certain I'll get it for a good price—I know most other bidders won't bid at all because of the lousy picture and I wind up with a better deal." If that's the case, then poor images really *do* cost sellers in the long run and could stand between you and your fortune.

18

Selling Strategies: Tried, True, and Groundbreaking

You've probably already noticed that this book is full of strategies for getting the best possible prices for items you sell on eBay—strategies for the most eye-catching images, the most enticing listings, the most successful sales policies, and much more. Think of this chapter, then, as the gold of auction mining: the time-tested strategies that will yield better results from your efforts.

Ask eBay experts about strategy, and they'll generally tell you the secret is not so much in the tool itself, but rather in the way that you use it.

Forget the come-ons you might see in which a CD-ROM peddler is promising to unveil all the closely guarded secrets of the eBay PowerSellers (those who maintain a sales volume of at least $1,000 per month); the secrets aren't really secret at all—they're simply well-founded business techniques that most newcomers have yet to apply. There are, however, a few unique approaches to marketing and selling at eBay, techniques you may never have figured could make a difference to your eBay bottom line. This chapter, then, offers the insights you've been waiting for, the methods and means to set yourself apart from the others as you edge ever closer to your financial goals.

IT ALL STARTS WITH TIMING

Okay. So maybe there actually is truth in that old adage "Timing is everything." Although it may sound a bit trite, when it comes to online auctioning, savvy sellers have found that strategic timing—in terms of *when* and *how long* an auction will run—can have significant impact on their ultimate success. The questions to answer, therefore, are these: What is the best day of the week to list or end an auction? How long should an auction run? Which is the magical hour for ending an auction?

Those are the questions; these are the answers.

The Long and the Short of It

Before listing, you need to calculate which day you want your auction to end. This in turn will dictate the starting day for your auction. As you recall from Chapter 7, eBay offers several choices for auction length, ranging from 1 to 10 days. Remember this, though: if an auction is too long (such as the 10-day epoch), it might be forgotten during its lengthy run. If it's too short, however (as in the 3-day quickie), it might not generate any momentum before it ends. In the past, the general recommendation would have been to run auctions for a 7-day stretch. Granted, this can be a long wait for sellers anxious to close a deal; however, by having an auction encompass a full 7 days, you can best reach people who browse the Internet and eBay only on certain days of the week (believe it or not, some folks still have limited access to a computer). Most important, the 7-day listing will span both weekend days (if started on a Saturday or Sunday) when auction traffic is generally higher.

> **eBay TIP:** Surely you'll hear others exclaim such-and-such day is the *best* day for auctions to close. Be sure to experiment with closing days to see what best suits your bidders and be willing to be flexible enough to adjust that closing day if certain situations (such as holidays) dictate. And how about those holidays? Most sellers agree that it's best to avoid ending auctions on a holiday (especially holiday weekends). Since many of us are either traveling or otherwise occupied by festivities, the traffic at auction sites will typically be light.

While the 7-day auction is still the longstanding favorite, the 5-day run is gaining favor. Why? Simply enough, with so many competing items to select from, not to mention the myriad other distractions the Internet offers, it's becoming a better choice to wrap up the auction sooner rather than later.

With a 5-day listing, you can launch your auction midweek and have it end on the preferred weekend close (more on that next).

And what about those 1-day rapid-fire offerings? Well, these are likely best for severely time-sensitive items such as event tickets. If your item will be null and void if you don't unload it right away, consider the 1-day fast track.

What a Difference a Day Makes

Although opinions vary, Sunday is still considered the best day to end an auction. Start and end your auction on a Sunday and you tap a full week and weekend's worth of exposure. Again, Saturdays and Sundays tend to bring out bidders, accommodating those who don't enjoy the luxury of surfing the Net at their workplaces. Start on Wednesday, in a 5-day scenario, and you'll likewise close on Sunday.

Are there bad days on which to end an auction? Well, Fridays can be challenging, since your listings won't benefit from the weekend surge. And folks who sneak off for early weekends might be away from their computers on Fridays and Saturdays. By ending an auction on a Sunday, though, you can still entertain those folks who've been away for most of the weekend but are ready to go online upon returning home Sunday afternoon or evening.

> **eBay TIP:** Incidentally, the 10-day auction was created to accommodate the national holidays, allowing a seller to list an item before the holiday occurred and maintain the auction activity for another week after the big event has passed. While this scheme seems good in theory, 10-day auctions haven't proven to be a boon to sellers, especially considering the 40¢ surcharge this invokes.

Tapping into the eBay Rush Hour

Perhaps the most crucial consideration in timing strategy is choosing the hour your auction will start and end. By and large, the best time to start or end an auction is in the evening hours when potential bidders are more likely to browse for extended periods of time, with a better chance to notice your new listings as well as be in attendance to bid during your auction's final minutes. Be sure to consider time zones in all this, offering West Coast citizens enough time to get home from work without making East Coast citizens stay up all night. (Hint: between 6 p.m. and 8 p.m. Pacific time is the safest bet.)

eBay TIP: As you decide on an ending time for your auction, keep in mind that eBay runs its auctions based in the Pacific time zone.

Choosing Bidder-Friendly Times

You can see that smart auction timing takes your customers' surfing and bidding habits into account, trying to accommodate their schedules. Don't forget to think globally. Yes, if you find that certain goods would be most attractive to bidders and buyers outside your native land, be sure to adjust your listing start and stop times to accommodate them in their homeland according to their clocks. When you give this sort of time consideration to your buyers, wherever they may be, you can expect to receive kudos for your efforts (I know I have).

USING COUNTERS TO CHART YOUR SUCCESS

One of the best ways to determine how well your auction listing efforts are paying off is to monitor the amount of traffic your items are attracting. A simple tool that's been available for some time is the *online counter.* When listing an item at eBay, you're able to select a free counter that will be displayed for all to see or remain hidden, if you choose, for your eyes only. Here's some insight into counter use and how to distill the information you might gather.

Why Count?

I once read the following sentiment about online marketing: "Fifty percent of my advertising doesn't work. I just don't know which fifty percent." Though relatively clever in content, there's truth to this statement, as sellers struggle to determine when and where their auction enticements are most effective. The best way to gauge the appeal of your listings and adeptness of your sales strategies is to quantify the public response—that's where counters come into play.

Counters can tally how many people have visited your eBay listings. Each time a particular item is viewed, the tally is incremented. In this way, you'll see how much relative activity an item is generating (how many looks), helping you to determine which items seem to be the most popular by way of comparing the counter hits. Immediately, you'll be able to identify those items that draw more attention from lookers and bidders and those that seem to languish undisturbed on the virtual shelf. This might provide valuable insight into which attributes of the listing (style, category, timing) are responsible for attracting the most traffic to your items, which item keywords seem to get the most search hits, which pricing strategies seem to lure more potential buyers, which days of the week see the most counter increases, and, overall, which combined approaches seem to be working best for you. Armed with these raw statistics, you're in a much better position to make well-reasoned adjustments as the numbers dictate.

Do the Numbers Ever Lie?

Understand that a high number of counter hits doesn't necessarily ensure a successful sale or higher auction bids. In fact, an item that receives a high number of hits but still doesn't sell might indicate your price needs revising, your description needs revamping, or perhaps your images need sprucing up. That is, if the item is getting a high volume of looks but those looks are being converted into actual bids or purchases, something is amiss; your enticement is excellent but something about the item or your policies is keeping you from closing the deal.

Be especially wary of an item whose images take an extraordinarily long time to display (did you overdo the HTML?). Visitors may have decided not to wait around, even though their attempt to view the item was tallied.

More to the point of counter accuracy, the free counters at eBay are often limited to providing simple *page views* (the number of times the item page has been looked at). While this is generally useful, the most granular and most telling statistic would be that of *unique visitor hits,* that is, how many *different* visitors have viewed the item (as opposed to the same visitor viewing your item page several times or more). Don't expect to get this sort of data integrity from eBay, though. Generally, to gain this sort of specific information, you'd need to purchase specially developed online tracking software and use it at a commercial Web site of your own (a topic of discussion taken up in Chapter 27). If you're not yet considering starting your own online business outside of eBay, it may be too soon for this.

Better Seen or Unseen?

Here's where the discussion often picks up—the argument over whether it's better or worse to include visible counters on your item pages (recalling that you can elect to have the counter visible only to your eyes). One faction argues that a visible counter can help motivate buyers and bidders, citing that a high number of counter hits will indicate to shoppers that the item is potentially high in demand; a subsequent buyer might be prompted to take the item quickly before someone else snatches it away. From the other side comes the argument that visible counters might dissuade a buyer or bidder for a couple of reasons. First, an item with a high counter value might indicate a belief that something's wrong with the item; if the current bid doesn't reflect a high value in concert with the high counter rate, something could be amiss. In a bidding scenario, a high count might foretell a bidding war that will likely ensue, a competitive showdown that many buyers choose to avoid. And if the count is low, well, that could also indicate a perceived problem with the item, or it might act as enticement to bargain hunters.

Either way, there are pros and cons to utilizing visible counters. It's wise to use invisible counters at the outset, as you can learn which items and sales approaches seem to be most popular without tipping off or otherwise influencing your bidders. Then, experiment with making those counters visible and determine whether they have a positive or a negative effect on your sales.

Strength in Numbers

Whatever your approach, using counters makes good sense and will help you learn more about online marketing as well as your growing online customer base (repeat buyers). And while some statistical data can be misleading, any sort of numerical results can typically aid you in honing your approach to improve your auction income.

THE POWER OF PERSUASIVE PRICING

With millions of items available every day, competition among sellers at eBay is stiff. Don't throw up your hands in despair, fearful that the only way to lure bidders is by dumping your great stuff at giveaway prices. Truth is, both high sell-through and healthy profits can be yours *provided* you're using the best pricing strategies.

Know How Your Items Fare

The preamble to proper pricing is to understand how your goods will measure up in the competitive auction marketplace. Therefore, consider these core tenets of smart pricing: present supply and demand, condition and completeness of your goods, your investment value in your goods, and your realistic sales goals. Research current and closed auctions to ensure your pricing strategies will complement, not contradict, current trends in auction sales.

You'll find this to be the critical information that determines whether what you want to sell is what the bidders want to buy—and at which price.

How Low Can You Go?

Naturally, bidders are looking for a bargain, and your task is to entice them with a low minimum bid that practically screams, "Take me home, cheap!" Half the fun of online auctions is the gamesmanship of back-and-forth bidding, and low starting bids will get the ball rolling. Once a bidding volley ensues, thwarted bidders often return to reclaim the item they've likely taken emotional possession of, frequently battling hard to bring home the win, even ignoring that the current market value might have already been surpassed.

If you've done your sales research thoroughly, you can safely attract those bargain hunters while ultimately achieving present market value (and sometimes beyond) for your item.

Is Higher Better?

Sometimes, higher-quality or highly desirable goods might be ill served by low opening bids, which could conjure the thought that "at that low a price, there must be something wrong" (similar to the psychology behind the eBay counter). A higher opening bid can work wonders to effectively communicate that your item is the real deal. It caters to the truly discriminating buyers— especially those who search specifically for higher-priced offerings—and showcases your knowledge and confidence in the fine goods you're offering. However, don't stall the bidding with *too* high a price. Rather, keep that starting price below present market value: try an opening bid price that falls between 50 and 75 percent of current market value. Bidders will see that you understand your item's value yet aren't opposed to allowing their competitive bidding to set the final price. Savvy buyers rarely let a desirable item sell too cheaply.

RESERVE BIDS

If you're unsure about getting a reasonable price or recovering your investment in an item, apply a reserve price to it. Establishing a secret reserve price (it's never displayed in your listing) is an option available to you within the Selling Format section of the Create Your Listing page. Reserve prices, as you'll recall from the discussion in Chapter 1, are preestablished sales price limits by which you're not required to sell your item at the auction's close if the high bid fails to reach your reserve price. This allows you to ensure you can protect your level of investment or belief of value in an item and not have to sell at a price you would consider too low. Although some bidders are put off at the mere sight of a reserve price auction, sometimes it's your best bet to avoid a significant loss. But like the high opening bid strategy, set your reserve slightly below market value whenever possible to allow for the auction process to ultimately decide the final sales price. If you get greedy or drop a reserve on *every* auction you list, you'll incur the stigma of being an overpriced seller who has little knowledge of (or faith in) the bidding market.

Buy It Now: A Quick, Noncompetitive Alternative

There's definitely a population of eager buyers who aren't interested in competitive bidding, nor are they inclined to wait for an auction to run its course. Instead, they prefer a quick purchase, plain and simple. Likewise, some sellers also prefer the fixed-price format of eBay's Buy-It-Now listings (see Figure 18.1) as a way to mitigate the risk of relinquishing items too cheaply, avoid use of the secretive and oft-maligned reserve price, and generally effect a rapid transaction. Recall that you were also given the opportunity to designate a Buy-It-Now within the Selling Format section of the Create Your Listing page (refer to Chapter 7).

If you're not certain when you should employ the Buy-It-Now feature, consider these situations:

- Your item is in demand and you've found the current market value to be acceptable; offer to let buyers take it at that price and be done with it.
- Your item is in *high* demand and you stand to gain above market value from a buyer who doesn't wish to lose out in the bidding wars any longer. Here, you can set a premium price for providing the opportunity for a quick and assured purchase (careful, don't price too high).
- Your item is of time-boxed demand (e.g., seasonal or trendy goods) and a fixed-price sell ensures the buyer of receiving it in a timely manner.
- You're in no particular hurry and can afford to set fixed prices to see if the market will bear a higher price.

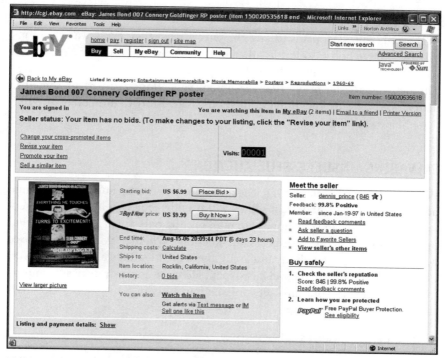

Figure 18.1 When the Buy-It-Now option is in use, you'll see the "take it" price listed just below the Place Bid area.

> **eBay TIP:** Remember that you can make use of the Buy-It-Now price within a traditional auction at eBay. Establish your opening bid, a reserve if you feel the need, and then suggest a Buy-It-Now price, too. Some bidders will decide it's best to take the item for the reasonable fixed price you're offering, resulting in a fast purchase for them and a quick sale for you. If not, the normal bidding can ensue.
>
> Usually, the Buy-It-Now option disappears once a bid is placed on an item that included the fixed-price alternative. However, if the seller also stipulates a reserve price in the listing, the Buy-It-Now price remains available until normal bidding meets or exceeds the Buy-It-Now price. Once the reserve is met, the Buy-It-Now option disappears.

Let the Bidders Decide

In the end, your best bet is to give the buyers what they really want: options. Whether they choose to battle other bidders for your goods or elect to buy your items outright, give them the opportunity to decide for themselves. Though this doesn't imply that *every* item you offer has to be presented in dual strategy, utilize the different methods in an effort to ultimately give bidders the power of choice.

SALVAGING UNSUCCESSFUL AUCTIONS

When you're new to auctioning, it's natural for you to step into eBay with high hopes for high bids, and most sellers will usually achieve a high level of success. However, when your hopes are high but the bids aren't, you might wind up with an occasional unsuccessful auction. Whether your reserve price wasn't met or even if nobody bid at all, there might still be a way to drum up a sale even after the final gavel has struck. Here are a few strategies to employ to bring success to your unsuccessful auction.

Ringing Up the Reserves

Believe it or not, one of the easiest postauction sales to make is when your auction's reserve price isn't met. Whenever you have an auction close without the reserve price being met, it's good customer courtesy to contact the high bidder as a form of closure. To help in this effort, eBay has provided the *Second Chance Offer*—it allows you to contact one or more bidders who bid on your item and give them the opportunity to make a purchase at their high-bid price. If normal bidding doesn't reach your reserve price by the time the auction ends, you can use the Second Chance feature (accessible from the closed item listing page or from within the Unsold area on the My eBay page) to appropriately contact underbidders to see if they'd still like to buy your goods.

---

 eBay TIP: Second Chance Offers are available through eBay only in cases where the reserve price wasn't met or a high bidder in an auction has failed to pay.

The Easiest Sale You'll Ever Make

Sometimes, though, the prospective underbidder or buyer may come knocking on *your* door. Via the "Ask the seller a question" link on the listing page, motivated buyers may contact you directly to see whether you're still interested in selling the item. Here's where you can determine whether you'll offer the item through eBay's Second Chance process or, just possibly, deal directly with the buyer away from eBay. Now, understand that eBay frowns upon direct deals like this—it cuts the site out of the action and earns eBay zero commission fees—so never go recklessly hawking your wares. However, if the buyer has a valid eBay user ID and you're comfortable selling direct after reviewing the buyer's feedback, then why not? Just practice the same care and caution as you would in any other transaction, stating your sales policies and accepted payment terms.

Though some buyers might try to swoop in and take advantage of you after a listing of yours closes without a sale (offering an offensively low selling price perhaps), many are legitimately interested in striking a reasonable deal. Reply promptly and be prepared to negotiate a bit—remember that if the buyer was interested in paying your original price, he or she would have bid during the course of the auction.

And don't be surprised if a high bidder gives you the always-welcome reverse suggestive selling routine: "Got anything else like this?" It's a real bonus when the bidders start asking you what you have to sell to them.

APPEALING TO BUYERS' SENSES

Here's a strategy you may never have considered: often, sellers overlook the importance of appealing to their buyers' senses. That is, in all the flurry of listing goods and managing sales, it becomes easy to overlook these small but significant nuances of selling items. Therefore, selling to the senses, so to speak, will help you improve your offerings, ensure high levels of customer satisfaction, and keep those buyers coming back for more. Here's how:

Sight

Clearly, first impressions are lasting ones. If an item you have to offer is dusty, dingy, or generally just a bit dilapidated in appearance, see if you can clean it up. And while brushing off the dust and wiping away the soil is typically a good idea, take care in your cleaning. Some sellers have damaged items in their efforts to add a bit of polish (e.g., attempting to remove old price tags or stains) and some buyers proclaim that removing an item's natural patina is a definite no-no. Therefore, clean when it makes sense—when there's no risk of devaluing the item—to give the item the best possible appearance (don't be bashful about asking around to find out how other sellers and collectors shine up similar articles). If you're not sure, provide a full disclosure of the item's present state and the potential for polishing, then leave it for the buyer to decide if a cleaning is in order.

Smell

Sometimes the nose knows what's inside a package long before the eyes ever get a glimpse. Take special care to please this sense, as buyers are often more than disappointed when an item brings along a stench that wasn't bargained for. If an item has a musty odor from moisture exposure, let it be known. If you're a smoker and your items have absorbed the odor, let that be known too. In fact, some sellers have found it an enticement when the ad plainly states, "Comes from a smoke-free home."

Otherwise, if your goods have a certain "air" about them that could potentially be offensive, be certain to state it up front.

Touch

Usually, touch isn't a sensation that proves to be too troublesome. Of course, items that are rough or sticky—and shouldn't be—necessitate full disclosure.

The same holds for furniture or other items that might have been worn smooth over years of use or could have the telltale rippling or warping that comes from moisture damage; these situations should also be properly explained at the outset. Many buyers will close their eyes and run their hands over an item to detect variations or imperfections that their eyes might miss.

Be sure there are no tactile surprises in store for your customers.

Sound

Naturally, when you're selling audio-related items (old records, tapes, radios, and so on), you'll want to fully describe the aural qualities of the goods. But beyond these obvious sound-related items, give consideration to sounds *any* of your items might make. If it rattles, is something broken? If it squeaks, does it need to be lubricated? Again, none of the senses should be taken for granted when selling to and satisfying your customers.

Taste

Okay, this is the one sense you might not need to cater to as attentively as the previous four. Still, some rock, gem, and coin collectors have stated that their taste buds can offer the final determination about an item's authenticity and lineage. You probably can't offer a taste test up front, but just be aware of this form of buyers' authentication.

Making Sense of It All

Although it might have sounded a bit far-fetched, appealing to your buyer's senses is just another consideration to be given as you manage your listings and strive for your fortune. Remembering that online sales prevent buyers from fully experiencing an item as they would in person, work to present as much positive sensory information as possible when listing your goods, and then be doubly certain that there will be no negative sensory surprises when the goods arrive. This is a strategy that will certainly set you ahead of your peers.

KEYS TO RELISTING

If, for all your efforts, your item simply doesn't sell, don't consider throwing it out just yet. Now knowing about the effect and impact of sales strategies, you're in the best position possible to reevaluate your approach while further refining your selling expertise. Therefore, always give consideration to an item's second life through relisting.

Review, Revise, and Remarket

On every eBay item page or from within the My eBay page for items sold or unsold, there is a text link that reads, "Relist this item." Click that link to navigate through the Create Your Listing pages as when the item was originally posted. All of the original listing information is still contained within the various fields, but when relisting, you might consider making some changes. Perhaps you need a change in approach and strategy as you prepare to reposition your item. To that end, consider these key relisting opportunities:

- Review your auction title for clarity and maximum-hit keywords (for buyers' searches).
- Review your auction category and determine whether it was the best choice, the only choice, or if there's a better choice available.

- Review your auction description to be sure it's informative, accurate, and enticing.
- Did you include an image of the item?
- Would using HTML increase the item's appeal?
- Was your minimum bid price or reserve price set too high? Can you adjust it down or forgo the reserve, trusting the current market to bring you a reasonable price?
- Was this the best time to list? Review the time, day, and season of your auction and determine whether an adjustment is in order.
- How many times have you relisted (if this isn't just your second go-round)? Is it possible there's simply no interest in your item at this time? (Yes, this is a rare but plausible conclusion at times.)

There is value in a failed auction: it communicates that your approach, somehow and somewhere, didn't quite work. Be open, perceptive, and flexible with each of your auctions. In many cases, it's a fine-tuning procedure in which you're stabilizing your business approach and adjusting your offerings. Relistings allow you to tinker with your listing approach until you can lock into your customer base in a way that has you bringing in the bids at a maximum success rate.

19

Building and Managing
Your Inventory

With expert sales strategies powering your auction results, you must now turn your attention to ensuring that your inventory of goods doesn't dwindle and dissipate. Some successful sellers have enjoyed terrific sell-through rates only to be caught unprepared when their stock of auctionable items virtually evaporates in short order. To make a long-term run at auctioning and online merchandizing, sellers need to establish reliable sources of replenishment or else face the dreaded out-of-stock dilemma. In this chapter, you'll learn how to keep your shelves fully stocked at all times and how to effectively manage that online storeroom to ensure your eBay income is never interrupted.

SETTING YOUR GOALS BEFORE STOCKING
YOUR SHELVES

While it's true that eBay is a terrific venue for cleaning up the house and yard and bringing home a few hundred extra dollars (easily), if you aspire to become a serious seller—to be in this for the longer term—you'll want to take a more focused approach to developing and growing your business potential. Once you get into that league, *inventory* fuels your fortune—and acquiring and maintaining that inventory by way of an inventory plan is what keeps you operating profitably, upward and onward. When establishing this inventory plan, be sure you have clear answers to these questions:

- Are you selling for the long haul or is this just a short-time stint?
- How much inventory do you already have (possibly made up of your own possessions)? What return might it bring? And how long will it sustain your selling activity?
- How much capital (expendable cash or access to it) will you need to establish your inventory of goods?
- What sorts of goods do you want to sell? Will you generalize or specialize in your inventory?
- At what prices can you purchase goods, and what profit percentage can you expect to achieve?
- How much demand might there be for the items you want to sell, and what kind of inventory turnover can you reasonably expect?
- How (and where) will you store your inventory, and does it require any special environmental conditions (in regard to temperature, humidity, etc.)?
- How many listings do you want to stage each week or month, and what levels of inventory will you need to support that?
- What is the lead time to replenish your inventory?
- Will the items you sell be seasonal (i.e., selling best at certain times of the year as opposed to sustained levels year-round)?

Yep, that's a lot of questions, but they'll need to be answered if you have intentions of launching and sustaining an eBay business. After having gotten the hang of auctioning and fixed-price selling at eBay, you'll want to seriously concern yourself with these inventory matters, ensuring that the goods you need are fully considered beforehand without having your aspirations of fortune depending on whatever items you might be able to hastily scrounge up.

IDENTIFYING SOURCES OF SUPPLY

Where do long-term sellers find all that great stuff to auction? Actually, it's rare for sellers to rely on a single source of goods; most have learned to seek out a variety of supplies (and suppliers) to keep their auctions running at full tilt. Here are some of the key places you'll want to investigate for potential inventory, including some you may have already considered and some maybe not.

Secondhand Goods

You've heard the stories: someone made a hundred bucks on a bauble they paid two bits for at the local flea market. Though it's common knowledge that online auctioneers have turned flea markets, garage sales, and thrift shops upside down in their quest for auctionable goods, the fact is that these are still very viable sources of inventory. With much of the initial auction fever having waned (casual sellers discovering that there's work required in steady auctioning), dedicated sellers are again finding buried treasures at these discard depositories. Though you won't want to rely solely on these secondhand venues, they're still worth a regular visit.

Inventory for Under a Buck

Surely, there's one of those funky dollar-type stores near you. If you haven't yet visited one, do so today—there are some decent finds within (and don't forget to visit www.99centwholesale.com, too). Often, manufacturers' overruns or discontinued merchandise can be found at these stores. Just because the retail market has turned its back on these goods doesn't necessarily mean the auction market has. Many sellers have admitted that these stores house some great items that cost less than a dollar yet can net profits of $5 or more (an easy profit with low overhead if you create a listing that you can relist time and time again). You'll have to be selective and you'll need to visit regularly, since much of the inventory changes from week to week. But with the frequent good finds to be had, it would be foolish to turn up your nose at these cut-rate supply headquarters.

The Online Source, of Course

One of the most convenient places to find inventory is on the Internet itself. Without ever leaving your computer you can research, locate, and procure the kinds of goods that you've found are selling well at eBay. Many importers and wholesalers maintain an online presence in an effort to reach a greater audience of buyers, as you are doing. Don't overlook the potential of searching

> **eBay TIP:** Some sellers can maintain steady auction activity by purchasing huge lots of merchandise by the pallet or boxful, often at incredibly low prices. They then sell each item individually for a healthy profit. If this is what you're interested in doing, read Chapter 20 for information on how to buy big.

Google.com or Yahoo.com by specific item keywords, which will usually turn up additional commercial and private sources. And remember to constantly peruse the auction listings themselves for even more low-priced inventory. It's commonplace for sellers to proclaim they've landed great bargains at eBay, and then, with a bit of sales strategy applied to a new listing of their own, turn the goods over in the same venue for a healthy profit (I do this constantly, by the way).

CARE AND STORAGE OF YOUR INVENTORY

Not all inventory is created equal, nor should all inventory be treated the same. As you continually research what sorts of things you might sell at eBay, you should also be sensitive to special requirements or considerations for the goods you'll handle. Matters of item size, item value, fragility, and so on will need to be considered as part of your work in acquiring, maintaining, and selling your goods. Therefore, take a look at this list of considerations as you determine whether your inventory will require any special care and handling:

- **How big (or small) will your items be?** If you're selling furniture or other large items, you'll be faced with the need for a larger storage area than if you're selling knickknacks.
- **Do your items require climate control?** All items are best stored in clean, dry environments, and some items will need special care in regard to humidity and exposure to sunlight.
- **Does your inventory require authentication?** If you're dealing in truly rare and collectible items, you might find your customers wanting irrefutable proof of originality before they'll drop big dollars. Authentication can cost extra and is a cost you'll need to figure into the overall cost of your goods to ensure that your eventual income will cover your outlay. (Incidentally, visit eBay's site map for a link to "Opinions, Authentication & Grading.")
- **Can your inventory be secured?** Though you needn't distrust friends or family, you will want to be able to close up your inventory area to ensure nothing is inadvertently moved or misplaced. And, of course, truly valuable items such as jewelry and the like should be locked up for safety's sake.
- **How large will your inventory grow?** Though you may start off with lower expectations, many sellers who find their rhythm tell of storage facilities that are quickly outgrown. Keep expansion in mind and be prepared to deal with overflow from your initial storage solution.

- **What will storage cost?** Some sellers have so much inventory that they have to move much of it to off-site storage facilities. Keep those costs in mind as you estimate your selling expenses and profit expectations.
- **How accessible will your inventory be?** If your items are stored off-site or in the attic, always work to keep them relatively easy to reach. Clambering over boxes or being unable to access an off-site facility could become inconvenient and time consuming. While maintaining a steady supply of hot-selling inventory is always the goal for the enduring online seller, never fail to plan how and where you'll store your goods before you commit to either a boxful or a boxcar load of items.

KEEPING TRACK OF YOUR INVENTORY

A well-organized inventory will be a key asset to you as you make your fortune grow. Employing the use of either a simple spreadsheet application (see Figure 19.1) or a hard-copy inventory ledger, here are the details you'll want to record:

- **Item number.** Develop a simple numbering scheme to make item identification easier—and make sure you always assign a number to incoming items.
- **Item name.** What is it?
- **Item description.** Detailed enough description that highlights unique attributes of the item.

Item #	Item Name	Item Description	Item Image	Purchase Price	Purchase Date
aur-17	Aurora Batcycle kit	Very good cond.; 1968 long box	c:\auctionpics\batcycle.jpg	$98.50	02/05/02
aur-18	Aurora Batmobile kit	Near mint cond; 1st issue purple; 1966 long box	c:\auctionpics\batmobile.jpg	$115.00	2/5/02
aur-19	Aurora Batplane kit	Mint sealed; 1967 long box	c:\auctionpics\batplane.jpg	$87.50	2/5/02
aur-20	Aurora Voyage Flying Sub	Very good cond.; 1968 long box	c:\auctionpics\flysub.jpg	$40.00	3/15/02
aur-21	Aurora Invaders Saucer kit	Near mint sealed; 1968 long box	c:\auctionpics\invaders.jpg	$60.00	3/25/02

Figure 19.1 The spreadsheet program on your computer makes keeping inventory records a breeze.

- **Item image.** Though this takes a bit more effort up front, an image will make identification all the easier. It will also be useful when it comes time to list your item—the image is ready to use whether it's a hard-copy photo that you'll scan or a link to a digital image that you'll later upload.
- **Item cost.** How much did you pay for it? (Don't forget to keep all of your receipts for potential tax-deduction purposes.)
- **When purchased.** This helps you keep track of how long the item's been in your inventory.
- **Where purchased.** You may have stumbled on a great source of inventory and will most likely want to visit it again.
- **Estimated resale value.** This can be subjective, but try to refer to generally accepted market values by reviewing price guides, talking with other sellers and collectors, and researching previous auction prices.
- **Storage area.** Where is it now? If you keep inventory in several places (as many sellers do), you'll want to minimize time spent hunting down an item. Of course, you should tailor this list of information to best meet your own specific needs, but be sure you have sufficient data to enable you to accurately identify, retrieve, and list any item in your inventory.

REINVESTING WISELY

The key to building any fortune is to put your earnings back to work for you. At eBay, this means using your auction profits and diverting some of that income back into growing your inventory. Knowing the goods you have today will not last forever, consider how you'll keep that supply of goods in steady replenishment. Though you may not have thought this out as you embarked on this fortune hunt, here are some things to think about as you reinvest in your auction future.

- First and foremost, invest only at a price that provides you the opportunity to make a reasonable profit upon resale.
- Tie your reinvestment decisions to what you've learned in your ongoing market research, electing to invest only in inventory that has a proven market.
- Target a percentage of your auction income for immediate reinvestment in inventory. If you're in this for the long haul, you need to let the business (rather than your personal funds) carry the burden of inventory reinvestment.

- Try to invest in goods that you can successfully resell within three months. Avoid having your operating profit tied up too long in inventory that may not provide the return you hoped for.
- Seek to build an emergency reinvestment fund for times when sales may slow or, better yet, when a rare opportunity to buy big presents itself. Yes, it takes money to make money, but if you've chosen your inventory carefully, maintained it faithfully, and reinvested astutely, you'll be halfway home on the path to your fortune.

With this information, you're ready to assess your current goods and determine your future acquisitions as you manage your eBay inventory. Begin with the goods that are readily around you and use those to gain much-needed insight into what sells well at eBay. Then, when you're looking at additional goods to sell, take the points raised in this chapter to guide you in your reinvestments. When you approach inventory in a well-informed manner, you're best prepared to maintain and grow that eBay fortune.

20

Buying for Resale

To be a truly successful seller and an expert in maintaining inventory, you'll need to become an equally adept buyer. By now you can see that one great buy or even an attic full of stuff isn't going to be enough to support your auction business (and it is a business) for an extended period. In order to ensure you can maintain an inventory of tempting and profit-bearing goods, you'll want to embody the traits of a savvy reseller and employ the uncompromising tactics of sound reinvestment to keep your business operating comfortably in the black.

THE RESELLER'S RESOLVE

To be a good reseller, it's important to approach that part of your eBay activity with only the purest resale objectives in mind. If you're not certain what criteria successful resellers apply to their inventory purchase, consider these differentiators:

- Resellers value an item for its ability to generate another sale, to broaden their offerings, and ultimately to entice more bidders.
- Resellers are in business to sell, and thus they should avoid becoming emotionally attached to their resale merchandise.
- Resellers will buy new and different sorts of items if they sense a trend beginning, if their return buyers continue to ask for such items, or if there's a viable opportunity to expand the appeal of their offerings to a larger buying public.

Though it may sound a bit cold to approach auctioning and inventory management in such a detached fashion, recognize that fortunes aren't made by buyers who keep all the items they've purchased or who make buys without a strong market to justify the investment. If you're in it to make a fortune, you're in it as a businessperson—cool and calculating.

CASTING A CRITICAL EYE ON REINVESTMENT

Operating under this sort of objective, profit-bearing mindset, approach each inventory purchase or profit reinvestment by first asking yourself a few questions about the sales potential of the goods you may acquire:

- Can you purchase an item or items at a price that ensures you a reasonable profit?
- Can you resell the item relatively quickly? You don't want your money tied up in inventory for too long.
- Is there demand for the item that has been proven in the online auction arena?
- If you're dealing in collectibles, do you know which items are more elusive and which are more common? You'll want to hunt down the elusive items to make larger profits.

(Hint: Talk with other sellers and dealers to learn what their customers are most eager to purchase, then explore the availability of those items for yourself.) Of course, there's no way to be 100 percent certain in every purchase you make regarding the resale potential of those goods, but by casting a critical eye on the items you might buy for turnover, you'll maintain that steely and objective mindset that will drive you to make better decisions before committing to a purchase.

CALCULATING MARKUP AND PROFIT

Now that you believe you've identified items that you're reasonably confident will sell, it's time to determine *how much* you can sell them for and *what profit* a sale will gain you. Sounds obvious, but so many sellers today tend to leave profit to chance. Instead of the passive approach, consider the following as you determine a necessary profit margin.

Determining Costs

- **Actual item cost.** If you acquire your inventory via onesey-twosey purchasing, your average cost per item might be higher than you think (this is especially true if you deal in a wide range of goods). If you purchase resellable goods in bulk, use your supplier's standard net cost as your acquisition cost. When special deals or discounts become available and reduce the per-unit cost, consider that immediate addition to your profit potential *without* altering your recorded average unit cost.

- **Acquisition cost.** Next, determine how much it costs you to acquire the goods, factoring in transportation or delivery costs, travel costs on your part, storage or other inventory care costs, and so on. Carefully track these costs, especially over an extended period, to arrive at an evenly distributed/attributed per-item acquisition cost.

- **Now, factor in your eBay listing costs.** Include listing fees and final value fees based on your average expected (and hopefully *sustained*) selling price. When you arrive at this final number, sum up the three to determine your most basic cost of goods sold.

Calculating Selling Price

Now comes the matter of determining the achievable selling price of an item such that will gain you the level of profit you desire. For example, if you want to achieve a 30 percent markup on an item, you would need to manipulate a simple formula as follows:

$$\text{Selling price} = \text{total cost} \times (1 + \text{markup percent})$$

Using that formula, if you have an item that bears a total cost of $5.50 (includes per-unit cost plus transportation, storage, listing, and any other costs incurred to get it to the point of sale) and you wish to earn a 30 percent markup, your selling cost would be calculated as follows:

$$\$5.50 \times (1 + 0.30) = \$5.50 \times 1.30 = \$7.15 \text{ selling price}$$

Once you figure your total item cost, you can work with various markup scenarios and compare those to the current market price (the demand for the goods where buyers will indicate the price they're willing to readily pay) to establish your per-item profit potential. Again, the more efficient and stable your acquisition costs, the better able you are to determine whether the selling price necessary for the profit you want is attainable.

On to Gross Margin Profit

Markup percent isn't the same as profit margin. If you crack open your collegiate accounting tomes, you'll recall that *gross margin profit* is the remainder after total cost of goods sold is subtracted from revenue. The actual *gross margin percent* is then calculated from that remainder. It's a bit more math, but it's not too difficult:

Gross margin percent = (selling price – total cost) / selling price

Using our previous example of the item you'd sell for $7.15, then:

Gross margin percent = ($7.15 – $5.50) / $7.15
Gross margin percent = $1.65 / $7.15
Gross margin percent = 23%

Ah! Now we have a working gross margin percent that's clearly different (and leaner) than a mere markup percent. At this point, you can use the gross margin percent calculation to experiment with setting the selling price of an item. If you want to achieve a 30 percent *gross margin percent,* the calculation would look like this:

Selling price = total cost / (1 – gross margin)

So . . .

Selling price = $5.50 / (1 – 0.30)
Selling price = $5.50 / 0.70
Selling price = $7.80

Take your selling price based on desired gross margin percent result back to the online marketplace to determine whether demand is such that you can achieve this sort of selling price (or higher). Now you're doing real business on your way to real fortune.

FINDING LOTS TO SELL

At this point you may be wondering where other sellers are finding the sorts of low-cost, high-profit items under discussion here. Actually, the goods are probably closer at hand than you think. First, consider the outlets in your local area (places like Cargo Largo or any of the dollar stores). If there are other closeout warehouses in your area, be sure to check those out. In fact, browse your local telephone book for wholesalers, liquidators, and importers.

To truly broaden your reach, though, go online to find even more suppliers of goods. Consider the following:

- **Dollar Days.** Wholesale closeout merchandise is always at your fingertips online when you visit www.dollardays.com.
- **Speedy Liquidators.** Serving as buyers and sellers of wholesale merchandise, visit www.speedyliquidators.com to see the wide offering of goods it has to offer.
- **5-Star Liquidations.** Located at www.5starliquidations.com, here is yet another outlet for wholesale consumer goods, with new merchandise arriving every week.
- **eBay.** That's right, even eBay is a great source for low-cost, high-quality goods that are ready for bulk purchase and immediate resale. Be sure to visit the Wholesale Lots link in the eBay categories to see who's selling lots (see Figure 20.1).

Of course, these are just a few of the outlets available to you when it comes to finding great resale merchandise. Be sure to visit your favorite Web portal (e.g., www.google.com) and perform searches using keywords like "wholesale," "closeout," "liquidators," and so on. You'll be amazed at the amount of inventory ready and waiting for you.

MORE INSIGHTS INTO BUYING ON SPECULATION

To continue our discussion of which items will yield the greatest return on your investment, let's delve a bit deeper into the matter of speculation. Good buyers are constantly on the lookout for that diamond in the rough, whether it be a hot new collectible or a timeless favorite. Moreover, they have learned how to snatch such items from a variety of sources without tipping off the competition (other sellers). The following key factors are at play when reinvesting in inventory really pays off.

Figure 20.1 The Wholesale Lots category on eBay will link you to even more brokers and manufacturers offering bargain-priced inventory.

Know Your Stuff

Knowledge is power, and it will be the strength of every one of your speculative purchases. If you'll be speculating on items about which you're already an expert (you know the commodity inside and out, including past activity, current trends, and future potential), you're already ahead of the curve. If your expertise is a bit thin, be sure to fully research what you'll buy. Use trade papers, collector's guides, the Internet, and even eBay itself to acquaint yourself with the item of investment. Become well versed in the history, manufacturing dates, variations, and reproductions (if any) of the items you will invest in.

Then research the sellers who are currently dealing in these goods (especially pertinent if you seek to acquire the inventory within the confines of eBay).

Determine how long a seller has dealt in this sort of item and what expertise he or she seems to have. If you're purchasing outside of eBay (e.g., from a dealer at a show, via a classified ad, or at someone's garage sale), you'll need to be prepared to make quick, on-the-spot assessments of authenticity and potential value. In these situations, if the item is inexpensive, you might not have much to lose in making the purchase. However, if it seems costly and you're just not sure, you might wish to pass, or at least get the seller's contact information for a chance at a later purchase—after you've done more homework. Never rush into a costly purchase lest you get burned.

> **eBay TIP:** If I had a dollar for every time I overheard someone visiting one of my garage sales excitedly mutter to a friend, "I can sell this for a lot more at eBay," I'd have an additional fortune in my coffer. Truth is, most of the items I drag out onto my driveway are those that didn't fare well at eBay; I've already tried that market and found the market isn't buying. These folks who think they're about to rob me blind likely haven't done *their* homework, or else they'd know that what I'm offering for a buck or two is truly a castoff. I just smile and gladly take their money, adding it to my accumulated fortune.

Remember Your Limits While Testing the Seller's Market Prowess

Regardless of how desirable an item is or how great its profit potential, you'll need to ensure you buy it at a price that allows a profit to be realized.

Although this is a bit repetitive of previous advice in this chapter, it's perhaps the single most important point that is forgotten during inventory purchases. Again, you're best served when you can obtain an item at a "wholesale price," that is, roughly 60 percent below the current retail value, always striving for the gross margin profit previously outlined. This doesn't mean you'll always get top profit percentages, and clearly it's your prerogative to earn less, but this margin should be your goal. How much you relax that margin target is driven by how much profit you wish or need to make.

How about a Haggle?

Of course, good haggling skills are a must in situations where you'll be making a direct purchase from a seller. Quickly assess how much the seller knows about the items and how fairly the items are priced. Never insult a seller with an obnoxiously low price—remember that seller might be trying to make the same profit you have in mind. After a bit of back-and-forth maneuvering, you may wind up with a better price than you originally anticipated—or you may need to abort the purchase if the seller is fixed on a price that offers little room for your own profit potential.

   If you're speculating at online auctions, your best bet is to set maximum bids—and not exceed them—that will allow you the profit margin you desire. While it's true that sniping often brings in good prices, it might also incite impassioned bidding on your part, causing you to exceed your investment limit. Good alternatives are to bid early in an auction and then forget about it, or use sniping services like eSnipe.com. Though you might be outbid often, you might also find sellers' invoices coming your way, bringing tidings of great deals. Of course, if you have the willpower to stay to your limit during a live snipe, enjoy the truest thrill of reinvestment and snipe away.

> **eBay TIP:** As a final but critical point, try to avoid rampant speculative buying. If you're grabbing everything in sight, you might lose sight of how much you're spending. Even if you're getting great deals, your outgo could quickly exceed your income. Try to keep a balance between sales and purchases, with the best situation being one in which designated percentage of your auction profits are reinvested in future speculative purchases.

ESTABLISHING THE PROPER FLOW FOR YOUR MERCHANDISE

A final consideration to guide you in inventory purchases is determining how, when, and at what volume you'll offer your goods. A sort of cousin to the timing strategy of listing items for auction, this is where, as you buy for resale, you determine the best time to offer the inventory you've invested in. For fun, I refer to this inventory turnover principle as knowing when to "flow, show, or stow your stuff." Here's how it works.

Flowing Your Inventory

Obviously, the key to profiting from an invested buy is selling when demand (and prices) are highest. Look for events (historical, film, media) that will make your item particularly sought after—then sell! Sometimes the best time to sell is immediately after purchase. If you're holding a trendy item that is virtually impossible to obtain, demand will be high *now*. However, if you hold on too long, the demand might bottom out and you'll be stuck with a fad gone bad (anyone remember Beanie Babies or Furbies?).

Showing Your Inventory

Some of your best sales happen when you're not actively selling. If you have some great items that you're holing up, pop them up for view on a Web site of your own. You can easily obtain free Web space from a variety of hosting sites (e.g., Yahoo!, Juno, AngelFire, or your Internet service provider). When you deliver goods to or correspond with customers, be sure to conspicuously provide the Web address of your site, then show off your cool stuff for any visitors to see. Frequently, customers and inquirers will ask whether the items are for sale, which could spell great direct-sale profits for you.

Stowing Your Inventory

Some items you speculate on will need time to mature to reach their highest value potential. If you're buying items like limited-edition sculptures, Christmas ornaments, or character icons, you might need to hold these for a while before their ultimate value can be realized. Figure that most pop culture items need around 20 years to reach full maturity—the point when younger folks of that day have also matured and now feel a tug of nostalgia for reminders of days gone by. Therefore, find good storage for these items—someplace dry, dark, and solid. Believe it or not, the time will click by sooner than you realize, and suddenly you're sitting on a nice nest egg of the items people are clamoring for.

The key to buying for resale is to be extremely knowledgeable about the potential profit that items can bring to you. When you consider buying in large quantities, you'll need to be relatively sure you can move that inventory within a reasonable amount of time (around three months), can free up your invested money, and can realize a profit that supports your fortune-finding goals. There is no secret to this approach, really, and there are very few secret stashes or stones unturned, as some might have you believe. The success in buying for resale is knowing what to buy, when to buy it, and when to sell it.

21

Identifying Trends: What's Hot and What's Not

The key to gaining the best possible profits at eBay is the market potential of your inventory. The past several chapters have dealt with those goods you'll sell and those additional goods you'll invest in to continue selling, but there is another faction of inventory that rounds out the keys to finding your fortune: locating those goods that are in demand at eBay and avoiding those that aren't. Unfortunately, there's no secret formula, nor are there any crystal balls in use that will ensure every item you'll be purchasing will be high on every bidder's want list (although a quick search of eBay for "crystal ball" may deliver interesting results). However, by applying the strategy and insights already discussed and adding a bit of perceptive prowess, you can develop your own method—perhaps even intuition—for finding what will be hot and what will be squat at eBay.

UNDERSTANDING ONLINE SALES MINING

Just as you wouldn't begin a treasure hunt without some sort of map or plan, you likewise can't expect to know which are the most desirable goods to go after until you've gotten some direction about where to begin looking. The trick to this planning is to begin with the information you have. Then go further by analyzing it and letting it lead you in the right direction. Sure, you can put your trust and hope into accidentally stumbling upon a fortune, but it makes better sense to leave little to chance, especially when you face the prospect of investing your profits in additional goods. When it comes to knowing what to sell, how to sell, and where to sell, it becomes imperative to actively drill deep into the online sales market and let the cyberstatistics guide you on your way to the best possible results.

Data on Demand

Perhaps one of the greatest contributions of the online marketplace (next to the ease with which we can all buy and sell goods) is its volume of real-time sales data, readily available day in and day out. This is the core of the data mining potential, enabling sellers like you to seek out products similar to yours and determine the mood of the marketplace for such items.

Start your mining by finding out who's selling the sorts of items you'll offer. First, check their minimum bid prices as well as their Buy-It-Now prices to see which sellers' strategies seem to be attracting the highest bids or most lucrative fixed-price sales. Next, check the bidding activity to see which items are commanding the most active bidding. When you zero in on the listings that are generating the greatest buzz, take note of the listing categories being used, which is an indication of where most buyers who browse might be congregating.

Beyond price and category, take a careful look at the listing title (watch for all-important keywords), the listing description, the images presented, the seller's sales policies, and the seller's feedback. In short order, you'll be able to ascertain which sellers are successful, which products are drawing activity and garnering the best prices, and what overall sales style seems to attract the most customers.

---

eBay TIP: Understand that *how* you sell an item is as important to your success as *what* it is you'll sell. Sometimes, goods that become hot at eBay are those that seem to languish, unattended by other sellers who fail to recognize the proper marketing that will hoist those items out of the bowels of the site and high up on the most-wanted lists. By minding the market climate for certain goods and then offering those sorts of items thoughtfully, strategically, and in a way that caters to current market desires, you stand the best opportunity to tap into current trends.

But what about other sales destinations on the Web? Be sure to expand your data mining to the various store venues (such as at Yahoo! Shopping and within the Amazon Marketplace) and search those listings, too (see Figure 21.1).

You may find it helpful to perform a search engine query to comb the entire World Wide Web in order to locate merchant sites run by folks just like

Figure 21.1   Yahoo! Shopping is your portal to search for product trends.

you. Standing in the customer's shoes, ask yourself how well each destination you encounter motivates you to inquire further and possibly compels you to buy. Check carefully to determine whether the site is being regularly updated or whether it appears to have been overrun by virtual cobwebs. Don't be bashful about contacting the shop owner via e-mail to ask specific questions about his or her operation and merchandise.

History Rarely Lies

The most telling statistics, naturally, are those found in the past. Again, the online marketplace has plenty of information to offer here. At eBay, take a careful look at completed listings, seeking out final selling prices as well as determining whether prices are holding steady or are experiencing upward or downward trends. Be particularly attentive to listings that seem to appear as spikes or dips in the market (with a final price being either unusually high or low); closely scrutinize these listings as you seek to determine what contributed to the spike or dip (was the item miscategorized, priced too high at the outset, poorly presented, or just not in demand?). This sort of sales history data is a bit more difficult to cull from fixed-price or independent merchant sites. Some sellers provide sales history (and you should, too, when you venture into the merchant realm) whereby you can ascertain what goods they've dealt with in the past and how much activity they've seen over a period of time. Again, inquire (politely) about recently sold items if you have questions.

Tallying Up the Counter Once Again

Another way to gauge the appeal of products and their accompanying sales strategies is to quantify the public response by way of a counter. Look for counters—either at eBay or at fixed-price venues—to ascertain the popularity or attractiveness of an item up for sale. Although these counters don't necessarily indicate *unique* page views or site visits, they are a good indicator of whether the seller's style and strategy seems to be successful with potential customers. If the counter numbers are low, then something in the seller's methodology could be amiss.

Mine Your Own Business

While you're actively sifting through the offerings of others around you, don't forget to carefully examine your own offerings as well. Keep close track of *your* sales history, determining where your items sell best, when they seem to be in greatest demand, and which transactions have encouraged customers to make return visits. By regularly watching others while monitoring your own results, you'll develop the conclusive data that will help you successfully navigate the ever-changing online marketplace and make wise decisions regarding which goods you should continue to invest in.

LEARNING TO ANTICIPATE THE NEXT WAVE

The crux of this discussion is how to find new material to put on the auction block that will have bidders clawing at one another for the chance of ownership. Naturally, you want to buy these items cheap and sell high to secure your fortune. The problem is that other sellers are trying to do the very same thing.

How do you beat them to the punch and bring in the hottest merchandise at the best profit potential? Moreover, how do you ensure that the items you buy won't be yesterday's news when you go to list them, leaving you with nothing but a cluttered closet of inventory? Good questions all. Here are some answers.

Perennial Favorites

Certain items always seem to do well in the auction market; you need to be aware of what those items are and whether you should be offering them. The real opportunity lies in your potential to specialize in a few hot commodities so you can develop that valuable expertise as well as being sure you're not running your auction activity in a sort of hit-or-miss fashion.

When you specialize, you not only have the opportunity to become intimately familiar with certain items (which your customers will definitely appreciate), but you also position yourself favorably to detect new buying or

---

 eBay TIP: When you're researching the hot items, be sure to review eBay's category listings page and notice the number of items in the various category headings and subheadings. Immediately, you'll notice in which categories the bulk of the items are being listed. To spot the current trends, further investigate headers and subheaders.

collecting trends before the mainstream populace catches on. In the competitive eBay selling world, this puts you ahead of your peers.

These perennial favorites, then, include such things as original advertising materials, books, coins, Depression glass, dolls, entertainment memorabilia, sports memorabilia, high-tech collectibles, and toys. Of course, there is much more that generally stays high on collectors' and buyers' must-have lists, yet the items just mentioned typically remain in high demand and can lead you to discover related items that are equally desired.

Trust the Experience of Others

While very few of us have a truly innate and infallible intuition for identifying those items that will lead the next megatrend, it is possible to get the jump on the competition by merely keeping an open mind to the input and experience of others. Therefore, recognize the tremendous value of forming relationships and even friendships with other sellers, collectors, and commodity experts. As you deal at eBay, you'll meet more experts than you ever dreamed possible—some being sellers from whom you might buy and others being buyers to whom you might sell. Almost everyone at eBay has some level of expertise about something, and by remaining diligent about upholding positive transactions with these folks you have the opportunity to also learn from them in ways that will help you understand what's hot and what's not.

Beyond eBay, recognize the value of being more attentive to what's selling in your local area. When visiting major retailers, take time to observe what seems to be selling well and what isn't. Take note of where marketing dollars are being spent and in what manner (i.e., from what angle) the seemingly popular items are being pitched. Of course, the proof of popularity is in the results, so take the time to observe which promotions are highly successful and which appear to be lost causes. This is perhaps one of the best ways to determine mass-market mentality—while riding the coattails of someone else's investment (i.e., the retailer's marketing dollar).

Next, visit smaller retailer establishments, and especially secondary market shops (those that resell used goods). Ask the store owners what buyers seem to be seeking and which items seem to be in short supply. In addition, be sure to read up on trends in the local and national trade papers and collectibles magazines. Search the Internet for specialty Web sites that cater to certain commodities and market trends. If these publications offer e-mail updates or product notifications, consider opting in to that distribution as an additional source of free information.

Distrust Your Bias

One of the biggest challenges to sellers eager to determine which items are popular in buyers' minds is maintaining a clear vision of what the buyers are really buying as opposed to what you, the seller, are most interested in. To develop a truly astute understanding of merchandising trends, you need to be able to recognize everything that is selling, not just those items that interest *you* the most. So often, a seller will look right past popular items because he or she has little interest in them. Consumers, however, may be buying up those goods at a fast and furious pace. To be successful in detecting trends, sellers need to develop a wider scope of vision, recognizing *anything* that is in demand, regardless of their own personal view of the goods.

FOLLOW THE FICKLE MARKET

When preparing to identify and invest in hot goods, be sure to anticipate how quickly the market can fluctuate. Ultimate success comes when you can buy before the market spikes and sell just as the market begins to peak. Be especially watchful for fads and trends that deliver great profits early on, then quickly bottom out as copycat sellers attempt to cash in—flooding the market and devaluing the price of the goods.

To this end, it's unwise to buy when the market is already peaking, when your investment cost may already be at a point that will prevent a decent level of profit and, as supply eclipses demand, actually results in future selling prices dropping lower than your original purchase price. Besides the surge in supply, anticipate the potential effect of current events and changing public opinion and how those might positively or negatively affect item demand and selling prices. Watch for upcoming events that could increase the value of some goods (such as new product launches, technology developments, and even movie releases) and likewise might render other items as cold as yesterday's breakfast.

GETTING THE JUMP BY PRESELLING

Sellers who have been successful in navigating product trends at eBay and elsewhere have learned another strategy in careful inventory management: the less they have tied up in inventory that might or might not sell, the more effectively they can profit as consumer interest spikes—and likewise avoid losses when demand dips. The secret is to offer items *before* the inventory investment has been made. But without inventory on hand, there's nothing that can be auctioned—or is there?

Whether selling items yet to be released or managing sales through a partnership with a third-party supplier or distributor, some sellers have learned that *preselling* items at eBay can be a smart move. It's not uncommon to find presale listings on eBay for items such as collectible figurines (see Figure 21.2), trading cards, toys, and even event tickets. It's not easy to effectively presell, though, and it requires special attention to ensure the item the high bidder wins *will* actually be available to successfully complete the sale. This advanced sales strategy has been noted to be highly effective in capitalizing on ever-changing market opinion. Consider the following if you're interested in managing your auction inventory using this more dynamic method.

Introducing Dynamic Inventory Management

Dynamic management of goods for sale (often referred to as *just-in-time* inventory—i.e., you receive the inventory you need only when you sell that

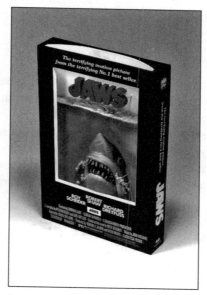

Figure 21.2 Just when you thought it was safe to visit eBay . . . this pre-sell movie poster replica is ready to bite at eager buyers.

item) can put you ahead of the curve in the marketplace. By establishing reliable inventory supply sources (wholesalers, distributors, or manufacturers), it's possible to let those sources manage the inventory for you, allowing you to order and presell unreleased and much-anticipated items, maintain a source of goods without having to purchase what you haven't yet sold, or even drop-ship (i.e., your supplier ships directly to your customer) items directly to your buyers without the need for you to see or handle the merchandise. It's the same method of supply-chain management that big businesses use every day.

The key to successfully selling items that you don't physically possess is being able to count on your suppliers to deliver the goods quickly and consistently every time a sale is made. This requires that you keep in constant communication with your suppliers to ensure that *their* inventory is on hand, is as described, and is always ready to ship. If the supplier is subject to constantly changing inventory (as is true of liquidators) or prone to frequent out-of-stock situations (back orders), then you'll be faced with having to inform your buyers that the goods they just won aren't readily available, if at all.

Therefore, if not managed and monitored closely, your source of presell supply might become a supply management nightmare that will frustrate both you and your customers.

Understand eBay's Rules

Understanding the real potential of managing auction sales and inventory in this dynamic method, eBay has come forward to establish how preselling is to be managed at its site. By site policy, eBay allows presales provided the seller can deliver the goods within 30 days of the auction's close. As a seller, you'll need to be absolutely certain that you can uphold this stipulation. Without proper compliance, it's possible that presale listings could be unceremoniously canceled without warning and your online efforts could be quickly thwarted.

Disclosing the Details

The key stipulation of eBay's rules—and one that every seller should commit to—is the full disclosure that an auction item is being offered on a presell basis and is not yet in hand from the seller's perspective. In fact, eBay's policy, goes so far as to require that sellers disclose presales information in an item's description (see Figure 21.3) using an HTML font size of at least 3 (no tiny print that might serve to mislead bidders or misrepresent the items up for bid).

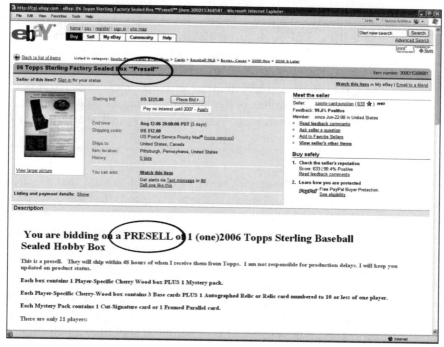

Figure 21.3 This seller clearly states in his item title that these very desirable and limited premium trading cards are offered on a presell basis.

More to the point of preserving your good reputation, it's in your best interest to be absolutely certain that bidders and buyers are fully aware that presell goods are not presently in your possession and that there may be a longer-than-usual delivery time due to the fact that the goods are on order or will be delivered by a third party. If you ignore such disclosure, you risk all sorts of postsale backlash, including buyer dissatisfaction, negative feedback, demand for refunds, and even escalation to eBay's Security & Resolution Center or to consumer protection agencies.

Ensuring Customer Satisfaction

Here's the heart of the matter of striving to offer hot items in a presale methodology: Do you stand behind everything you presell? Are you committed to the customer's 100 percent satisfaction? If so, then you'll need to go to extra lengths to ensure that your customers will be absolutely delighted with

> **eBay TIP:** Visit the Federal Trade Commission's Web site for more information related directly to the matter of proper guidelines and legal statutes for offering presale items. The FTC's *Business Guide to Mail or Telephone Order Merchandise Rule* (which incorporates preselling online) can be found at this Web address: www.ftc.gov/bcp/conline/pubs/buspubs/mailorder.htm.

their presell purchases. Although it's within your right to state that all sales are final, such a policy isn't well suited to the sale of goods that you don't own at the time of listing. Whether an arriving item is different from how your supplier (and ultimately *you*) described it, arrives damaged or late, or doesn't arrive at all, you must absorb the fallout to avoid alienating your customers.

Be ready to accept returns and deliver refunds. If shipping inventory back to a supplier, you might need to navigate some special return procedures, and you might be required to pay a return or restocking fee of some sort. If you intend to pass along any fees to your customers, you should do so only in cases where a customer has changed his or her mind about the purchase, not in cases of product misrepresentation (which is *your* liability).

Although some sellers have tried to blame problems of item delivery, quality, or content on their suppliers, it becomes the sellers' ultimate responsibility to guarantee that whatever they sell is "as advertised" in all aspects of the phrase. If not, buyers have the right and responsibility to take protective counteraction.

Although no one can unfailingly predict every trend and market shift when seeking to identify the next big wave of hot items, there are nevertheless many steps that can easily be taken to home in on buyers' wants and needs. By continuing your regular auction research, testing strategies and methods to present goods, and carefully investing in the goods you'll sell (sometimes on a strategic presell basis), you can unlock the potential to read the market and keep up with (and ahead of) the auction-going trends.

22

The Forbidden Zone:
What You Can't Sell at eBay

While you've now seen that practically anything and everything offered at eBay will find a buyer, there are some items that for good reasons shouldn't (and according to the site's rules, *can't*) be offered for bid. Certain goods deemed inappropriate, immoral, illegal, or in unforgivably bad taste are off limits at eBay. Therefore, familiarize yourself with the sorts of items you can't sell, and equally important, the sorts of items you shouldn't buy at eBay.

ITEMS eBAY FORBIDS

No doubt while listing an item for sale at eBay you have seen a text link that describes the sorts of things eBay has prohibited. Simply put, if you attempt to sell this stuff and are caught, the eBay Patrol may shut down your auctions, might revoke your registered status, and could possibly turn you over to law enforcement agencies for actual prosecution. Yikes! Make no mistake: when eBay says *forbidden,* it is serious. In actuality, eBay states that some items fall under one of three categories: *prohibited, questionable,* and *potentially infringing.* Right away, be sure you understand what is absolutely forbidden to list. Here's the rundown on these illicit items:

- **Alcohol.** Alcohol is generally forbidden for auction because of the complex taxation, import, and licensing rules that govern it. Unless you're bidding at a licensed site with sellers authorized to deal in alcohol (e.g., Winebid.com), the rules generally in force state that alcohol auctions will be promptly closed by eBay.

- **Firearms.** Though firearms are sometimes considered a type of collectible (for period pieces), eBay has had to unequivocally forbid auctioning of any mechanism originally designed to fire some sort of projectile. There are, however, some sites (e.g., ArmsBay.com) that are properly licensed and specialize in auctioning such items.
- **Fireworks.** These are illegal in many U.S. states and in many other parts of the world. They are therefore not eligible for auctioning.
- **Drugs and drug paraphernalia.** Illegal goods, plain and simple.
- **Human body parts and remains.** Yuck, right? At eBay, it started with the human kidney auction back in 1999. Since then, no body parts. However, at eBay the rules do state that selling skulls and skeletons for educational purposes is allowed.
- **Animals and wildlife products.** Excluding, perhaps, a warehouse find of vintage sea monkeys, dealing with the sale and shipping of live animals is typically left to the pros (animals handlers and such). Adhering to edicts set forth by the U.S. Fish and Game Service, eBay does not allow the sale of live animals or animal parts unless expressly noted (sale of some taxidermic items, pelts, etc., might be allowed if strict conditions are adhered to). If you're considering this sort of item, read the full disclosure of what's allowed (and what isn't) before you venture forward.
- **Stolen or counterfeit goods.** They're stolen. They're illegal. They aren't allowed for auctioning. This should be obvious. Here's a quick list of some prohibited items:

> Catalog and URL sales
> Counterfeit currency and stamps
> Credit cards
> Embargoed goods from prohibited countries
> Gift cards
> Government IDs and licenses
> Links
> Lock-picking devices
> Lottery tickets
> Mailing lists and personal information
> Multilevel marketing, pyramid schemes, and matrix programs
> Plants and seeds
> Postage meters

Prescription drugs and devices

Recalled items

Satellite and cable TV descramblers

Stocks and other securities

Surveillance equipment

Tobacco

Travel (allowed but limited due to local travel regulations)

If you disagree with the banning of these items or simply want to learn more about why they're disallowed, visit eBay's site map and drill into the links that more fully explain these items and why they've been prohibited.

The lists of questionable and potentially infringing items are significant, yet they aren't *completely* forbidden, depending on the situation. As a seller, it's your duty to understand the site's rules about these additional items and to make sure that what you sell isn't illegal, infringing, or even unnatural. Again, carefully review the explanations eBay has provided to ensure you don't stray into the forbidden zone.

> **eBay TIP:** If ever you're unsure whether the item you're about to list is forbidden, simply visit the eBay page "Prohibited and Restricted Items—Overview" at http://pages.ebay .com/help/policies/items-ov.html.

WHO SAYS THESE ITEMS ARE FORBIDDEN, AND WHY?

Why has eBay gone to such great lengths to blacklist so many items from sale? Well, aside from some of the more obvious items, eBay cites these reasons:

- Since eBay never actually possesses the goods for sale, it is unable to verify the legality or appropriateness of questionable or potentially infringing goods.
- Many goods that might be sold are subject to local statutes that differ from state to state and country to country.
- For health, environmental, and agricultural reasons, some goods would violate import or export statutes.

- In some cases, eBay might actually incur liability for the sale and subsequent effects of certain goods.

DEALS, STEALS, AND GRAY-MARKET GOODS

Taking the informed buyer's perspective, it's important to understand whether items you might bid on are forbidden or questionable. Certain products are perennial favorites of backroom sellers. When you're buying, you might be surprised to find that you could be bidding on illicit goods. What kinds of things might be offered by unsavory sellers? Here are the most common examples:

- Computer software
- Electronics (small and midsized)
- Music (CDs and cassettes)
- Movies (VHS and DVD)
- Pornographic material (though not necessarily stolen, often the content of some of it *is* illegal)
- Knockoffs (illegal copies of name-brand items)
- Printed matter (undisclosed copies or restrikes)

Of course, there are more ways to proliferate bad merchandise than you'd probably care to imagine, but those listed tend to be the most common, due largely to their relative ease of handling as well as their profit potential. When you're buying, it's up to you to identify items that might be bogus or stolen (and therefore forbidden).

When you search the auctions for items to bid on, exercise the following due diligence to make sure you're not courting eBay contraband:

- Check the seller's feedback rating first! Are there any comments that might indicate trouble?
- Compare the potential selling price of the item to what the market usually bears; if it's *too* cheap, remember the old saying about things that are too good to be true.
- Pay close attention to the item's description, and determine whether any key information has been omitted. Is the description blatantly incorrect in terms of the item being described? Is the description evasive in a way that makes you wonder whether the auction's on the level?

- Contact the seller to ask questions. If you don't receive a reply, or if you receive a very curt and uninformative reply, think twice about bidding. (If nothing else, this could indicate that the seller might not be very responsive and might not manage the postauction activity to your liking—a warning flag to a different problem.)
- Study the seller's policy: Does it contain harsh or potentially unreasonable terms (short payment period, no returns or guarantees, and no good explanation for the policy)? Does the seller seem to be in an unusual hurry to sell and wrap up business?
- Most important, be knowledgeable about the items you might bid on and be aware of their potential for being stolen or illegally reproduced. It's not such a good deal if you end up with inferior merchandise that isn't even worth the bargain price you paid.

THE ABCS OF COPYRIGHT

Copyright is usually a gray area in the minds of folks who buy and sell stuff, either at online auctions or elsewhere. It makes up the bulk of the "potentially infringing" category of goods. Whether it's music, software, promotional materials, or similar items, copyright may be an issue more often than most people realize. First, the official definition of copyright as presented by the U.S. Copyright Office goes like this: "Copyright is a form of protection provided by the laws of the United States (Title 17, U.S. Code) to the authors of 'original works of authorship,' including literary, dramatic, musical, artistic, and certain other intellectual works. This protection is available to both published and unpublished works."

But what does that mean to you as you buy and sell at eBay? Simply, it means that any copyrighted material duplicated for multiple sales and yet not being sold by the originator or licensee of the work is most likely infringing on a legal copyright registration.

Who's licensed to sell copyrighted material? The answer depends on who has been authorized to distribute the work by the copyright owner (the originator of the work). Typically, that means someone who has been granted a license to reproduce and sell the work in a "tangible medium of expression" (e.g., a CD, a DVD, a book or magazine, a poster or lithograph, or even a dramatic work).

Are infringing items, then, being regularly offered at eBay and elsewhere online? Absolutely. Can the legal copyright owners or licensees claim infringement? Absolutely. Does every infringing sale get noticed and acted upon? No. But don't let the sheer volume of items being exchanged lull you into a false sense of security (or obscurity). These days, people are diligently hunting down bootleggers and frauds who make a living on the originator's work without a license and without sharing the income with the originator. Musicians, filmmakers, writers, and the like are all working to take a bite out of infringement, and auction sites especially are working alongside them to keep trading legal to the greatest extent possible. That's why copyright is such an important matter.

YOUR CHECKLIST TO AVOID POSTING INFRINGING ITEMS

Here are some guidelines to use to determine whether the items you wish to auction will be deemed lawful and legitimate:

- Avoid selling unlicensed items manufactured by you or others that bear legally registered logos or trademarks that you don't have permission to use.
- Avoid selling counterfeits (knockoffs) made to specially resemble licensed items, including the use of logos, markings, or other trademarked details.
- Avoid selling promotional items that are marked "Not for resale."
- Avoid selling bundled software that is delivered with computers.
- Avoid selling live recordings (audio or video) for which you do not have express permission from the performer or license holder.
- Avoid selling items that are unreleased, or beta, versions not intended for public use or display.

DOESN'T EVERYONE INFRINGE JUST A LITTLE?

The question is, will you get caught for selling copyrighted material when you're not the owner or aren't licensed to do so? Maybe and maybe not. Perform a search of eBay and you'll likely find a generous offering of such material with nary a mention of the original copyright owner or licensee. Quite often, copyright owners will turn a blind eye to such things, realizing the amount of work it would take to track down, halt, and prosecute every violator.

Believe it or not, some content owners see the secondary market that exchanges copyrighted material as potentially good for business. Though legally this is discouraged and disallowed, the word-of-mouth potential and greater dissemination might bolster public awareness for an artist, a musician, or whomever (recall the great Napster uproar of 2000, when some recording artists called for the song-sharing site to be shut down while other artists proclaimed the exposure was free publicity). Provided it's not a situation that truly gets out of hand and becomes outright piracy, some content owners will consider it part of the business and a form of free marketing (of course, you don't know which copyright holders are inclined to this lenient sentiment).

Be cautious, though, since some content owners are adamant about protecting the rights (and potential income) of their work. In fact, many such owners are working directly with eBay to monitor listings and to identify infringing items. If such items are found, the penalty to the infringing seller can be as simple as a *cease and desist* order (a slap on the hand that instructs the seller to discontinue such sales both now and forever)—but it might involve stiff fines or even imprisonment. In more blatant cases of piracy or fraud, content owners are working with federal agencies to conduct sting operations to ferret out and fully prosecute hard-core offenders.

WHAT IS eBAY DOING ABOUT COPYRIGHT INFRINGEMENT?

The eBay site became significantly more involved in policing its listings amid claims of rampant fraud and illegal and infringing sales back in 1998. To maintain a safe and legal trading environment and to prevent its portal from becoming an absolute nest of thieves, eBay has taken these steps to keep its listings on the up-and-up:

- It has posted explicit policies regarding items that are disallowed for auctioning.
- It provides listings of prohibited, questionable, or infringing items as guidance to sellers who want assistance in determining if their items are potentially problematic.
- It actively monitors certain categories of items in search of illicit goods.
- It regularly shuts down auctions of disallowed items.
- It regularly suspends sellers who are in clear violation of site policies in these matters.
- It has teamed up with organizations such as the National Consumer's League, content owners, and the FBI to take further steps against violators.
- It maintains its right to turn over user information to official agencies when requested as part of an investigation or potential prosecution.

- It has even solicited the help of the auction community to assist in identifying and reporting offending listings.

THE AGENCIES THAT TAKE ACTION

Who's getting involved in bringing auction offenders to justice? You might be surprised to learn how visible online auctions have become in the prosecutorial community. Here's just a small list of organizations that are presently involved in scrutinizing listings and their proprietors while simultaneously assisting buyers and eBay itself in matters of the goods for sale and the proper practices in selling them:

- Better Business Bureau (BBB) Online
- Federal Bureau of Investigation (FBI)
- Federal Trade Commission (FTC)
- International Trademark Association (INTA)
- Motion Picture Association of America (MPAA)
- National Consumer's League (NCL)
- Recording Industry Association of America (RIAA)
- Software and Information Industry Association (SIIA)

Clearly, with the heightened visibility of online auctions, many national law enforcement agencies, content owners, and consumer organizations are just as active at these sites as are bidders and sellers (though clearly for different reasons).

THE AUCTION VIGILANTE

Communities of involved members are what make many auction sites successful. However, some people have gone a bit overboard in deputizing themselves to strike out and rid the auction streets of targeted "undesirables." Although their intentions might be good, their methods of attack may be muddled and can become as undesirable (sometimes more so) as those they purport to be policing.

To start, understand what creates an auction vigilante (what I often referred to as the *Net cop*):

- Some users feel the need to step in to help eBay deal with wrongdoers (a good intention, initially).

- Some users respond (sometimes overzealously) to the site's appeal for community members to get involved in helping police the auction place.
- Some users feel eBay doesn't do enough to thwart auction misdeeds.
- Some users feel eBay can't or won't act fast enough to execute justice online.
- Some users feel the need to be needed; an exaggerated desire to be wanted or perceived as important.
- Some users are bored and want something to do—seriously.

Even though you're minding your own business and attempting to steer clear of trouble, a Net cop might tap you on the shoulder and inquire about your purpose for being here. Here's how you may be approached:

- You may get unexpected e-mail messages from strangers who don't seem to be potential bidders inquiring about an auction and the item's origin.
- You may hear from an anonymous user (using a vanilla e-mail account such as HotMail) informing you of an auction site's policies or current laws that conflict with an item being auctioned.
- After you bid in an auction, you may get a message warning you about the seller and urging you to reconsider and withdraw the bid.
- After you post an auction, you may receive a threatening message warning you to halt the auction or risk being turned in to auction administrators and even law enforcement.
- If a host site cancels an auction, you may get a message from another user claiming responsibility for the cancellation.

Clearly, the activities practiced by Net cops range from helpful advice to unwanted harassment. Take the friendly contact as just that: friendly. However, if you're uncomfortable with how some unannounced vigilante has gotten involved in your business without being authorized by an auction site or official agency, here's how you can respond:

- Ignore the contact. Remember, some people are just bored or looking for an excited response. File the message away for the time being and go about your business.
- Politely respond to the senders and ask their purpose and authorization for contacting you. They might be trying to help you or they might be trying to rattle you.

- Report any bothersome, harassing, or threatening messages to the hosting site immediately.
- Report any individual (or e-mail address) to proper authorities whenever you suspect someone is posing illegally as a law enforcement or agency official.

Although this information paints Net cops in a pretty poor light, there are some involved community members who are responsible and conscientious when patrolling the auction sites. In fact, eBay generally encourages all community members to become involved and not turn a blind eye or deaf ear to obvious misdeeds (recall that this is the core tenet of ensuring eBay's Feedback Forum remains successful). Just remember to keep it within reason and turn matters over to the properly authorized individuals if a real problem arises. Although you may never have considered all this, these are the ins, outs, ups, and downs of dealing in forbidden items at eBay. Be familiar with, not fearful of, the site's policies and guidelines, and always be aware of the items you'll offer and whether they cross the sometimes-fuzzy line of what's considered illicit at eBay.

PART IV

TAKING YOUR eBAY BUSINESS TO THE NEXT LEVEL

23

Becoming a Business and Managing High-Volume Sales

By this time you're probably realizing your fortune will be acquired not by selling any *one thing* at eBay but by selling a *high volume* of *anything.*

This section of the book brings us full circle to the original discussion of how you will define *fortune* and how willing you'll be to invest effort and resources into earning that fortune, whatever your timetable. Every one of us would like to get rich quickly, and at eBay, though you might not become rich overnight, you can hasten your results by moving a higher volume of goods through the auction space.

This chapter, then, begins the next phase of your fortune-finding trek— helping you to get more results from your auctioning efforts by further exploring your motives and commitment, then helping you gain more from your listing activity by showing you how to list more items in less time. If you're ready to take the next step, this chapter guides you in your journey.

PASTIME, PART-TIME, OR ALL THE TIME?

Although you might not be ready to proclaim your ultimate purpose just yet, this is the perfect time to look at your future and determine what you're looking to gain at eBay and what you're willing to invest to do so. The common question from newer eBay users is whether this can be a reliable single source of income. The answer: it depends. Many factors determine how you will approach an auction business, including those driven by the economy and marketplace and those driven by your own personal motivations. The good news, though, is that auction at eBay is such an adaptable enterprise that you can pretty much make of it whatever suits you best, either casually buying and selling or feverishly moving merchandise (and you can flip-flop between these modes whenever you like). To provide some food for thought, consider how auctioning can fit any lifestyle, and weigh the opportunities and challenges you may face as you decide whether you'll do this for fun or profit.

The Happy Hobby

If you've defined fortune as being the opportunity to buy and sell as you choose, lounging about in your bathrobe and slippers, earning a few hundred dollars here and there, and finding some great items for yourself along the way, then you've adopted the hobbyist's approach to auctioning. This approach is perfect for those who wish to use eBay as a pleasant pastime that can yield some very promising rewards in terms of gaining a modest amount of income, acquiring some terrific items, and enjoying the aspect of interacting with interesting people along the way.

Are there drawbacks to the hobby approach? From a pure business standpoint, a hobbyist is not able to take advantage of certain tax breaks that the bona fide businessperson can. According to the U.S. Internal Revenue Service, tax deductions for business expenses can be legally claimed only if the effort maintains an operating profit for every five years of activity, and income activity must be properly reported using the appropriate small-business/sole-proprietorship income tax filing (see Chapter 25 for more about

eBay TIP: Though your initial intentions may be to operate as a hobby, don't be surprised to find yourself drawn into the profit potential of eBay and other online selling. Many of today's ardent sellers began as hobbyists but found the fortune awaiting them too good to pass up. The benefit, though, of beginning from a hobbyist's mindset is the approach allows you to slowly ease your way into the entrepreneurial fray and deliberately decide when and where to ratchet up your efforts. In this way, many hobbyists develop real-world expertise and are better poised for success when they turn their attention to becoming more serious in their auction endeavors.

taxes). Further, if a hobbyist attempts to fake it by claiming to be a business in order to deduct expenses, the IRS likewise stipulates that if said business reports an operating loss for more than two years in every five-year period, that operation will be deemed a hobby, ineligible for deductions and possibly liable to pay taxes and/or penalties on undeclared income.

The Part-Time Proprietor

When the business bug first bites you, the natural response is to investigate running your entrepreneurial effort on a part-time basis. This approach is best for those who aren't willing to take the high-stakes gamble of forsaking all other forms of income to rely solely on auction and other online income. I usually recommend that eager entrepreneurs (and hobbyists-turned-home-businesspersons) operate on a part-time basis for at least 6 to 12 months. All the while, keep that day job, whatever it may be, for these good reasons:

- You can be more at ease venturing into self-employment if you maintain the safety and security of drawing a regular paycheck to protect your everyday living expenses.
- A part-time endeavor will be relatively risk-free as you determine whether online merchandizing will suit you in the long run.
- You'll be able to safely determine whether you have the motivation and mindset to maintain and manage a home-based business before fully committing yourself.
- You'll be able to take advantage of company benefits from your regular employment while testing the waters of self-employment to determine whether the income you gain will be able to support the cost of those benefits.
- You'll have the opportunity to begin keeping business records at an activity level that allows for experimentation and change as you seek the method that best suits you.
- Your part-time profits can be stashed away as a financial foundation to be reinvested in a full-time venture, should you decide to make that transition.

Truly, taking a part-time approach when courting an online business makes sense in order to avoid the anxiety of having to ensure fast and steady income to support your living expenses. Working at it part-time also enables you to use the extra income as just that—extra—while also permitting you to increase or decrease your activity, as needed.

The Full-Time Fortune

If you're ready to make a go of it, then lace up your shoes and get ready to run. Many have been quite successful operating an auction business full-time, especially those who had previously developed a good understanding of the sorts of activities required to maintain a steady income. If this is to be your path to fortune, be sure to understand what sorts of activities full-time sellers engage in, day in and day out, week after week:

- Stage and photograph new items to sell.
- List plenty of items regularly (at least 100 items every week).
- Source and acquire new inventory regularly.
- Keep clear and concise business records to measure outlay versus income (to determine whether a true profit is being realized).
- Keep current with product trends and market shifts in demand.
- Attend to bidder inquiries quickly.
- Monitor and manage current listings (especially if changes are required in midlisting).
- Respond to completed listings and engage the buyer to begin the payment-for-goods transaction.
- Prepare and package items sold.
- Arrange for carrier drop-off or pickup as needed.
- Follow up on postlisting invoices and late payments.
- Return to the start and do it all again (and again and again).

Certainly, this isn't an insurmountable list of tasks, yet it's no cakewalk, either. There's much to do to maintain a full-time auction endeavor, yet if your heart and mind are properly focused, this can be the fortune fantasy so many would-be entrepreneurs have dreamed of: a business you can run from your back room that can be as far-reaching as the fabled four corners of the globe. To make the transition from part-time to full-time business, you'll need to prepare yourself to commit to the ways and means of going into business for yourself. Here are some of the prerequisites you'll need to ensure your success:

- Be sure you are extremely well versed in the methods and manners of online auctioning and fixed-price selling and are clear about the tasks and duties you'll need to manage along the way.
- Ensure your credit is good with banks and other financial institutions while paying down as much outstanding consumer debt as possible before cutting off any existing flow of regular income.

- If you have a spouse or other partner who's currently employed, determine whether that person's regular income can serve as a backup or safety net to your business start-up and whether you can be added to his or her benefits package.
- Ensure you've established a financial cushion of 6 to 24 months' living expenses to fall back on in case your start-up efforts are slow to gain momentum.
- Leave any previous employment on a positive note, and seek a letter of recommendation from your manager or supervisor (this might be useful if you decide to apply for a business loan).
- Set realistic business goals, and track your progress every step of the way to ensure you're executing to plan.
- Believe you can do it!

Make no doubt about it, going into business for yourself can be the most stressful, yet most rewarding, of experiences. If you're fully prepared, if you have created a sound plan and have the appropriate level of funds to back you up, you're ready to take the plunge. In fact, those sellers I've spoken with who regretted going into an auction business full-time confessed they hadn't planned properly before making their move. These days, it's clear that eBay and other forms of e-commerce aren't simply fads and aren't showing any signs of weakening in their mass appeal. Therefore, be deliberate in your preparations and recognize that you have time to fully consider a thorough approach to online selling; you'll be in the best possible position to make the leap if you've taken the proper steps in preparing to earn your full-time fortune.

BULKING UP YOUR BUSINESS WITH BULK LISTING

Now that you've given full consideration to how you'll approach growing your eBay business, consider how to most easily increase the volume of item listings at eBay. No matter what volume of activity you wish to maintain in your auctioning, the simple fact is that you can earn more for your effort if you can list more items in less time.

One way to achieve greater results for your listing efforts is to employ eBay's bulk listing tool, Turbo Lister. This application allows you to create bundles of item listings in a single screen, thus avoiding the need to navigate the numerous steps in listing a series of single items. If you want to make more items available in just a fraction of the usual time, Turbo Lister is the tool for you. Here's why bulk listing makes sense:

- Bulk listings can be created offline, as eBay's Turbo Lister application runs directly on your computer without requiring an active Internet connection. You can create bulk listings while on the go, too, using a laptop if you like.
- Bulk listings can be assembled whenever you choose and at a pace best suited to your needs.
- Bulk listings can be uploaded in a single effort to start immediately, or they can be scheduled to start at a later date or time.
- Bulk listings allow you to combine similar items to simultaneously list and effectively cross-sell your goods.

DOWNLOADING TURBO LISTER

The best news about bulk listing at eBay is that Turbo Lister is completely free to download and use. Here's how to do it:

- Go to eBay's site map and seek out the Turbo Lister link within the Selling Tools section.
- Upon arriving at the Turbo Lister page, click on the Download Now button to install the program on your computer (see Figure 23.1).

In the subsequent pop-up window, choose to save the Turbo Lister file. The file, "setupUS" will be saved to your computer (for easiest use, simply save it to the default-suggested location of your computer's desktop folder. Once complete, find and double-click on the "setupUS" icon within your desktop folder (or graphically visible on your actual Desktop screen) and select Run in the pop-up window to initiate the actual installation. Now simply follow the instructions within the Install Wizard screens to successfully install the program onto your computer—it's easy.

Upon successful installation, you'll see a new icon on your computer's desktop from which you can easily launch Turbo Lister (see Figure 23.2).

The first time you launch Turbo Lister, you'll need to provide your eBay user ID and password, then verify your registered contact information (see Figure 23.3). On subsequent uses, it's only necessary to provide your eBay password to begin creating bulk listings.

To begin creating your first listing, click on the New icon (the starburst image) at the top of the Turbo Lister screen (see Figure 23.4).

Creating a Turbo Lister item is actually an exercise in creating an inventory listing that you'll later launch as an eBay listing. Just as you directly created a listing in Chapter 7's "Create Your Listing" example, here you'll pro-

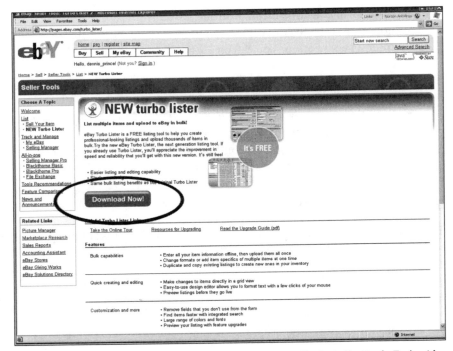

Figure 23.1 Click the Download Now button to easily install eBay's Turbo Lister program on your computer.

vide the same information—item title, description, pictures, listing format, shipping and payment details, and so on—and then you can also provide a Custom Label in the Inventory Information section. Complete the Create New Item form (as shown in Figure 23.5) and click the Save button when you're finished.

eBay Turbo
Lister 2

Figure 23.2 The Turbo Lister shortcut icon is ready on your desktop; just double-click to launch.

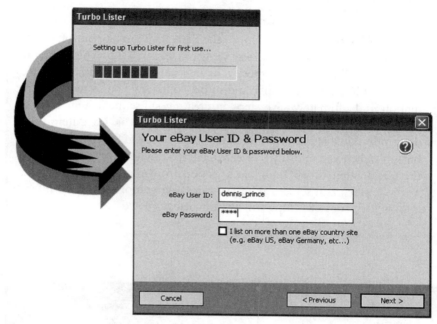

Figure 23.3 Upon first use, you'll see the setup indicator followed by the pop-up where you'll provide your eBay user ID and password.

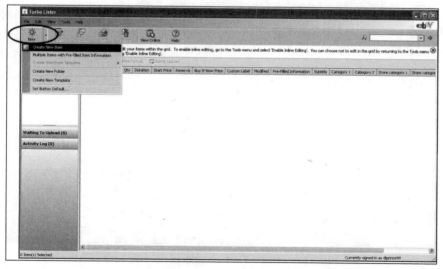

Figure 23.4 Begin creating items in Turbo Lister by clicking the New button at the top of the screen.

eBay TIP: Notice the Save As Template button at the bottom of the screen shown in Figure 23.5. This shortcut allows you to specify listing settings—format, duration, shipping and payment details, and so on—allowing you to recall information and ultimately save steps in creating subsequent item entries. Specify all the non-item-specific information—that is, leave item title, description, images, and so on blank—then click the Save As Template button. When you're ready to create an actual item listing, simply select the Create Item from Template selection from the New icon on the Turbo Lister main screen. When you do, a large portion of the information for your new listing will already be completed.

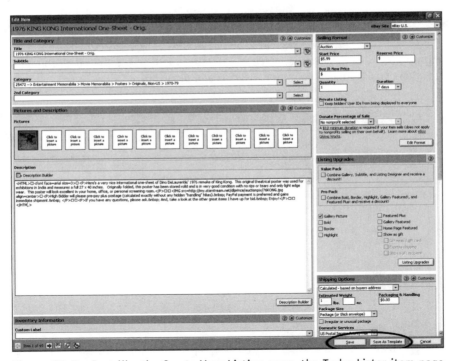

Figure 23.5 Just like the Create Your Listing page, the Turbo Lister item page allows you to easily specify item and/or template details.

> **eBay TIP:** Turbo Lister will assume that you wish to use eBay's iPIX image hosting service and will invoke the tool to select images directly from your computer. If you'll be using images that are stored elsewhere, such as at a Web site of your own, you can change the iPIX default choice by clicking the Customize button and selecting the "Self-hosted pictures" option (see Figure 23.6). By doing so, you can specify the Web location where eBay should look for and select the images you'll specify.

Continue to create additional listings in this manner; each time you save you add another item to your Turbo Lister inventory. With listings now resident in your Turbo Lister Item Inventory (see Figure 23.7), select those you wish to upload to eBay. (Simply click on the item to highlight it or hold down your mouse button and drag down the list to highlight multiple items.)

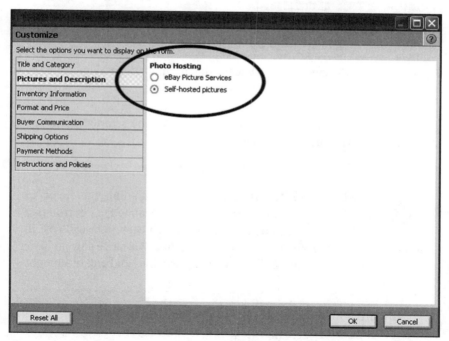

Figure 23.6 Click Customize in the Pictures and Description area to change the image hosting option.

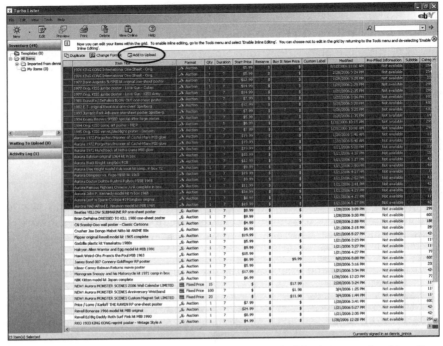

Figure 23.7   With many items now ready to launch, it's time to upload to eBay.

Click the Add to Upload button to transfer the selected items to the Waiting to Upload queue (see Figure 23.8).

> **eBay TIP:** Before actually uploading the items to eBay, make use of Turbo Lister's Calculate Fees button (see Figure 23.8) to determine how much each item will cost in insertion fees. If the fees are higher than you like, you can easily go back and modify some of your individual listing specifics and enhancements.

Now, from the Waiting to Upload item collection display, you can click on the Schedule button to specify a date and time you want your items to launch. (Some sellers work from Turbo Lister midweek and schedule to launch on the weekends, and some also elect to stagger the start time of each

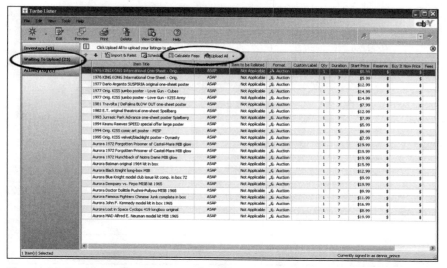

Figure 23.8 Upon choosing to upload items, Turbo Lister will move copies of those items to the Waiting to Upload area, ready to launch at eBay.

listing to allow the same bidders to snipe bid more than one item ending throughout the day.) If you want all your listings to start immediately, simply forgo the scheduling option. When you're ready to upload your items, click on the Upload All button to enact the item transfer.

Turbo Lister now connects to eBay to transfer those items in your Upload queue to that actual site (see Figure 23.9). When the upload is complete, click either the Go to the Pending Listings . . . text link (if you specified a later date/time) or Go to My eBay . . . link (if you selected immediate auction launch) to view the results of your upload, there finding your items listed simultaneously just as if you had listed them one by one directly on the site.

 eBay TIP: With Turbo Lister you can schedule and upload up to 3,000 items at a time. Now that's bulk listing!

Clearly, bulk listing makes it easy to manage a large volume of items and allows you to schedule and otherwise stagger when your auctions will

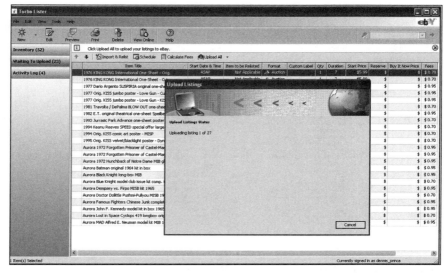

Figure 23.9 The Upload Listings status window indicates your items are being transferred to eBay.

begin. While creating your listing collections, keep these important considerations in mind:

- List similar items so that multiple-item bidders can find related goods to maximize cross-selling potential, or list a wide variety of goods to provide a range of items to attract more single-item bidders.
- Upload or schedule listings to coincide with peak bidding days and times.
- Always calculate listing fees before uploading to ensure you're aware of the costs.
- Try to stagger the ending day of listing collections so you'll be able to tend to end-of-auction activities one collection at a time.
- Be certain you have fully prepared all shipping materials and other supplies to quickly package and queue sold items that will be awaiting payment.

As you move forward on attaining your fortune in auctioning, you'll see that efficiency will play a key role in helping you earn the most for your efforts. Bulk listing will, in effect, exponentially reduce the amount of time it would otherwise take to list high volumes of goods using the single-item listing method. By taking advantage of Turbo Lister's offline operation, you'll be able to construct your batches of listings without being connected to the Internet, allowing you to plan your next wave of listings whenever and wherever you might be.

24

Establishing an Auction Workplace

Regardless of your volume of business, organization will be key to your success in any sustained level of auctioning. These days, efficiency seems to underscore everything, allowing for better opportunities, greater savings of time and money, and the ability to do more with less. Here is where you can effectively establish a rhythm and routine to your eBay activities. Although you needn't go overboard in organization, you will find that a little extra efficiency can significantly add to your eventual success (and profit).

ESTABLISH YOUR OWN AUCTION OFFICE

Many have dreamed of a workplace away from the workplace. However, when it's time to get serious about keeping the online income flowing, it's time to set up an efficient operation. A first step is to establish an *auction office*—a dedicated space where you'll tend to your online endeavors week in and week out. If you never considered where such an office might be located, here are a few ideas that could be right under your nose (or just down the hall and to the right):

- **The extra room.** If your home or apartment has an extra room used for storage, clean it out and use it as a virtual storefront instead. The extra room converted to a home office is typically the most desirable situation for managing auction activity: it's a self-contained work area that can go undisturbed and can be closed off from the rest of the living space when not in use. Remember, too, that a room used specifically for a business can oftentimes be deducted from your taxes as a percentage of your rent or mortgage and your utilities.

- **Attic or basement.** These natural extra spaces are prime choices for home office conversion. Sometimes special considerations need to be taken when using an attic or basement (consider adequate headroom, lighting, and protection from excessive heat or moisture), and you may want to use some bug bomb before occupying the space.

- **A cozy corner.** If you can't commandeer an entire room for your eBay business, is there a special area of a room where you can set up shop? Workspaces can be located in the corner of a living room, dining room, or family room (any room, for that matter). Typically, it takes only about six to eight square feet of dedicated space for your business, especially considering the incredibly compact nature of computer tools these days.

- **A spare closet.** Believe it or not, standard wardrobe closets make excellent work areas. A typical six-foot closet provides ample floor space for locating a desk, a chair, and the other office tools you'll soon learn about. The bonus of a closet, much as with a spare room, is that it usually has doors that you can close to hide the workspace from view when it's not in use.

In this mobile-technology, laptop-laden culture, you might ask, "Why set up an office when I can be on the go?" Sure, that's an option, but typically not a good choice for a long-term auction business. Mobile computing and communication should definitely be employed in your office design, but the entire office-in-a-briefcase propositions from some manufacturers and resellers may look great in advertisements and be impressive at the cybercafés, but there are some drawbacks of not having an established workplace:

- **Connectivity.** Connecting to the Internet (which is at the core of online merchandizing, right?) can be twitchy when it comes to mobile computing. Repeated tries at connecting to the Net with a cell modem are definite time wasters. While you should make use of wireless technology within your own work realm, relying on riding someone else's hot spot to run your business simply isn't advisable.

- **Continuity.** If you look at someone's messy desk, you'll wonder how that person gets anything done. However, the occupant is typically quick to proclaim that he or she knows *exactly* where everything is and *exactly* where he or she last left off. A mobile environment doesn't support starting and stopping very well. After every use, the work needs to be packed up and put away, usually disrupting a natural flow in progress. Plus, it's easier to lose important information (whether physical or virtual) in a transient environment.

- **Convenience.** Although mobile computing is much ballyhooed as convenience in the palm of your hand, there's not much convenience to *having* to work from the palm of your hand. Serious auction-goers need to be able to spread out, to know that their office space is always ready and waiting for them, and most important, to know that it's *their* space and can be cordoned off from other hands.

ALLOWING FOR NECESSARY OFFICE AMENITIES

As soon as you locate your prime office real estate, ensure that it will have the basic amenities you'll need to get into business and stay productive.

- **Online access.** There has to be a phone line or cable line available or there's no getting onto the Net. Be sure live access is nearby, preferably on the same wall where you'll locate your work surface. Of course, with the improved reliability of wireless routers, you have greater freedom to locate your work space in the most effective area, without regard to butting up against a cable or data line wall jack. If you go the wireless route (and I recommend you do for reasons I'll soon explain), be sure your router is located in a safe place that provides the best possible transmission conditions (refer to the manufacturer's recommendations in positioning your router).
- **Proper lighting.** Mom was right about eyestrain: it'll mess you up. Though a PC monitor has a glow all its own, you'll need decent overhead lighting as well as desk lighting to keep your eyesight from suffering and to keep all your work materials within easy view.
- **Elbow room.** Though it's not necessary to have a 20- by 20-foot office to be effective, you do need a certain amount of space to work in. An overly cramped work area is not only difficult to keep in order, it can become physically uncomfortable. Be sure you have a work surface that offers at least a 4- by 3-foot work area (the more the better). Think about the PC monitor, the printer, the telephone, and many of the other office tools you'll need and want within easy reach.
- **Air circulation.** In most situations, this isn't much of a problem. However, if you're eyeballing the attic, the basement, or a converted garage, be sure you can maintain a comfortable room temperature

and airflow. Avoid areas subject to extremes in temperature, static air, moisture, or dust.

AUCTION OFFICE TOOLS

You've got your space; now it's time to fill it with the tools you'll need (and some you'll want) to shift your business into higher gear. To start, consider these to be the bare essentials:

- **Computer.** This was discussed in Chapter 2, yet it's worth repeating here. Be sure that your dedicated auction computer is located within your auction office.
- **Printer.** Although it's an electronic age, there's still a need for printed matter (e.g., invoices to include in shipments). These days, printers are being bundled with PC packages and can be had, PC and all, for around $400 to $500. If you buy a stand-alone PC, expect to pay an additional $60 to $150 for a printer, depending on your specific needs and wants. For your auction business, a simple color printer (inkjet or laser) will meet your needs for years.
- **Telephone.** The phone in the kitchen may be just around the corner or down the stairs, but having a phone in your work area is a real convenience and time-saver. Keep a phone pad and pencil nearby, too.
- **Internet access.** Again, this was discussed earlier in this book, but remember that you need to be able to access the online world from within your auction office.
- **Wireless router.** If you'll be working from home and you have several others living in your household, it's conceivable that each of you will have one or more computers you call your own. In my situation, I maximize my efficiency by using a slim-line desktop computer connected directly to the Internet, as well as a wireless notebook computer that gives me wireless connectivity via the router. When working in my shipping area, I can use the wireless notebook to keep the business flowing in real time without excessive back-and-forth running about. Others in the household also catch a ride online by accessing the Net via the wireless router. Everybody's happy!
- **A second phone line.** Time was when folks hooked up second lines to support a teen's talking habits. Today, second lines are almost required if you'll be sharing the work space with others in the house-

hold who may need to use the phone for old-fashioned reasons—like recreational chatter.

- **Hands-free phone system.** Though you might not consider this as much more than a showy little upgrade, using a phone earpiece or headset really makes a difference. By keeping both hands free to type, maneuver a mouse, or whatever, you can stay productive while you're on hold or even in the middle of a conversation. Speaker phones and PC phones achieve the same thing, but the sound quality is often compromised for both you and the person on the other end.
- **Postal scale.** Consider purchasing a postal scale for your auction office; these devices are handy and ready on demand. You have many to choose from: some simply weigh items and indicate postage cost, while others have digital readouts and can print metered postage via a phone hookup.
- **Answering machine/voice-mail account.** Help buyers make voice contact with you even when you're away. An inexpensive answering machine or voice-mail account will help buyers leave those important messages without enduring the aggravation of phone tag.
- **A comfy chair.** Sounds silly until you wind up saddle sore and back weary from squirming in an unsuitable seat.

STAGING YOUR AUCTION ITEMS

Remember the earlier discussion about your auction office and your dedicated auction work space? Besides serving as a constant home to your auction tools (the PC, printer, and all the rest), your auction space also can serve as your auction staging area. When you list your goods and treasures for sale in the virtual marketplace, your glowing descriptions aren't enough—you have to deal with the goods themselves in the physical world before, during, and after the auction. Why might you need a dedicated staging area?

Here's why:

- A staging area provides space to examine, categorize, and catalog your auctionable merchandise.
- A staging area can serve as a miniature photography studio (discussed in Chapter 17) where you can take digital pictures of your items.
- A staging area can also serve as a safe storage area to keep items clean and free from damage or loss (especially important if they're currently being bid on or ready for shipment).

- A staging area, if established properly, can provide further organization to your auction business, eliminating clutter and enabling you to deal with your merchandise faster and more efficiently.

A staging are doesn't necessarily need to be in the same place as your auction office (remember, you can harness the wireless router and a wireless notebook computer to maintain virtual continuity). Many auctioneers use different rooms or storage areas for their staging and storing needs. Whichever approach you choose—one location or dispersed—be sure your staging area meets these basic requirements:

- It should be clean, dry, and free from temperature extremes.
- It should be clearly identifiable as a devoted staging and storage area that will prevent others from moving or removing merchandise you intend to sell or are currently auctioning.
- It should be spacious enough to accommodate the goods you intend to auction without being crammed or overstuffed—the leading cause of postauction damage.
- It should be easily accessible to you, allowing you to get to your merchandise without needless climbing over stacks of boxes, crouching in crawl spaces, and creeping up shaky ladders.

Remember, the key to becoming organized and staying that way is to develop work areas that are easy to work in and to work with.

ESTABLISHING A SHIPPING STATION

Although shipping supplies and methods were discussed fully in Chapter 12, consider that effort and how it fits into the methodology behind establishing an auction office. Free yourself from rummaging for the last roll of tape or endlessly searching for the right box for an item. Beyond where you stage, list, and manage auction items, you likewise need a *supply room* that will be well

eBay TIP: If your shipping area is organized, you'll always know when to order new packing supplies. Remember, you can order free packing materials from shop.usps.com.

stocked with all the goods you need to make an easy transition from listing an item to packing an item.

Although you might be anticipating this by now, be sure your supply room has the following qualities:

- **It's a dedicated area.** No, you don't need a 10-bedroom home or condo to be an organized auctioneer. A single auction office located in a spare room can serve multiple auction uses (office, staging area, supply room). In fact, if you can find a large enough living space, the best auction environment is one where *all* of your auction activity can be contained within a single space. If not, find another corner where you can set up a supply shop.
- **It's a clean and well-lit area.** Cleanliness and good lighting will work in your favor as you pack up those items that customers have already paid for and that they are anxiously awaiting.
- **It's large enough to allow organization.** Again, a mansion isn't necessary, but you'll do better if all your supplies aren't stacked in a cramped corner or dumped into a carton that requires upending to get to what you need.
- **There's adequate work space to pack items.** It's where you'll keep your supplies and where you should expect to use them, too. Make sure you have enough room to work.

ORGANIZING YOUR SUPPLY ROOM

The goal of organization is to have what you need when you need it and within easy reach. As you establish your supply room, envision the actual flow of work: picture an assembly line process (moving from left to right) or a single-item packing station where all packing materials are within reach (boxes underneath, box fill above, tape to the left, labels to the right). Though it might sound a bit silly, the organization of your supply room will allow you to develop a repeatable and time-efficient packing process that will round out the establishment of your fully functional auction office.

25

Record Keeping: The Best Methods and Tools

At this point, you're probably grinning at the premise that you are truly in charge of your own business. In seeking your online fortune, it's become clear that you can pull down a regular income selling almost anything at eBay. While you daydream about your newfound freedom—the satisfaction of finally being able to work as you please and manage your affairs as best suits your needs and desires—there is one thing you can't escape: the need to keep accurate records, analyze profit and loss statistics, and pay taxes. No, the dream hasn't come to an abrupt end, though some folks would rather endure a root canal than face the tedious task of sorting out their business affairs. But fear not—keeping records and keeping track of your auction exploits isn't such an arduous task, provided you establish good habits up front. This chapter explains how easy record keeping can be and how facing Uncle Sam come April 15 can be a relatively painless process.

KEEPING UP WITH KEEPING RECORDS

Although it's been said a clean desk is a sign of a sick mind, the online seller who's well organized will generally have an easier time with record keeping. Though much significance is given to proper pricing, impressive images, and compelling item descriptions, keeping track of your online sales, bidder and buyer information, and everything else that comes with selling at eBay is paramount if you want to maximize your potential for success. No doubt about it, record keeping requires discipline, but if you consider this aspect of your business venture at the same time you plan what sorts of items to list and where you'll obtain your inventory, you'll stand the best opportunity of establishing an efficient operation. With a well-thought-out plan up front, you'll find it's easy to hit a stride in your offline duties, and you'll take the pain out of keeping track of your actions.

Why Keep Accurate Records?

Before getting into the principles of good record keeping, you may be wondering why it's important to keep accurate accounts of your work outside of the need to pay the government its due. Simply put, if you don't keep accurate records, how will you ever know whether you're succeeding in making your fortune? If your business begins to suffer a financial downturn, will you be able to quickly recognize what is happening and make corrective adjustments based simply on your feel for how things are going? And how will you be certain that the financial decisions you make are well founded and well planned if you're never empirically certain of the impact of those decisions?

Those who seek a profitable enterprise must look to good records to tell the story of how effectively their operation is running and how quickly they might be able to realize their financial goals.

IDENTIFYING THE KEY DATA

If you're convinced that good record keeping is vital to your efforts, you may wonder what sort of data you should keep. To help you get started, the following auction-related information will be the foundation of your record-keeping objectives.

Inventory and Assets

- **Inventory purchases.** Record all inventory you purchase or otherwise acquire that will be sold at eBay (or elsewhere, for that matter). Record *when* you acquire the items, *where* you acquire them, and at *what cost.* Keep all related receipts in an organized filing system, and if you don't receive a third-party receipt, write one up yourself on the spot to capture the date, place, and cost of the items (see Figure 25.1).
- **Capital equipment purchases.** If you're purchasing a dedicated PC, printer, camera, office supplies, or other such items that will be used directly in your auction business, properly record each of these pur-

```
Microsoft Excel - Book1
File  Edit  View  Insert  Format  Tools  Data  Window  Help
                                                      Arial          10    B  I
A17          =
```

	A	B	C	D	E
1	**Item Name**	**When Purchased**	**Where Purchased**	**Purchase Price**	**Comments**
2	Aurora Batcycle kit	02/05/06	Kit-Kat	$98.50	Small axle piece missing; replace
3	Aurora Batmobile kit	02/05/06	Kit-Kat	$115.00	Box top has one split corner; some
4	Aurora Batplane kit	02/05/06	Kit-Kat	$87.50	Mint, sealed
5	Aurora Voyage Flying Sub	03/15/06	Antique Trove, Roseville	$40.00	Complete, water damage to box top
6	Aurora Invaders Saucer kit	05/25/06	Model & Toy Show, Sac	$60.00	Mint, sealed
7					
8					
9					
10					
11					
12					
13					
14					
15					
16					
17					

```
Inventory Overview  Inventory Suppliers
Ready                                                             NUM
```

Figure 25.1 An inventory spreadsheet is easy to create and easy to maintain, as shown in this example using Microsoft Excel.

chases by logging the item name, cost, date of purchase, place of purchase, and business reason for the purchase.

- **Inventory sales.** Here's where your tax liability comes into play and where you need to be excruciatingly accurate in your record keeping. Whenever you sell an item, record sales price, sales tax (if applicable), and date of sale.

Hosting Venue Expenses

- **Standard listing/insertion fees.** By now you're well acquainted with the insertion fees levied at eBay. This is part of your cost of doing business and is critical information to record to determine how profitable your business is.
- **Special feature fees.** Although you could lump these costs in with the standard insertion fees, recording and tracking these separately will help you recognize whether these additional costs are really paying dividends based on your final price obtained.
- **Final value fees.** These constitute the final piece of the puzzle with regard to direct expenses incurred when listing items at eBay. Again, it's a good idea to separate out the costs of listing and ultimately selling an item at eBay so you can track and adjust (where possible) your direct cost of sales.

Transaction Fees

- **Shipping and handling.** When you're buying for resale or buying equipment and supplies, be sure to capture any transit and delivery costs you paid.
- **Insurance and tracking.** If you paid for these services when you made your purchase, be sure to record these fees as well.
- **Money fees.** When you're using an online payment service, escrow, or purchasing money orders, be sure to record the cost of sending or receiving payments. (Remember, as a seller using PayPal, you're regularly paying Business or Premier account fees as well as per-transaction fees; record those.)
- **Travel.** If you're hunting for inventory or simply driving to a carrier's office to drop off or pick up packages, record the cost of travel, be it by plane, train, or slow boat.
- **Supplies.** When you purchase supplies specifically for managing your auction business, you need to record those costs as well.

General Expenses

- **Internet fees.** If you're paying for online access, be it DSL, cable modem, or dial-up service, those costs are generally attributable to your business.
- **Storage and insurance fees.** If your inventory is stored offsite and/or you're paying specific fees to insure that inventory, you should also track these costs.
- **Home office deductions:** The IRS permits you to claim a percentage of your costs of maintenance, mortgage interest or rent, utilities, and other direct and indirect expenses if your home office is used *regularly* and *exclusively* to operate your business. Naturally, there may be additional costs and activities you'll want to track for your specific needs. Also, be sure to consult your tax advisor should there be items that could legally benefit you, and these should be recorded as well.

ESTABLISHING A RECORD-KEEPNG PLAN

Everyone will have different ideas about the best way to organize records. Because of this, you'll find there is no one right way to manage your sales data (although stuffing it all in a shoe box is definitely the wrong way). When devising a record-keeping strategy, review these key considerations to ensure your personal method is efficient and effective:

- Adopt a method that's easily repeatable and that can be useful for both high-volume and low-volume selling.
- Be sure your method is efficient to the degree that *you* won't be tempted to abandon it in the near future. Record-keeping methods can be enhanced, but if you find yourself changing over to a new style every other month, you may have developed something too complex.
- Keep it as simple as possible. You don't have to keep every single bit of data. Decide on the most pertinent information that will serve you for one year's time and go with that.

Of course, you can choose from many tools to help you manage your online sales records: paper-based ledger systems, PC-based spreadsheets or database applications, onsite inventory management systems, or third-party software packages. Whichever means you settle on, be sure you're comfortable with it, have the proper storage facilities for such records (physical or electronic), and have some sort of backup or recovery method in case the unforeseen occurs.

ADDING EFFICIENCY TO THE TASK

Most less-than-organized sellers confess they spend more time digging for past sales information than they care to admit. That time is lost opportunity, plain and simple. Avoid this by establishing a filing plan, be it hard copy or electronic, and sticking to it faithfully. If you'll be dealing in the real world of paper, using clearly marked files will allow you to store and retrieve information in mere seconds. By logically ordering your various records and receipts in a simple cabinet of hanging file folders, you'll be able to keep all of your pertinent data easily within reach.

If you want to go electronic when filing data, there are a few simple applications and online destinations that will help you get organized and stay that way:

- **Spreadsheet applications.** I prefer Microsoft Excel for my spreadsheet needs, though MS-Access (a database utility) runs a close second. With Excel, I've been able to enter my pertinent sales and purchase data (refer to Figure 25.1) easily and without any complications. All of the data is easy to view and even simpler to sort and analyze.

- **Online service sites.** Over the years, two sites in particular have continued to be valuable to me in my business exploits: www.quicken .com/small_business (see Figure 25.2) and www.irs.gov/businesses/ small/index.html. Both of these sites have been indispensable to me in the information they've provided and the downloadable tools I've been able to sample (though I admit that I have found that Excel meets most of my record-keeping needs in the single package).

- **Quicken.** This well-known electronic budgeting and bill-paying tool has a Web site that caters directly to small business owners or otherwise self-employed businesspeople. I guarantee that you can spend hours poring over all the information and advice it has to offer—all

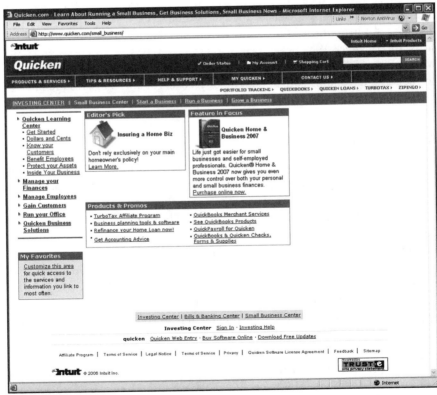

Figure 25.2 The Quicken Web site dedicated to small businesses offers answers to almost every question you might conjure up.

time very well spent. Likewise, the IRS provides numerous tips, forms, and even self-paced online training sessions to help entrepreneurs like you get your business running well and properly managed.

- **E-mail tools.** As much as I've encouraged you to excel in all your communications, you now need to be equally adept in filing and storing records of customer interactions. Practically all of the e-mail tools available today feature an embedded filing system. Create sensible file folders ("Items Listed," "Items Sold," "Payment Pending," etc.) and keep your messages stored appropriately.

> **eBay TIP:** The programs and Web destinations on these pages are the ones that have been of greatest help to me in my activities. They may or may not suit your needs or desires. Choose whichever electronic tools work best for you, but try to refrain from using *too many* tools. There are so many business helpers and organizers available today, but your business will be best served if you can focus on one, two, or three (at the most) to manage your activity. Any more than this and you could end up spending more time servicing the tool than servicing your business.

AN IMPORTANT NOTE ABOUT SECURITY

Just a quick note about controlling your records: be sure you have *exclusive* access to your business records—meaning that you shouldn't allow access to someone else in the household who might unwittingly reorganize or otherwise disrupt your organization system. It's a safe and practical measure to be able to lock your physical files, and be sure to use password protection for your electronic tools, too. If you work with a partner, be sure you both agree on the organization methods and communicate fully whenever a change or enhancement might be useful.

RECORDS THAT PAY REWARDS

As any good businessperson knows, a base of customers can be your best asset for long-term success. To an online seller, understanding who your best customers are and occasionally notifying them of the availability of the things they desire can leave the two of you feeling quite happy and successful.

To this end, keep the following customer-related information:

eBay Item #	Item Name	Start Date	End Date	Final Price	High Bidder	Payment Type	Shipping Method	Ship Date
3320400494	PS Allosaurus	2/9/2006	2/16/2006	$345.09	xxxxxxxx	PayPal	USPS Priority	2/19/2006
3320400502	PS Flying Rep.	2/9/2006	2/16/2006	$140.25	xxxxxxxx	PayPal	USPS Priority	2/18/2006
3320400512	PS Spiked Dino	2/9/2006	2/16/2006	$136.27	xxxxxxxx	Money Order	USPS Priority	2/25/2006
2921800977	PS Giant Bird	3/16/2006	3/23/2006	$145.00	xxxxxxxx	PayPal	USPS Priority	2/18/2006
2170187223	PS Cro-Magnon	3/16/2006	3/23/2006	$122.77	xxxxxxxx	Money Order	USPS Priority	2/24/2006
2170673835	PS Neanderthal	3/16/2006	3/23/2006	$147.29	xxxxxxxx	Per. Check	USPS Priority	3/3/2006

Figure 25.3 Sales information as shown in this spreadsheet excerpt can be vital to sorting out a complication or misunderstanding with a customer.

- The customer's name and contact information (address provided, e-mail, etc.)
- The dates of your auctions and other supporting transaction dates with the buyer
- Method of payment you received
- Method and cost of shipping used, plus any tracking numbers

Beyond providing you with the ability to keep in touch with your past customers, good auction records can also be critical to sorting out a potential snag in an auction transaction. A buyer could contact you weeks or months after you believe the deal was closed, possibly raising concerns or becoming confrontational. Although this is not necessarily a reason to suspect a scam, your ability to quickly present detailed records and accounts of an auction transaction via your spreadsheet of information (see Figure 25.3) or stored e-mail messages will be your best tool for proving you held up your end of the bargain.

Though you wouldn't use their information irresponsibly or inappropriately, keeping track of the folks you've sold to in the past and their contact information will ultimately pay dividends, as it helps you recognize potential repeat customers, possible deadbeats, or those who have expressed interest in the sorts of items you offer.

DECLARING INCOME AND PAYING TAXES

Every year around January 31, you should have collected your W-2 forms as you prepare to report your annual taxable income. But, there's likely one income form you haven't collected—your *online income statement*. While the IRS continues to eyeball the online sales venues, you'll be best served to keep your nose clean in reporting your auction income. To that end, here are some tips on how and when you should report income and what sorts of expenses you might legally deduct.

Always Consult a Professional

At the outset, understand that the information provided here is intended to guide you toward a better understanding of legally reporting income. Taxation rules can differ from state to state and even town to town, so always consult a licensed tax preparation expert to be sure you fully understand the tax liabilities, allowances, and limitations as they might pertain to your particular situation.

Gains and Losses

The rules are simple: whenever you make a profit, taxes must be paid. Even if you decide to infrequently sell off prior investment pieces such as fine art, vintage automobiles, or antiques, any profit over and above your original purchase price is deemed by the IRS as taxable income. Conversely, if such a sale fails to recoup the original investment, you'll be faced with a loss that could be deemed a "declarable loss" (again, consult a tax professional in these matters). Naturally, you'd prefer to see your gains exceed your losses, as would our government.

Making Estimated Payments

If your approach is to regularly buy and sell items at online auctions, you're unquestionably operating a business designed to make a profit.

If you're this sort of happily self-employed businessperson, recognize that you're responsible to make quarterly estimated tax payments based on the income to be realized for the tax period. Required payment dates are April 15, June 15, September 15, and January 15 of the following year. These payments are filed using Form 1040-ES (OCR). But there's a catch to paying these taxes on your business: besides paying a regular tax on any profit, you're also responsible to pay an additional 15.3 percent to cover Social Security and Medicare contributions. When it comes time to file your annual tax return in April, you should consider reporting your business's activity using Schedule C, Profit (or Loss) from a Business or Profession, with your Form 1040.

Declaring Business Expenses

More good news is that whenever your business incurs expenses while striving for a profit, those are probably deductible costs that can offset a portion of your net gain. Though some folks try to claim questionable expenses (vehicles, vacations, etc.), the following expenditures are generally acceptable deductions:

- Listing fees
- Business-related postage costs
- Phone and Internet connection fees
- Supplies
- Computer programs
- Office furniture and equipment
- Business-related training and educational expenses
- Tax preparation fees
- Legal fees
- A percentage of rent or mortgage if you have a separate office of a specific size

These are just some of the common deductions you can legally claim as you operate your business. Be sure to consider other expenses that you incur as part of keeping your business alive and thriving, and consult your tax advisor to see what additional deductions you may be letting slip through your fingers (and into Uncle Sam's hands).

26

Cutting Costs, Controlling Expenses, and Improving Your Profitability

Here's an adage you may not have heard before: in order to make a fortune, you first have to save a fortune. Similar to the venerable "penny saved, penny earned" axiom, a large factor in becoming truly rich is your ability to retain that which you acquire. By controlling selling fees and other expenses, you'll be in better control of your overall business performance and bottom-line profit than if you rack up costs indiscriminately and unmonitored. No, you don't need to become an absolute tightwad, and you needn't relegate the special features in your auction listings to the bare-bones minimums (that would be poor selling strategy in some regards). This chapter helps ensure that you remain aware of the fees and costs associated with online selling and discusses how you can apply effective strategy to keeping those costs down while fortifying your fortune.

CONTROLLING eBAY FEES

When making your first listings, you may have been surprised and maybe even concerned about the number of various fees eBay levies. While it's true that almost every little enhancement seems to have some sort of associated cost, it should be comforting to know that many of these listing-related costs can be reduced and managed with a bit of foresight and careful planning. You won't be able to escape every fee, but you can reduce and avoid many that really don't add much to your profit potential and exist largely to chew into your bottom line.

The Fees You Can't Avoid

Be realistic—you *will* pay some sort of listing fee when you sell at eBay. The days of free online auctioning are long gone (those sites dried up back in the late 1990s due to low traffic and sparse listing volume). Still, some cantankerously contend that eBay is getting rich because of its tariffs. Nevertheless, it's important to understand that the fees you pay provide the capital needed to fund useful new features, costly infrastructure (hardware and software maintenance), and user services and tools.

Much like your own business, as eBay continues to grow, it needs to reinvest to ensure it can satisfy the needs and wants of the more sophisticated online seller. The listing and usage fees wind up being a small price to pay for the ability to list, sell, and collect at so large a site, and the advanced methods and tools (such as Turbo Lister) become worth the cost when you consider the time, effort, and, yes, money *you'll* save in the long run. Internet and online auction history have already proven that free sites simply cannot compete and perform at these levels.

The Little Things That Can Cost Big

While it's reasonable and affordable to manage basic eBay insertion fees, there *is* a lot of fluff in there, and you *can* cut costs by carefully selecting which features and services you'll use in your listings. In fact, after doing some research and investigating, you might find that although some adornments and extras add plenty of eye candy, they also might offer little true return on the investment.

Cast a frugal eye on the following questionable, and often costly, eBay listing enhancements:

- **Title enhancements.** Be it bold, highlighted, or whatever, few bidders really pay much attention to the visual style of your item's title. Save by making selective use of capital lettering (not exclusively, though) to highlight a key element of your item title. Make sure you use plenty of good keywords, since most items are found via the all-important keyword searches discussed previously in this book.
- **Special icons.** Whether it's a birthday cake, a Christmas tree, or a firecracker, when it comes to added title icons . . . who cares? When did

you last leap at an item because of the cutesy little picture that accompanied it? Again, save the buck.

- **Home page featured placement.** This is one of the most expensive listing options at eBay and, unless your item will gain you thousands of dollars in high bids or has a tremendously high profit volume, it's best to bypass this one if you're trying to cut costs. Again, it's typically the keywords that get noticed, not the site real estate where your item is listed.

- **Cross-category listing.** This ability to have a single listing appear in two categories simultaneously will almost double the fee you pay and yet may not truly pay off in the end (recall that the additional category can be selected during the initial step of the listing process). Revisit your research methods to determine the *best* category to list under, and be willing to use a different category if your research indicates a better home for your goods. Besides, if you double-categorize, how will you know which category was ultimately responsible for your success?

Learning to Choose Fees Wisely

Of course, this isn't to say that *all* fees are inherently evil and detrimental to your eventual profit. Just as it makes perfect sense to pay reasonable fees for site and service usage, it's also prudent to occasionally make use of features and enhancements when the situation calls for it. For example, consider the following:

- **Gallery picture.** Recall how I demonstrated the use of the Gallery Picture when creating your item listing. While it's a costly little adornment, the impact it has on drawing buyers' attention from a search result list is well worth the investment. This is the key feature I'll always include in my listings.

- **Reserve prices.** Don't be penny-wise and pound-foolish: If you need the reserve to protect you from losing on your investment, by all means use it. However, recognize that eBay has skillfully hiked its insertion fees based on opening bid *or* reserve price, charging you the highest insertion fee possible, treating the reserve price as if it were an opening bid amount. Therefore, if you use a reserve price, try to choose the lowest value possible to keep your listing fee low, too.

- **Opening bids.** Of course, if current demand for your item easily will gain you your target price without the use of a reserve, then list in the lowest fee bracket and let the bidders work their magic. Beyond this, be sure to work the opening bid fee structure to your best advantage, seeking to list at the top end of the lower brackets to reduce your fees. That is, if you want to start bidding for your item at $25.00, the insertion fee will be $1.20. Start that same listing at the comparable $24.99, and the insertion fee is cut in half, incurring only a $0.60 levy. Pay careful attention to the fee breakdowns (see Table 26.1) as you compare the opening bid amounts and how those map to insertion fees.

---

 eBay TIP: Yes, eBay does have a tendency to adjust its fees. To ensure you're working from the most recent fee information, visit http://pages.ebay.com/help/sell/fees.html.

- **Relisting.** Well, it's typically free (at eBay, you're refunded listing fees if you get a sale), and the benefit is that you can make changes to the item title, description, and category to find your buyer on the site's dime. Take advantage of that.
- **Online payment:** Some sellers might not be happy that fees are levied by online payment sites, but remember that buyers who can pay with credit cards (via services like PayPal and Bidpay) will invariably spend more than if they must surrender their cash on hand. If your

Table 26.1   Study the eBay Insertion Fee schedule to choose opening bid or reserve price values that can result in the lowest possible insertion fees.

INSERTION FEES

Starting or Reserve Price	Insertion Fee
$0.01–$0.99	$0.20
$1.00–$9.99	$0.40
$10.00–$24.99	$0.60
$25.00–$49.99	$1.20
$50.00–$199.99	$2.40
$200.00–$499.99	$3.60
$500.00 or more	$4.80

items sell at good prices, make it easier for your buyers to pay by offering the online payment opportunity, then collect their higher bids at the relatively low cost to you. (Some sellers even go so far as to insist that if a buyer wants to pay through an online payment service, then he or she—and not the seller—will have to fork over the necessary fees. Obviously, such a practice will cause some bidders to say thanks, but no thanks. It's also against eBay's rules.)

Is It Cheaper to Have a "No Sale"?

Just when you thought sniping was the reigning king of online auction controversy, along comes *fee avoidance,* the frowned-upon act of manipulating auctions and luring bidders off the venue to make a sale without paying site fees and commissions. But just as eBay is in the business of making money, well, so are you. Read the site's terms of service carefully on this issue; however, to date there's still no penalty assessed if you're contacted by a buyer who inquires about an item that fails to meet the reserve or possibly asks whether you have more of the same to sell. It's a fine line, though: if the *seller* initiates offline transactions or additional sales, a swift site warning could be forthcoming, as well as possible suspension, since such actions are considered acts of fee avoidance.

eBay TIP: Not surprisingly, eBay openly counsels registered users to report incidents in which sellers make unsolicited contact with a buyer for the purpose of selling items outside of the auction site. Long-time eBay sellers and buyers know there is nothing wrong with this practice, from a person-to-person perspective, provided the contact isn't coercive or continuous (i.e., spam). Some buyers and sellers manage mutually agreeable deals in this manner, are able to review one another's eBay feedback ratings, and often develop long-lasting business relationships (even friendships) as a result. Since eBay receives no commission for such sales, it's certainly not promoting such ad hoc transactions.

In the interest of your sales and overall profit-to-cost ratio, be sure buyers can easily contact you (provide an e-mail address or Web site link in your item description) to assist them with any inquiries they may have, informational or otherwise, during an auction or otherwise offsite. If a potential buyer initiates a potential transaction, then that's just simply good for business and could (not unfairly) save you some operating costs in the process.

> **eBay TIP:** Amid the various fees you'll be hoping to reduce or dodge altogether, don't forget to load up on the freebies such as carriers' gratis shipping supplies, eBay tools like Turbo Lister, and even free advice from the eBay Discussion Forums (see the site map under "Community"). Many services and supplies are yours for the taking, provided you know where to look.

SAVINGS THROUGH SIMPLICITY

Sometimes the simplest things can pay off in ways you might not expect. When it comes to online selling, simplicity and consistency in managing your sales can help boost your savings potential in the following ways:

- Simple listings are usually cheaper in regard to insertion fees, and with limited enhancements, the simpler listing is immediately less costly.
- If you'll be using HTML to add a bit of dazzle to your listings, using an effective style and then committing that to a repeatable template will save time in creating new listings, while the HTML itself will add splashy features free of charge (as opposed to enlisting eBay's fee-based eye candy).
- While you want to offer options within your sales policy, adhering to shipping methods that are relatively simple to you (such as choosing carriers that are geographically nearby or selecting a carrier that offers all of the shipping options you'll support) makes it easy for you to anticipate your postauction activities without having to reinvent your methods at every turn.
- A simple, straightforward, and streamlined postauction process likewise makes it easy to anticipate your upcoming activities, and, when operating to a proven routine, you stand to gain time and efficiency through your repeatable methods.

> **eBay TIP:** While not all materials necessary to your business are free, don't forget to search eBay itself for additional goods and equipment you might need, such as office supplies, furniture, equipment, and even decor. Plenty of bargains may be found at eBay, so don't forget to search for good deals for these often-mundane goods when *you're* in the buyer's seat.

TIME-SAVING STRATEGIES THAT WILL SAVE YOU MONEY, TOO

From the equipment they use to the methods they manage, many eBay sellers are surprised to learn how much time they've lost in their *inefficient* endeavors. While you're focused on saving money, consider some of the following simple yet effective efforts that will help you reclaim your most precious, non-renewable resource—time.

Time Is Money

For starters, begin your profit boosting by closely examining your use of time. Take two to four weeks to carefully log your time (be diligent here) to see how much you're really getting accomplished each day. You might learn that you're surfing the Net too much or chatting the day away with friends. And if you're sitting around waiting for that ancient computer or lazy dial-up connection to chug you around the Internet, it might be time to upgrade.

The overall goal here is to ensure you can reduce the time it takes to complete your online merchandizing tasks. Set firm working hours, use listing and e-mail templates, carefully schedule trips into town, and whatever else you can do to save time as you tend to your online business. Develop an efficient work plan that keeps the profits rolling in and makes the best use of your working day.

Intangibles That Inject More Savings

Your approach to your auctioning can save you countless hours every year. Turn your attention to tuning up your business behavior, which is often the element that can bring the greatest returns in the long run.

- **Establish working hours.** Whether you choose to work hours on end or to segment times of the day, put a schedule in place when work is to be done—and stick to it. So many home business enterprises fail due to lack of discipline in setting regular working hours.
- **Stay in your office.** With so many products and resources now available online, you can eliminate wasted time running errands. Today, you can order packing supplies online, you can buy postage online, and you can research your customer market online, all without ever having to stray away from your work space.
- **Limit interruptions.** If your friends keep calling to chat, switch over to the answering machine. If incoming e-mail throws you off track, close your e-mail window. Take control of whatever might be distracting you from completing your tasks; don't let distractions away at your productivity.
- **Develop a weekly work schedule.** Monday is packing day. Tuesday is record-keeping day. Wednesday is listing day. Whatever schedule works best for you, establish a routine so you can anticipate the next day's duties and avoid wasting time pondering, "Hmm, what should I do today?"
- **Focus on the task at hand.** While you're working at eBay, it's all to easy to become distracted and surf off to read, play, or shop. Stick to your task until it's done, *then* play.
- **Take a break.** Take regular breaks not only for your physical well-being (get out of that desk chair once in a while) but also for your mental well-being. It's been proven that regular (but not excessive) breaks serve as a proven mental reenergizer, allowing you to return to work with a refreshed perspective and renewed motivation.

Recognize the importance of keeping focused on your online sales goals to bolster your profitability, but don't forget to give yourself a break from time to time to keep your perspective fresh. When you can step back and objectively view your efforts and the results of them, you'll be better able to apply cost and expense controls while gaining improved visibility of even more areas where you can add efficiency.

27

Creating Your Own Online Storefront and Presenting Your Business as a Brand

While the eBay experience is invigorating for bidders and largely profitable for sellers, the real fortune to be had is found when you diversify your assets. In online selling terms, this means going beyond eBay itself and incorporating a more permanent commercial presence online. These days, creating an online store is easier than ever, while the financial results you stand to reap will definitely elevate your business into the big leagues.

CREATING AN eBAY STORE

Your commercial Web experience can begin right within eBay itself, where you may create an eBay store. From eBay's home page, click on the eBay Stores link under the Specialty Sites header (see Figure 27.1), then, on the eBay Stores main page, click on the Open a Store button to begin the store-building process (Figure 27.2). When you build your store, remember everything you've learned about eBay listings—the best content, keywords, style, and business methods—and apply that to your store. By doing so, you'll be establishing a consistent approach to your business that will resonate well with your customers (plus, it leverages so much of the excellent work you've already done!).

As you might expect, the mechanics of creating an eBay store are quite involved, and it's not feasible for me to explain all the details to you in this particular book. However, you will find that, when you're ready, venturing

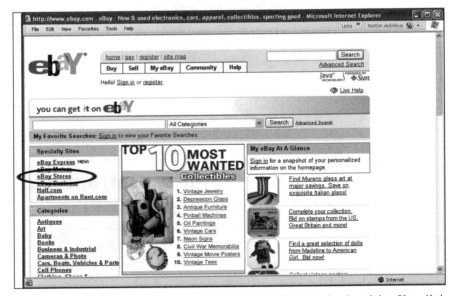

Figure 27.1 Access the eBay Stores area by clicking on the Specialty Sites link from the eBay home page.

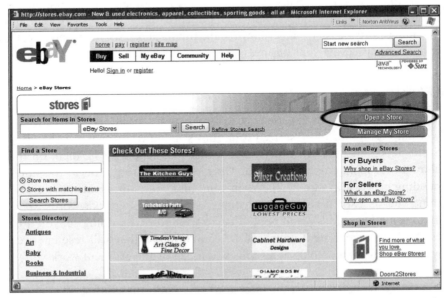

Figure 27.2 Click the Create a Store button to begin your store-building adventure.

into creating an eBay store can be a boon to your bottom line, since eBay stores include the following compelling features:

- The ability to showcase auction and fixed-price items all in one place
- Your own eBay store Web site address (e.g., www.stores.ebay.com/ your_store_name_here)
- Your store's name and link highlighted in all of your eBay listings
- Your store name featured in eBay's store directory, where buyers can browse or search for your store
- A built-in store search engine for your customers' use
- A store newsletter feature to facilitate publishing news and updates to your customers
- A store icon next to your eBay user ID so buyers can easily visit your store
- The ability to create custom item categories within your own store

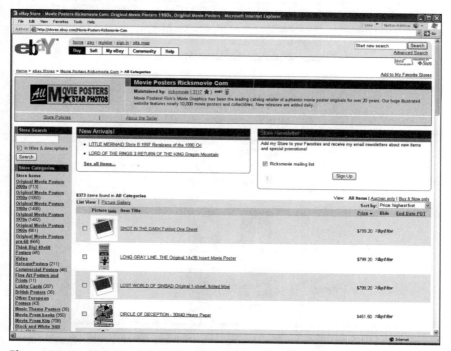

Figure 27.3 RicksMovie is a favorite eBay store of mine and has proven to be highly profitable for Rick and his staff.

Do eBay stores really make a difference? According to Rick (from Rick's Movie Graphics, a purveyor of fine movie memorabilia and other collectibles), his eBay store, RicksMovie, has proven to be a boon to furthering his online commercial presence and feeding his business fortune (see Figure 27.3).

CREATING A STORE OUTSIDE OF eBAY

When venturing into the creation of an online store, don't just settle for an eBay shop. Broaden your horizons and increase your potential sales reach by creating a bona fide Web site all your own, open and ready for business in the wide expanse of the Internet. Although this chapter can't provide all the details of setting up such an operation (that's a topic for another entire book, and I highly recommend McGraw-Hill's *How to Sell Anything on Yahoo . . . and Make a Fortune*), consider investing the time in establishing your own Web site. Many eBay sellers have done this with great success over the years

Figure 27.4 RicksMovie.com is active and in front of prospective customers' eyes every day on the World Wide Web.

and have further increased their moneymaking potential by maintaining an active presence both inside and outside of eBay. Pay a visit to Rick's commercial Web venue, www.ricksmovie.com (see Figure 27.4) to see how he and his team have effectively extended their reach beyond the confines of eBay and into the prosperous expanse of the entire Internet.

DEVELOPING YOUR BRAND, BOOSTING YOUR BUSINESS

Perhaps you now have presence in the auction realm as well as in the online store space and though your business is brimming with terrific products, you seem to struggle in developing a repeat customer base. Before you wonder whether your diversification efforts have been to no avail, recognize that you might be in need of a brand—a name, a look, and a style that shoppers will remember and associate with your high-quality goods and superb service. Don't leave it to chance to have customers find you out there in the marketplace. Instead, consider developing an effective brand to position your business's name in the forefront of customers' minds, wherever they may find you.

Developing a Name That Sells

Choosing an effective business name is no simple task (just ask the large corporations that spend millions of dollars on such efforts). It's not necessary, though, to seek out an advertising firm to develop a winning name. According to some of the greatest marketing minds, an effective business (or product) name should have the following characteristics:

- It defines the benefit of your product or service.
- It's easy to remember.
- It's not too similar to any other established business name or brand.
- It differentiates your business from your competitors.
- It's multinational.

Of course, the online realm requires that a few extra considerations be taken into account when developing a cybermoniker. First, keep the name as short as possible, yet try to ensure it is mentally and verbally pronounceable. Try to eliminate use of special characters (such as hyphens, ampersands, etc.)

as well as numbers; these are the sorts of characters customers tend to forget easily.

> **eBay TIP:** Notice how Rick was careful to name both his eBay store and his Web site "RicksMovie." Since he's grown active customer bases in both realms, his buyers can easily find him and his products inside and outside of eBay by remembering just one simple store name. *That's* effective.

Above all, select a name that's appropriate to your business or product. If you're in the business of selling books, choose a fitting name like "Book-World" or "RareBooks." More colorful names work well (consider "Reflections-Past" for an antique mirror business), though you'll need to be careful the name isn't so esoteric that it's difficult to associate with your products. Expect that securing a desired online name could take some work—many choice domain names have been duly snatched up in previous years' dot-com frenzy. At the very least, acquire an e-mail address with your business name (e.g., RareBooks@aol.com).

Adding Visual Recognition

Once you have a great business name, consider creating a uniquely recognizable business logo. (After all, where would eBay be without that highly recognizable upsy-downsy emblem?) Be it an evocative artistic representation of the name, an identifiable color scheme, or some sort of clever character, logos can be as big as the name in perpetuating a business's brand. If you develop a logo design, be sure to make it plainly visible (but not obnoxiously so) whenever and wherever you have items for sale.

Delivering on Your Business's Name

It's one thing to have a brand name that rolls easily off your customers' tongues or a business logo they recognize at first glance, but it's another thing to ensure that brand unequivocally delivers the sorts of goods it implies. While you shouldn't relegate yourself to selling only one specific product (such as antique stoves, mirrors, or carnival glass), make sure you're *always* well stocked with items promised by the name. Once you are certain you can deliver what you advertise, it's easy to include additional items of interest that might likewise tempt your visitors' shopping and collecting tastes.

Developing Market Mindshare

Effective branding ultimately leads to firmly establishing a spot in your customers' minds. To make sure your branding can be working for you at all times, use it in all of your customer correspondence. If possible, overlay your business name in the corner of every item image you post (many photo editors allow the addition of the semitransparent watermark). Include invoices or thank you notes that bear your brand in all of your shipments.

Better Business for a Better Brand

Recognize that your *style* of business will make or break your brand. Keep your online destination tidy, well-organized, and informative. Be sure you've developed considerable expert knowledge about your featured commodity so that you can easily and reliably assist customers in their quest for information as well as merchandise. Establish operating policies that meet your customers' needs, taking into account the unique needs they might have related to your product offerings. And keep your inventory fresh and enticing by actively rotating the goods for sale.

Having done all this, your business name will likely mean more to your customers, and they'll be eager to return time and time again. And every time they specifically seek out your business (whether online or elsewhere), your business name will become further ingrained into their consciousness. *That's* a successful brand.

Using Counters to Track Your Brand's Success

As mentioned in Chapter 18, counters provide you the opportunity to determine how many visitors are shopping at your Web site. Whereas the counters you used in your eBay auctions provided data only on the number of page display visits (i.e., the number of times anyone—even the same person during multiple visits—viewed your listing), a successful business Web site will profit from a more sophisticated form of counting and even monitoring customer visits. Begin by understanding the sort of specific data that should be collected and analyzed. Most successful Web enterprises track the following:

- Which areas of your Web site are visited most?
- On which days of the week do the majority of visits occur?
- How long do visitors spend at your Web site (and in which areas of the site do they linger)?
- How many errors occur at your site (pages that don't display properly or other such programmatic-type problems)?

To help Webmasters and businesspersons like you gain a better understanding of who's visiting your site and what happens while they're strolling your virtual aisles, programs known as *Web traffic analyzers* have been developed. Here are a couple you might like to learn more about:

- **OneStat.** Created for small and medium-sized business sites. Learn more about this analyzer by visiting www.onestat.com, where you'll find a free trial version of this popular tool.
- **Surfstats.** Another Web analyzer that's also available for a free trial download; go to www.surfstats.com.

AUCTIONS VERSUS STORES: WHICH PRICE IS RIGHT?

Online sellers, you'll find, all operate under their own preferences and pronouncements of the best ways to do business. When it comes to listing formats and selling strategies at eBay and beyond, the lines are often drawn within the community between the fixed-price approach (store and buy-it-now offerings) and the dynamic-price approach (ascending price auctioning). It's unlikely that you'll attempt to start up your own auction venue at a commercial Web site, yet it's highly important that you take this opportunity to further explore the differences between the pricing methods. Although purported by some to opposing formats, some of the most successful offsite sellers have pursued the opportunities of both pricing formats to determine whether both methods can successfully coexist within any seller's business plan.

Understanding Fixed Pricing

To begin, online selling in and of itself has proven to be one of the most promising opportunities for traditional offline (brick-and-mortar) sellers, though many have yet to venture into the online realm. With all the buzz about eBay and auctioning, some traditional sellers have become confused regarding their options and opportunities in fixed- versus dynamic-pricing models.

In a nutshell, fixed-price selling is exactly how sellers do business in their offline (real-world) sales establishments—they present an item, put a selling price on it, and, for all intents and purposes, they have established the equivalent of an online fixed-price listing. The method here is the same; only the venue (virtual) is different.

Dynamic Pricing Defined

The dynamic format, then, is characterized by the back-and-forth bidding that ensues when an item is up for bid in an auction environment. It's no secret that the gamesmanship of this competitive bidding has made eBay the multi-billion-dollar success it is today. Of course, different auction formats, including Dutch auctions, reserve auctions, and so on, can sometimes cloud the definition. Generally, the dynamic format reflects ascending price bidding, wherein the final price equals the highest bid at the auction's close.

When Fixed Becomes Dynamic and Vice Versa

What some sellers tend to overlook is how the fixed format can *become* dynamic, and vice versa. For example, if an item at an eBay store or other commercial site does not sell, the seller can reduce its price or have a limited-time sale, therefore dynamically altering the price at which it will be offered. Sellers can modify prices as they see fit, either in response to present market demand, to generate additional activity at their online Web store, or for any other reason that will suit their customers' wants and needs.

Similarly, the dynamic format has evolved into a sort of hybrid fixed format, thanks to the addition of the Buy-It-Now sales feature at eBay. A seller can offer an item to the bidders in dynamic format, yet also dangle a fixed selling price should anyone care to offer that price and close the auction immediately. In effect, this serves as an auction stopper, but it also works as an effective method for a seller to tempt bidders by offering a reasonable price—perhaps the same price they'd offer in a fixed format—instilling a sense of urgency to take it at that price before the opportunity is gone or the bidding goes even higher.

Dynamic Pricing Risk

A generally held misgiving about the dynamic format is the perceived lack of control over the price. In a fixed format, the price is the price, plain and simple, and is not subject to a whimsical or mercurial market. Really, the only risk is whether the item will or will not sell at that fixed-format price. Fixed-price sellers can safely venture into the dynamic format by using either high opening bids, reserve prices, or those Buy-It-Now prices, all of which could equal the original fixed-format price. The concern that usually arises is whether an item up for bid (in dynamic format) without price protections makes for risky business, the seller being uncertain whether the bidding will result in a fair market value in the final high bid. No doubt that's a definite risk, but one that can be mitigated to a reasonable extent provided the seller has researched the current market value and would be satisfied to receive such a price. Nonetheless, the dynamic format doesn't *guarantee* a fair final price.

> **eBay TIP:** While I've fallen victim to the downside of a bidding war on occasion, more often than not I've gained much better prices than I had originally expected, thanks to the impassioned battling of bidders who were each determined to win— the win sometimes being more important than the final price.

The Value of Fixed-Price Sales History

There's a key intangible at work that has yet to be touched upon: in a fixed-format Web store, sellers are able to maintain and make public their history of past sales. Just as leading high-end auction houses Sotheby's and Christie's do, Web store sellers can provide a record of their past sales, allowing their customers to see the sort of goods sold in the past. This is viewed as a definite plus in the fixed-format environment since it works to visibly demonstrate the expertise and knowledge of the seller based on the goods and prices he or she has managed. And eBay's short-duration dynamic listings, archived for only 30 days after an auction, can't quite offer that sort of recap of previous business.

To some discerning buyers, this is important background information that will drive their decision to purchase or not. Realistically, for the reasons just stated, if yours is to be a Web store devoted to high-end goods, you likely wouldn't want to rely solely on the dynamic (auction) environment. However, if you have less-significant items to offer, if you want to sell trendy items that can provide healthy profits for a limited period, or if you temporarily seek to move some inventory that is otherwise languishing in a Web store, take advantage of the high traffic within the dynamic environment of eBay. At the least, you should expect to sell the item at a reasonable price, and in the best scenario, your low-end to midrange items might spark a bidders' battle.

Whatever the outcome, the dynamic venue can then lead your ultimate buyer and possibly some of the underbidders back to your fixed-format Web store, where you stand to gain additional sales and hopefully some repeat business as well. To wrap up this brief discussion, a recommended approach is for Web sellers to offer at least one high-quality item within the dynamic environment—eBay, that is—at all times. The potential for attracting more viewers, which translates into increased clientele, is too valuable to pass up. This sentiment alone suggests that a thorough understanding and strategic use of both formats simultaneously makes good business sense to the seller who hosts auctions as well as a Web store.

10 TIPS FOR IMPROVING YOUR FIXED-PRICE SALES

While eBay has the tools available to help you build your store, that help runs short when you want some advice on *how to run* your online shop, at eBay or elsewhere. To conclude this chapter's discussion of store building and brand boosting, here are 10 timely tips to help you gain better visibility, greater customer satisfaction, and maximum return on your fixed-price sales efforts:

1. **Be seen in everything you do.** Whenever and wherever you auction or otherwise sell items, be sure to conspicuously advertise your online store or your auction goods, providing links to both whenever you list goods for sale.

2. **Make sure your store inventory is easy to browse.** Categorize your fixed-price goods in meaningful ways that will help customers zero in on exactly what they're looking for. For example, if you sell clothing, you could organize your wares by men's, women's, and children's, breaking shirts, pants, skirts, and so forth into subcategories. Don't just dump an unsorted inventory in a heap and hope that visitors will have patience to comb through it all (many won't).

3. **Be accessible.** Don't make it difficult for your customers—especially new customers—to get in touch with you. Be sure your contact information is clearly visible wherever and whenever you have

items listed. If your e-mail address or other contact information can't easily be found, you've likely lost a customer.

4. **Keep a customer list.** Once you've satisfied a customer, keep the relationship alive by adding his or her name to your customer list. Use the list to inform your buyers of upcoming sales (and auctions) of items that might be of particular appeal. Of course, *always* allow customers to opt out of such notification if they choose.

5. **Make your terms known.** Be clear, concise, and complete when posting your business terms and policies. Shipping options, insurance, return policies, and guarantees all need to be clearly spelled out and easy to find.

6. **Diversify your listings.** Whether or not you specialize in a particular type of item, be sure to list items in multiple venues (there are sites other than eBay) and use multiple selling formats (fixed and dynamic). The more you can diversify your location and sales methods, the better chance you will have of attracting an equally diversified clientele.

7. **Exhibit your expertise.** Don't be bashful. Make liberal use of About Me pages wherever possible and showcase your sales history, your related experience, your business credentials—everything that tells your customers why you're the seller with whom they can feel confident. And don't forget to post a picture of your most valuable asset—*you!* Customers like to see who they're dealing with.

8. **Give 'em more than just goods.** Most successful sellers offer generous amounts of additional information to their patrons. Post additional articles, images, and interesting information that will help your shoppers learn more about the goods they seek—the goods you're selling.

9. **Maintain customer wish lists.** As you develop your customer base, get to know what else they're looking for. By keeping their wants in mind, you'll improve your ability to sell more goods faster (essentially, a *presale*) and you'll further enhance your customer relationships.

10. **Post customer testimonials.** With their permission, visibly post the comments of your satisfied customers. Not only will they feel special about seeing their name in print, you'll also help new customers get a better sense about your commitment to total customer satisfaction.

Unlike auction listings, an online store should advertise more than just the items you're selling—it should reveal the details of how you run your business, how you manage your sales, and how you serve your customers. Make sure your online store incorporates these top 10 keys to success, thereby offering your customers an easier and more satisfying experience when visiting your nonauction offerings.

28

Keeping Up with Changes at eBay

Within a relatively short span of time, eBay has logged an active and eventful history of its own. With regard to events, developments, shakeouts, and shake-ups, online auctions in general have seen so much activity that it might appear they've been around for *decades* (though it's been just over one decade at this writing). If you've been around the Internet and auctioning for at least six or seven years, you've seen many would-be auction sites try and fail in their efforts to compete with eBay.

Within eBay itself, you can expect to see ongoing changes in the form of new features and perhaps modified site policies or fee structures (just as this revised edition reflects the newer elements installed since the original 2003 book). While it's never been a problem to adapt to such changes, it's a good idea for you to keep up-to-date on the latest and greatest eBay has to offer to keep your business running smoothly and your fortune flowing.

How will you keep up with what's going on and what's coming up at eBay and elsewhere online? The purpose of this final chapter is to direct you to the sources of information where you can monitor upcoming changes to your online oasis. The good news is that, thanks to the Internet itself, you can find a wide variety of information sources right at your fingertips.

MINING THE eBAY COMMUNITY BOARDS

Many sites host forums where members can meet and chat about the site, its members, and its direction. Good sites will have moderators who respond to member questions and comments while also posting notices of upcoming

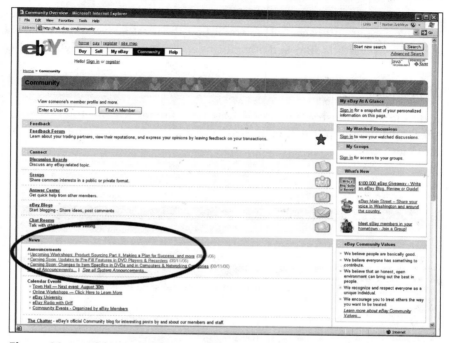

Figure 28.1 Visit eBay's community page regularly to keep up with news and announcements.

services, upgrades, or special events. Be sure to click on the Community button within eBay's main toolbar to access the community page, then pay close attention to the News and Announcements sections to see what's upcoming at eBay (see Figure 28.1).

KEEPING CURRENT WITH OTHER ONLINE SOURCES

Of course, the Internet offers a virtual sea of information, much of which provides numerous perspectives of online buying and selling. Be sure to visit sites like the following which come from both amateur and professional reporting forums.

Vendio.com

Formerly AuctionWatch.com, Vendio has established a reputation as a leader in online business support, useful buying and selling tools, and general auction and e-commerce advocacy. With current events in mind, be sure to visit Vendio's community pages, where you'll find the most active and insightful discussions regarding eBay and other forms of e-commerce. (See Figure 28.2.)

Internet.com

A division of industry-leading analysis firm Jupiter Media, Internet.com offers plenty of information regarding tech trends and online business activities.

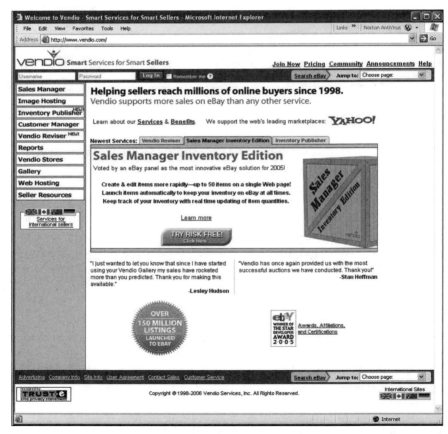

Figure 28.2   Vendio.com offers numerous buyer and seller tools, and it features the most active and informative community discussion boards next to eBay itself.

Nasdaq.com

When you're serious about maintaining a profit margin and growing a business, you'll want to remain aware of the overall market for your industry. Yes, online auctioning is an industry, and it's tracked closely on the stock market.

Nasdaq.com tracks all the publicly traded e-commerce venues (eBay's symbol is EBAY) and provides extremely useful analyses and press releases that keep you informed of how well the site is doing in relation to the entire e-commerce industry.

CNET.com

If you're looking for more news and information about technology and the online world, C/NET offers generous helpings of insight and analysis. C/NET's Top Tech News features and special reports keep you up-to-date on the latest happenings at eBay and elsewhere.

Wired.com

This site offers more tech news you can use, with a bit more attitude thrown in. It provides the down-and-dirty perspective of online business and other technology developments. It's great.

Portal Searches

With so much having been written about eBay and online auctions, don't forget to log on to your favorite Web portal site (such as Yahoo!, Google, or AltaVista) and search for auction-related keywords like "eBay," "online auctions," "e-commerce," and so on. There are plenty more sites out there that have reported on and are continuing to follow eBay and auction trends and developments; a search from a portal can help you uncover additional information you might otherwise miss.

THE POWER OF PRINT

Finally, don't forget to visit your favorite magazine stand or bookseller to find additional information about eBay and various other auctions. Remember to review the trade papers, which, besides reporting on collectible and commodity trends, also keep close watch on developments in online selling and auctioning. Also look to print publications such as *BusinessWeek, Industry*

Standard, and *Entrepreneur* for regular stories and features that pertain to the online marketplace. Hopefully, this book has brought you up-to-date with all that is happening at eBay and all that is good for your online business. Your fortune is waiting for you, and by staying informed of new trends and established traditions of dealing in goods on the Internet, you'll be in the best position to sustain a profitable enterprise for years to come.

Index

About the Author

Dennis L. Prince is a well-recognized and long-trusted advocate for online auction-goers. He continues his tireless efforts to instruct, enlighten, and enable auction enthusiasts and business owners, improving his readers' chances of success every step of the way. His perpetual passion for online auctioning and adherence to good business practices has earned him recognition as one of the Top Ten Online Auction Movers and Shakers by Vendio.com (formerly AuctionWatch.com). His insight and perspectives are regularly sought out by others covering the online auction industry. He has been featured in *Entrepreneur* magazine (2003) and *Access* magazine (2000) and has been a guest on highly rated television and radio programs such as MSNBC's *Countdown* with Keith Olberman, TechTV, BBC-Radio, and C/Net Radio.

Besides his previous books about eBay and Internet commerce, his vast editorial contributions to industry stalwarts like Vendio.com (formerly Auction Watch), Krause Publications, Collector Online, and Auctiva have earned him a well-regarded reputation in his ongoing analysis of the online auction industry. He likewise maintains active interaction with his ever-expanding personal network of auction enthusiasts, power sellers, and passionate collectors, both online and offline.